THE BIG BOOK OF
BRITISH FILMS

THE BIG BOOK OF
BRITISH FILMS

ROBIN CROSS

a Charles Herridge book

SIDGWICK & JACKSON

© Copyright Charles Herridge Ltd 1984

Published by Charles Herridge Ltd
Woodacott, Northam, Bideford, Devon EX39 1NB

Typeset and printed by
Devon Print Group, Exeter

ISBN 0 283 99135 6

Distributed by Sidgwick & Jackson Ltd
1 Tavistock Chambers, Bloomsbury Way,
London, WC1A 2SG

CONTENTS

Britain Awake   6

Britain Asleep   54

Into the Sixties   128

Finally – a tribute to the
players   182

Acknowledgments   189

Index   189

1 BRITAIN AWAKE

In 1946 Dilys Powell recalled a wartime visit to a remote Welsh mining village: 'A mobile van had arrived; the village hall was thrown open; and at the end of the day's work miners and their wives sat rapt and silent through a documentary record of the making of an airscrew.' Replying to a questionnaire sent to him in 1943 by the Wartime Social Survey, another member of the Welsh mining community, a young face worker, boasted: 'In 1942 I saw 300 films, in 1943 I saw 382 and in 1944 I reached the grand total of 430. I hope I can beat that total in 1945.' The villagers, ignorant of the commercial cinema, and the young Stakhanovite of the stalls, reflected two ends of the rich spectrum of wartime cinema in Britain. Escapism and entertainment took their place alongside information and moral uplift and, as the war progressed, came to mirror the hopes and fears of the British people, their shifting attitudes towards themselves and their enemy, and their visions of the future. If, as A.J.P. Taylor has written, 'In the Second World War the British people came of age', the same can be said of British cinema.

During the 1930s the British film industry rode a switchback of boom and slump which by 1939 had left it in one of its periodic states of crisis. The dominating figure of the decade was Alexander Korda, the nearest thing British films possessed to an Irving Thalberg or a Darryl Zanuck. Born Sandor Kellner in 1893 in a small town in Hungary, he arrived in England in the winter of 1931 by way of Hollywood and Paris. A journalist and film director in his native Hungary, he had been forced to leave in 1919 with the coming to power of Admiral Horthy's military dictatorship. After a spell in Vienna and Berlin he went with his film star wife, Maria Corda, to Hollywood. He worked for First National and Fox, for whom in 1927 he made *The Private Life of Helen of Troy*, in the process

discovering a formula that brought him fame and fortune in the 1930s. He left Hollywood in 1930, having broken with both his studio bosses and his wife and, after a brief period in Paris working for the French subsidiary of Paramount, he arrived in England and established London Films.

Korda's first films were 'quota quickies' made for Paramount. The 'quota' had been established by the Cinematograph Act of 1927 in an attempt to halt the drastic decline in British film production which followed the First World War. By 1926 only five per cent of the films screened in British cinemas were British-made. Coming into force in 1928–9 the Act established a renter's quota of 7½ per cent and an exhibitor's quota of 5 per cent for the first year, rising by stages to a 20 per cent quota for both sections of the industry in 1936–8. The Act certainly increased the quantity of British films – the first twelve months of its life saw production rise from 26 films to 128 – but in the long run it did nothing to improve overall quality. Small independent producers were paid £1 per foot to churn out shoddy little B features, many of which were screened before the audience arrived, merely to fulfil the quota. The American majors also used the system to dispose of some of their 'frozen' assets in Britain by making quickies through their British subsidiaries. The result has been aptly described as 'an undergrowth of poverty-stricken parochialism'. Nevertheless, the quota quickies gave some major talents the chance to cut their teeth in the film industry. Michael Powell recalled making a 1931 4-reeler for Fox, *Two Crowded Hours*, starring John Longden, Jane Walsh and Jerry Verno: 'It was played for laughs and thrills and we were paid £1 per foot by Fox, which meant that we got £4,000 on delivery and so we obviously made it for £3,000.' Among Korda's quickies of 1932 was *Men of Tomorrow* which starred Robert Donat, Emlyn

Williams and Merle Oberon, whom Korda married in 1939.

The Films Act of 1938 extended the quota system, lowered the percentages and attempted to improve the quality of domestic films by providing for a minimum cost of £7,500 to enable a film to qualify for quota recognition and a scale of quota privileges which were based on production values. These measures encouraged a brief period of American investment in major films produced in Britain – *A Yank at Oxford*, *The Citadel* and *Goodbye Mr Chips* – which was brought to an end by the outbreak of war. They demonstrated that, given the right conditions, British technicians were capable of achieving a glossy finish equal to that of Hollywood.

Alexander Korda was anything but parochial. His eyes were fixed firmly on the international market, and his first major success, *The Private Life of Henry VIII* (1933), starring Charles Laughton, received its world premiere at the newly opened Radio City Music Hall in New York, opening in London two weeks later. Made for a relatively modest £60,000, the film's first release grossed £500,000 and immediately transformed Korda into the man who was going to save the British film industry single-handed. The mood was infectious, and even the level-headed critic C.L. Lejeune felt able to speculate on the battle that was about to break out between British studios and Hollywood for domination of the world market. With backing from the Prudential Assurance Company, Korda set about the construction of an ambitious complex of studios at Denham in Buckinghamshire. In 1935 he became a full partner in United Artists, the major distributor in the United States of the films made by independent producers. In the following year United Artists acquired a half share in Britain's Odeon chain of cinemas. This guaranteed Korda an outlet for his films in Britain and gave Oscar Deutsch, chairman of the Odeon circuit, a rudimentary version of the vertical integration of production/exhibition which was enjoyed by the Hollywood majors.

Along with the rise of Korda went a boom in the film business. In 1936, 212 films were produced, with the figure rising to 228 in the following year. But as Michael Balcon pointed out after the war, it was an artificial boom created by a rapid influx of speculative capital which was not offset by a corresponding outflow of commercially successful features, or even films which gained an overwhelming international 'prestige' for Britain.

Despite his foothold in America, Korda was unable to break successfully into that lucrative market, a failure which was to be repeated a dozen years later by another British mogul, J. Arthur Rank. Moreover, Korda's success carried with it the seeds of destruction. His biographer Karol Kulik has written: 'Korda's particular model for making films and the way he had them financed both made and destroyed the British film industry. He gave the British cinema its first taste of international success and then undermined it all by trying to pull himself and the industry up too quickly.'

A man who could make money in millions was also capable of losing it in equal amounts. While this kind of flair has often been viewed with sympathy – even admiration – in the warm sunshine of California, no such indulgence was forthcoming from the Victorian Gothic halls of the Prudential's headquarters in Holborn. In 1937 Korda was forced to initiate pay cuts at London Films, and shortly afterwards he lost control of Denham studios, renting the space back from the Prudential and J. Arthur Rank. In 1940, his credit exhausted, he left Britain for Hollywood.

During this period of upheaval, Twickenham studios went bankrupt, the Gaumont–British studios at Lime Grove, built in 1926, were closed down and Gaumont–British, which had lost £100,000 in 1936, pulled out of film production to concentrate its attention on its chain of 305 cinemas. All down the line smaller companies folded up and studios ceased operating. In 1938, 228 British films were registered under the Films Act; the 1939 figures showed a slump to 109.

Korda and Internationalism

The 1930s did not see the establishment of a 'national' cinema in Britain along the lines of those in France and Germany. Korda's prestige films frequently boasted strong English casts but the men behind the cameras at Denham reflected his international outlook, a legacy of his peripatetic life in the 1920s. Key members of the Denham set-up were Korda's two brothers, Vincent and Zoltan. Vincent was a superb art director and Zoltan the director of the studio's hymns to an empire already lost in an Edwardian past: *Sanders of the River* (1935), *The Drum* (1938) and *The Four Feathers* (1939). Other collaborators included the Hungarian scriptwriter Lajos Biro, the French cameraman Georges Périnal and the American Harold Young, who edited *The Private Life of Henry VIII* and went on to direct *Catherine the Great* (1934) and *The*

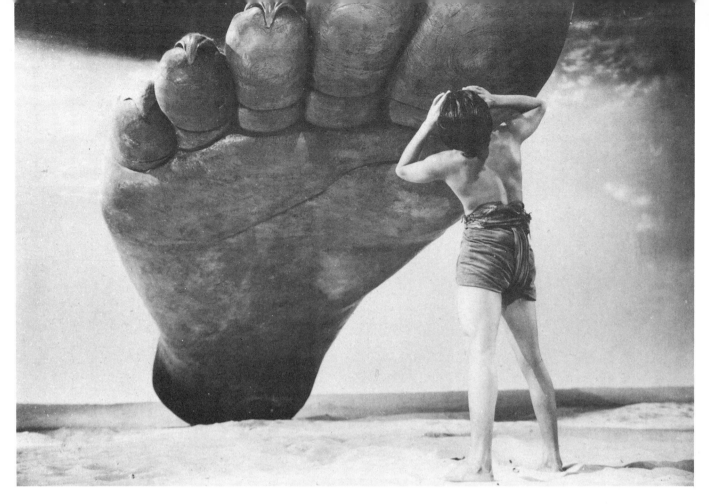

Not Monty Python but fantasy from Alexander Korda. Sabu is overshadowed by the giant foot of Rex Ingram's Djinn in *The Thief of Bagdad* (1940). The film boasted a characteristically international array of talent. Directing credits were shared by Michael Powell, Ludwig Berger and Tim Whelan, with additional contributions from Alexander and Zoltan Korda and William Cameron Menzies. The screenplay was by Lajos Biro with additional dialogue by Miles Malleson. The cameraman was Georges Périnal and the editor Charles Crichton, who later became an Ealing director.

Scarlet Pimpernel (1935). *Fire Over England* (1936) was produced by a German, Erich and directed and photographed by two Americans, William K. Howard and James Wong Howe. Early in 1937 Joseph von Sternberg came to Denham to begin filming *I Claudius*, with Charles Laughton in the title role. It was abandoned after one month of filming, but the remaining fragments hint at the clash of Korda's, Laughton's and von Sternberg's monster egos. The American production designer William Cameron Menzies directed *Things To Come* (1936) and that prodigal genius Robert Flaherty spent a year on location in India shooting miles of spectacular footage for *Elephant Boy* (1937), some of which was incorporated in the final version produced by Zoltan Korda on the backlot at Denham. In 1935 René Clair came over from France to direct *The Ghost Goes West* and his compatriot, Jacques Feyder, the most successful 'international' director of the 1930s, directed *Knight Without Armour* (1937) at Denham with Marlene Dietrich and Robert Donat. A film industry joke, current at that time, was that the five Union Jacks flying over Denham Studios represented that studio's five British employees.

Korda, however, was only pursuing a course – albeit on a far grander scale –

followed by other British studios. An American, William Beaudine, the grizzled veteran of countless Bs, directed three Will Hay comedies for Gainsborough in the mid-30s. *Boys Will Be Boys* (1935) was the first film to give full rein to Hay's most famous characterization, the seedy, ignorant schoolmaster; *Windbag The Sailor* (1936) brought Hay, Moore Marriott and Graham Moffatt together for the first time; and *Where There's a Will* (1936), in which Hay plays an impoverished solicitor, anticipates his best film of the 1940s, *My Learned Friend* (1943). In 1937 Beaudine gave way to the French director Marcel Varnel, whose second film with Hay was the classic *Oh, Mr Porter* (1938).

Will Hay brings us nearer to the native British cinema built around the personalities of those immensely popular entertainers, Gracie Fields and George Formby. In their rough and ready films there was a community of interest between the stars and their mass audience, unlike Korda's invitation to upward identification with his aristocratic heroes and heroines and the upper-class flag-bearers of an empire in which most ordinary English people no longer had any deep interest. Both Hay and Formby went on to make wartime films at Ealing Studios, whose head of production was Michael Balcon.

Balcon's career encompassed all the ups and downs of the 1930s. In 1925 he had given Alfred Hitchcock the chance to direct his first feature, *The Pleasure Garden*, at his Gainsborough studios in Islington. Later, as head of production at the Gaumont–British studios at Lime Grove, he brought in Hitchcock to direct *The Man Who Knew Too Much* (1934), *The Thirty-Nine Steps* (1935), *The Secret Agent* (1936) and *Sabotage* (1936). During this fertile period Balcon also masterminded Jessie Matthews' rise to stardom in *Evergreen* (1934) and *First a Girl* (1935), both directed by Victor Saville. After the Gaumont–British crash of 1937, Balcon spent a brief and intensely unhappy time as MGM's British head of production. He produced *A Yank at Oxford* (1938), and then walked out on MGM and into the welcoming arms of Ealing Studios, succeeding Basil Dean, whose successes in the 1930s had included a string of Gracie Fields musicals, *Sing As We Go* (1934), *Look Up and Laugh* (1935) and *Queen of Hearts* (1936).

Another film maker for whom the war came at a crucial period in his career was Carol Reed, who in 1939 was 33 years old. His future collaborator, Graham Greene, had already singled out his first film, *Midshipman Easy* (1935), and later *Laburnum Grove* (1936)

for special praise in his film column in 'The Spectator' – significantly both were made for Basil Dean at Ealing. Reed's warm and well-observed *Bank Holiday* (1938), which followed the experiences of a disparate collection of English holidaymakers, provided a model for one of the most popular contrivances of 40s cinema, the 'portmanteau' film.

The Phoney War

When war came in September 1939 it seemed for a short time that Hitler and the National Government had conspired to compound the crisis precipitated by Korda's extravagance and the South Sea Bubble speculations of the mid-30s. One of the most powerful and terrifying images of the decade had been the mass bombing raid in William Cameron Menzies' *Things To Come*, a nightmare made real by the destruction of Guernica. British civil servants had drawn their own apocalyptic conclusions from the lessons of the Spanish Civil War: the death toll in London during the first days of an aerial bombardment in a European war would be measured in tens of thousands – one estimate was 200,000 casualties in the first two weeks; panic-stricken hordes of Londoners would pour out of the shattered

Goodbye to all that. Thorold Dickinson's whimsical detective story, *The Arsenal Stadium Mystery*, released in the winter of 1939. A tense moment between Anthony Bushell (centre), Brian Worth and Esmond Knight in the Trojans' dressing room as the crack amateur team prepare to run out against mighty Arsenal. Bushell is the victim of an unusual professional foul when he is murdered on the pitch. The mystery is solved by Leslie Banks' eccentric Scotland Yard detective, who dons a different piece of headgear for each stage of the investigation.

capital into the countryside where the Government had laid contingency plans to turn them back with machine-gun fire in what nowadays would be coyly termed 'a worst case scenario'. Visions of mass death in crowded cinemas led to their being closed and a number of them – for example, the Tivoli in the Strand – were set aside for the storage of coffins. On a more practical note, a large amount of studio space was requisitioned for use in the 'shadow factory' programme and for storage. In 1939 there had been 22 studios using 65 sound stages – by 1942 the number had fallen to 9 studios and 35 sound stages. At Pinewood the sound stages assumed the unglamorous role of warehouses for sugar and flour. A 'hush hush' unit from the Royal Mint was also established at Pinewood, prompting the inevitable jibe that for the first time the studio was making money. Denham studios were scheduled for requisition in the early days of 1940, but this was prevented – whether by accident or design is not known – by Gabriel Pascal's *Major Barbara* (1940), which was running way over schedule. Throughout the war Denham continued to make films rather than Spitfires. The call-up and wartime shortages were also to take their toll. By the winter of 1940 Ealing had lost about a quarter of its relatively small workforce of 200. Ultimately, about two-thirds of the film's pre-1939 technicians were called up. Sets were built from salvage wood, packing materials, hessian and plaster. Obsolete equipment was nursed along by expert servicing. Coupon allocations had to be wheedled from the Board of Trade for costumes. One evocative photograph of the period shows an Ealing music sound track being rehearsed by musicians in overcoats and mufflers. All this was in keeping with the philosophy of 'make do and mend' which lasted throughout the war and into the peace that followed.

Another victim of the opening week of the war was the BBC's fledgling television service. It had been transmitting since 1936 to viewers in the south-east and in 1937 some 50,000 viewers had watched the coronation of George VI. Television went off the air for the duration of the war but only a fortnight after their abrupt closure, cinemas and theatres were reopened. However, the imposition of the 'blackout' extinguished the neon-lit façades and prominent illuminated towers of everyone's local Odeon. Post-war fuel shortages ensured that the cinema lights did not come on again until 1949.

The mood in Britain at the start of the war was captured in a short documentary produced by Alberto Cavalcanti for the GPO Film Unit. *The First Days* showed the population of London reacting to war with characteristic mildness and restraint. A small group of suburbanites huddle round a car in the road to listen to Chamberlain's announcement that 'we are at war with Germany'. Barrage balloons billow slowly up into the sky. When the first air-raid siren sounds people file obediently into the shelters, shepherded by a warden whose 'principal equipment is friendliness, the wartime equipment of all Londoners'. A streetcorner sandbag shelter in the East End is called the Rock of Gibraltar, complete with a model cannon and cheerfully insulting messages for Hitler. There is one short sequence which hindsight has bestowed with a sad irony – the camera tracks along a worried queue of aliens waiting to register while the commentator bumbles on about London's 'broad culture and tolerance'. (The wholesale internment of 'enemy aliens' at the beginning of the war – many of them refugees from Hitler – is a stain on the smug British belief in civil liberty.) 'Funny, it takes a war to give us a bit of peace and quiet', muses a working class mother after the evacuation of her children. Perhaps most moving is the quiet, simple, unemphatic 'goodbye' which the commentator repeats three times over scenes of departing troops. *The First Days* ends with a diffident barrage balloon drifting off the screen in a cloudy sky – a suitably uncertain image for an uncertain period.

As days turned into weeks, the dreaded aerial bombardment failed to materialize. The 150,000 British troops who had crossed to France saw no action. Visiting the front line, Prime Minister Neville Chamberlain asked querulously, 'The Germans don't want to attack, do they?' It was not until December that the British sustained their first casualty, one Corporal T.W. Priday, whose patrol had the misfortune to bump unexpectedly into some Germans. In Britain there was an air of unreality. The RAF were dropping leaflets rather than bombs on Germany. News pictures were published of babies in gas masks being wheeled to the shelter by similarly equipped nurses. This seven-month period became known as the Phoney War, an affair apparently not run by soldiers but by conscientious civil servants.

The civil servants, however, had only the vaguest notions of how to integrate the British film industry into the war effort. Before the outbreak of war, Michael Balcon had submitted a memorandum to Whitehall outlining 'How to put films to work in the national interest in wartime'. He merely received an acknowledgement slip.

The men at the newly formed Ministry of Information (MoI) had a gentlemanly distaste for the very notion of propaganda. In May 1940 the first Minister of Information, Lord Reith, was succeeded by Duff Cooper. A month later, as France's armies disintegrated under the German blitzkrieg, the hapless Cooper wrote of the Ministry, 'ex-ambassadors and retired Indian servants abounded, the brightest ornaments of the Bar were employed on minor duties, distinguished men of letters held their pens at the monster's service'. Duff Cooper was driven to wonder if the Ministry could serve any purpose at all.

Determined not to disturb the relative calm of the Phoney War, civil servants hovered anxiously over the making of Korda's *The Lion Has Wings*, the first feature film of the conflict, released in November 1939. By Korda's standards it was a cheapie, costing a mere £30,000, which the great man raised on his life insurance policy. It was shot in 12 days by a trio of directors – Brian Desmond Hurst, Adrian Brunel and Michael Powell – and finished in five weeks.

The Lion Has Wings was a remarkable hotch potch, combining an illustrated lecture on Nazism, delivered by the newsreel commentator, E.V.H. Emmett, with dramatised documentary and staged scenes in which a 'typical British couple' (Merle Oberon and Ralph Richardson) face up to the realities of the war. This consists principally of Merle telling Ralph, 'We must keep our land, darling...we must keep our freedom. We must fight for the things we believe in – Truth and Beauty...and Kindness.' Generous amounts of inspirational footage from Korda's *Fire Over England* were thrown in, with Flora Robson addressing the troops before they sailed out to deal with the Armada. An RAF bombing raid on the Kiel canal was contrasted with the sight of a German air fleet turning for home on sighting the serried ranks of London's balloon barrage. Although the mood of the film was dreadfully misjudged, it took up one theme which was to become a staple of many British war films – the difference between Germany and Britain at war, the former all jackbooted uniformity, the latter a combination of mildness and quirky good nature. At one point the film cuts between Hitler in a paroxysm of demagogy at Nuremberg and the shy George VI

singing 'Under the Spreading Chestnut Tree' at a Boy Scout jamboree. The point was lost in Germany where an American journalist reported from Berlin that the film was being run as a comedy.

Adapting Traditional Themes

In the absence of a constructive lead from the MoI, film makers followed their own instincts, subject only to the prevailing restrictions. They drew on the traditions established in the 1930s with a stream of espionage stories which adapted the thriller modes of the previous decade. In *Traitor Spy* (1939) Bruce Cabot, the swarthy veteran of *King Kong* and a host of G-Man B features, played an undercover agent in the pay of the Germans infiltrating an 'anti-submarine' factory. He comes to a sticky end, burning to death in a house in the Waterloo Road, which was later to provide the name and location of one of the best films of 1944.

Michael Powell's *The Spy in Black*, starring Conrad Veidt and Valerie Hobson, was released in August 1939, just before war broke out. Set in World War I, it pitted U-boat commander Veidt, attempting to penetrate the great naval base at Scapa Flow, against British agents Hobson and Sebastian Shaw. The torpedoing of the battleship *Royal Oak* at Scapa Flow in September gave the film a great deal of useful, if unsought, publicity, and it enjoyed a considerable success in the United States under the title *U-Boat 29*. *The Spy in Black* was the first collaboration between Michael Powell and the emigré Hungarian screenwriter, Emeric Pressburger. Their next film, *Contraband*, once again starred Conrad Veidt, this time as a Danish merchant captain charting a dangerous course between the British contraband control and the U-boat menace. Forced into a British port, he follows one of his passengers (Valerie Hobson) to London and helps her to expose a German spy ring with the help of some friends from a Danish restaurant. Ironically, *Contraband* was released during the month Hitler occupied Denmark. It was also the first film to use the blackout as a dramatic device, in a tense chase sequence in which Hobson edges to safety along a high, narrow girder.

Carol Reed's *Night Train to Munich* (1940) went from blackout to 'whiteout', providing a climactic chase through a cardboard Alpine set at the Gaumont–British studios in Shepherd's Bush. War broke out during the filming of *Night Train to Munich* and many years later Reed recalled the effect this had: 'At the

The thriller format adapted for wartime entertainment. Conrad Veidt and Valerie Hobson find themselves in the clutches of a Nazi spy ring in Michael Powell's *Contraband* (1940).

Early wartime images of the enemy often descended into caricature, playing up the Nazi 'thug element' as demanded by the Ministry of Information. Albert Lieven, destined for a long career as a German heavy, threatens Margaret Lockwood with the bullwhip in Carol Reed's *Night Train to Munich* (1940).

beginning it was called "*Gestapo*" and it was rather serious. But when the war came on we felt it was wrong to make something so heavy at such a time, so we made it more amusing, in the vein of *The Lady Vanishes*.' With a screenplay by Frank Launder and Sidney Gilliat and the casting of Margaret Lockwood, Basil Radford and Naunton Wayne, the film might well have been called *The Lady Vanishes II*. Starring opposite Lockwood was Rex Harrison as Dicky Randall, a debonair British agent who poses as a Nazi to spirit a Czechoslovak inventor (James Harcourt) out of Germany. Margaret Lockwood played the inventor's daughter, used by the Germans as a decoy to trap the British agent. Basil Radford and Naunton Wayne, as the cricket-obsessed Charters and Caldicott forever stranded in the continental railway system, are on hand to lend bluff assistance when the going gets rough.

Night Train to Munich succeeds in sustaining the mixture of sprightly humour and tension which distinguished Launder and Gilliat's work in *The Lady Vanishes* (1938). In one scene Caldicott attempts to warn Dicky Randall that his cover has been blown. Recalling that in his student days Randall was very partial to doughnuts he slips a message, telling him he's 'batting on a sticky wicket', under a doughnut on a refreshment tray. Suddenly he is assailed with doubt – was it rock cakes, perhaps, that Randall favoured?

Charters and Caldicott's first appearance in the film provided Launder and Gilliat with a marvellous opportunity to pour gentle scorn on one of the prime articles of Nazi faith. Having failed to secure the latest *Punch* from the station bookstall, Charters picks up a copy of *Mein Kampf*. Back in the compartment he tells Caldicott: 'Bought a copy of *Mein Kampf* – occurred to me that it might shine a spot of light on all this how d'you do. Ever read it?' Caldicott replies, 'Never had the time. I understand they give a copy to all the bridal couples over here.' Charters again, 'Oh, I don't think it's that kind of book, old man.' Later in the film, *Mein Kampf* is put to symbolic good use in blindfolding a trussed-up Gestapo man.

The Genteel Amateur

Similar plot devices – along with the underlying assumption of the superiority of the genteel English 'amateur' to the blinkered thuggery of the Nazis – were used in Leslie Howard's *Pimpernel Smith* (1941). Here Howard plays Horatio Smith, the very model

Raymond Huntley, Francis L.
Sullivan's Goering look-alike
and Mary Morris on the look-
out for Leslie Howard in
Pimpernel Smith (1940).

of an absent-minded professor of archae-
ology, pottering along the university clois-
ters, reciting 'Jaberwocky' to himself and
trailing knotted handkerchiefs to remind
himself that there are crumpets for tea. But he
has a secret *alter ego*, a modern version of the
Scarlet Pimpernel (a role Howard played in
1934) who runs an escape line for scientists
and writers threatened with imprisonment in
Germany. He arrives in Germany with a
group of students, ostensibly to locate the
traces of a lost 'Aryan' civilisation, but his real
mission is to smuggle a crusading Polish
newspaper editor back to Britain.

On the surface Horatio Smith is a typical
'soft' upper middle class Englishman, languid, whimsical, given to bouts of self-
deprecating humour. At one point he
remarks, 'I am not a spectacular person; a
natural ability to melt into the landscape has
proved remarkably useful.' Underneath, he is
infinitely tough and resourceful. He infiltrates a German concentration camp diguised
as a scarecrow – literally melting into the
landscape. A guard takes a few casual pot
shots at the 'scarecrow', wounding Smith in
the process; he remains silent and motionless
as the blood runs down his arm.

His German adversaries are uniformly
crass and brutal, and his principal opponent
(Francis L. Sullivan) is a combination of
Goebbels and Goering with all the emphasis
on the style and bulk of the latter. Guzzling
chocolates beneath vast murals of acceptably
'Aryan' art which display sprawling vistas of
monumental buttocks and thighs, Sullivan
struggles to come to grips with 'the British
secret weapon, their sense of humour'. Scrat-
ching his head over back numbers of *Punch*
and the novels of P.G. Wodehouse and, inevitably, 'Jaberwocky' itself, he professes
himself mystified. Later in the film he is given
a sharp lesson in this elusive national trait
when he comes face to face with Howard at
an embassy reception. 'Shakespeare is a
German – Professor Schutzbacher has proved
it once and for all,' he blusters. 'Well, you
must admit that the English translations are
remarkably good,' replies Howard.

In similar fashion to *Night Train to Munich*,
the Germans have baited a trap for Howard
with the newspaperman's daughter (Mary
Morris, one of the most beautiful and intelligent leading ladies in British films of the 40s).
Howard, who up to this point has been at
pains to display a whimsical misogyny typical of pipe-puffing academics, falls in love
with her. In a charmingly understated scene,

The image persisted. Robert
Morley enjoying himself as the
absurd von Geiselbrecht in
Ealing's *The Big Blockade*
(1942), directed by Charles
Frend. Charles Goldner is the
emissary from Mussolini seated
on the left. *The Big Blockade* was
an uneven mixture of drama
and documentary aimed at
explaining the meaning of
economic warfare. The
President of the Board of
Trade, Hugh Dalton, put in an
appearance, and there was a
typically confused exposition
of the complexities of the
Navicert system by Will Hay's
puzzled trawler skipper.

Reginald Beckwith finds himself at a temporary disadvantage in Anthony Asquith's *Freedom Radio* (1941).

Wilfrid Lawson's man of God is made ready for the lash in a studio-bound concentration camp in the Boultings' *Pastor Hall* (1940).

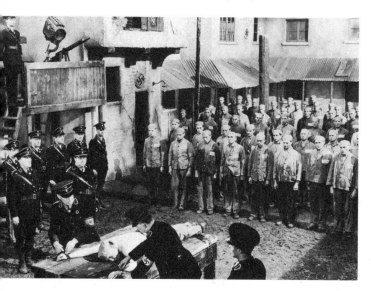

Billy Russell as Hitler in Maurice Elvey's *For Freedom* (1940), which reached a climax with the battle of the River Plate. The film's use of men from *Exeter* and *Ajax*, and prisoners from the *Altmark*, gave a hint of the documentary influence that was to dominate the films of the mid-war years.

he declares his love by tearing up a photograph of a classical Greek statue, the perfect woman of his imagination.

With father and daughter both safely over the border, Horatio Smith is left alone on a remote station platform with Sullivan, who informs his tormentor that, as they speak, German armoured columns are massing on the Polish border. 'Violence, power and strength will rule the world,' he bellows. 'Then why are you sweating, General?' is the mild reply. Howard escapes with effortless panache, leaving the preposterous Sullivan blazing away at a will o' the wisp of cigarette smoke. From the shadows, a quiet voice tells him, 'I shall be back, we shall all be back.'

Pimpernel Smith's beguiling message could not hope to survive the climate of 'total war' which followed the fall of France in June 1940. Horatio Smith's call-sign was a softly-whistled version of 'There is a Tavern in the Town', and there was, ironically, a certain element of 'whistling in the dark' in the film's suggestion that Nazi Germany would collapse under the weight of its own absurdity or be mocked out of existence by men of conscience.

Resistance

A number of films of the early war period dealt with the theme of German resistance to Nazism, albeit more hopefully than realistically. *Pastor Hall* (1940), made by the Boulting brothers' Charter Films and directed by Roy Boulting, was based on the career of Martin Niemoller, a German cleric who had defied the Nazis in the 1930s. Niemoller had originally been a Nazi sympathiser before seeing the light but Wilfrid Lawson in the title role

played a kindly, apolitical man of God – all too aware of the failings of his little flock – who is driven to speak out against the regime as he witnesses the destruction of his happy village community by the arrival of an SS unit led by cold-eyed zealot Marius Goring. Despite some rudimentary sets and occasional lapses into heavy-handed symbolism – the arrival of the SS unit in the village's main street is preceded by a flock of sheep – *Pastor Hall* is a typically thoughtful piece from the Boultings with a splendid central performance by Wilfrid Lawson, progressing from doubt to outrage and finally open defiance. He is ably supported by Seymour Hicks as a hard-drinking Junker of the old school, whose make-up turns him into a kind of hammered-down Hindenburg, a representative of a more 'honourable' Germany. Lawson is sent to a concentration camp, where he is helped to escape by one of the guards (Bernard Miles), a former member of his congregation. Miles is killed in the escape and Lawson turns down the efforts of his family to smuggle him out of the country, dons his canonicals and descends on his church. Thrusting aside a new incumbent – a weasel-like Nazi appointee who preaches the faith on strict party lines – he delivers a

rousing sermon before walking out into the square to face a fusillade of bullets from the waiting storm troopers.

In Anthony Asquith's *Freedom Radio* (1941) Clive Brook was a Viennese surgeon who sacrifices his life in the establishment of a German resistance radio network as Hitler invades Poland. Crisply played, and directed with Asquith's customary polish, the film was praised for its 'unrestrained heroism', but it bore little relation to anything that was happening in Greater Germany. Asquith's subsequent *Uncensored* (1942) merely transposed the setting to Belgium, where we find cabaret entertainer Eric Portman running a resistance newspaper, *La Libre Belgique*.

Films which were set in occupied Europe and dealt with the activities of the Resistance almost invariably had a slightly bogus ring about them, often compounded by the addition of a romantic sub-plot. In *Secret Mission* (1942) agents Hugh Williams and Roland Culver penetrate a vital German headquarters in France by posing as champagne salesmen with forged papers from von Ribbentrop. In *The Adventures of Tartu* (1943) Robert Donat impersonated a member of the Rumanian Iron Guard in order to obtain the formula of a new poison gas being developed in Czecho-

Finlay Currie, Deborah Kerr and Hugh Williams in Harold French's *The Day Will Dawn* (1942). Williams played a dissolute racing journalist sent to Norway at the outbreak of war as a foreign correspondent. Currie and Kerr were a local father and daughter who helped him locate a vital U-boat base and guided in a combined bombing and commando raid.

15

Secret Mission (1942), directed by Harold French. James Mason's Resistance fighter Raoul de Carnot expires nobly amid the general gloom displayed by Brefni O'Rourke, Nancy Price, Hugh Williams and Roland Culver.

Downed Flight Sergeant Bernard Miles takes a crash course in the Dutch national drink in Michael Powell's *One of Our Aircraft is Missing* (1942). The film followed B for Bertie's crew as they journeyed through Holland after being shot down on a bombing raid, and is notable for eschewing both the customary love interest, and music. Godfrey Tearle's elderly rear gunner watches Miles' discomfiture with some amusement.

Sally Gray and Anton Walbrook in Brian Desmond Hurst's *Dangerous Moonlight* (1942), whose immense popularity owed much to Richard Addinsell's Warsaw Concerto.

slovakia. Michael Wilding and John Clements were a very British pair of Yugoslav guerillas in Sergei Nolbandov's *Undercover* (1943). While Clements takes to the hills, his doctor brother (Stephen Murray) stays behind in Belgrade to gather information, posing as a collaborator. This was a favourite device of the period. In Vernon Sewell's *The Silver Fleet* (1943) Ralph Richardson played the owner of a Dutch shipyard who agrees to complete two submarines for the Germans as a cloak for his patriotic activities. The Resistance steal one of the submarines and sail it across the Channel, while Richardson sabotages the second, sacrificing his life in the process.

Night Train to Munich had made light of some of the unpleasant aspects of Nazism, and in *Pimpernel Smith* a concentration camp sequence is merely the pretext for another feat of legerdemain by Horatio Smith. Marcel Varnel's *Neutral Port* (1940) pitted crusty old sea dog Will Fyffe in a personal vendetta against the U-boat threat. Brian Desmond Hurst's immensely popular *Dangerous Moonlight* (1940) was an old-fashioned romance dressed up in wartime clothing. Anton Walbrook played an exiled Polish concert pianist who leaves the United States to join the Free Polish Squadron. Shot down in the Battle of Britain, he loses his nerve and his talent for music, but recovers both with the help of his American journalist wife, Sally Gray. The original story was devised by Terence Young (later an efficient director of James Bond films) while he listened to a concerto on the radio in an army training camp. The film's theme tune – the Warsaw Concerto, a bravura pastiche of Rachmaninoff by Richard Addinsell – became a huge hit, prompting many imitators.

History as propaganda

Like the nation itself, the films of the early war period searched for their bearings in a mood of optimistic uncertainty that, during the Phoney War at least, was captured in the hopeful refrain of the Crazy Gang song, 'We're gonna hang out the washing on the Siegfried line, if the Siegfried line's still there.' If the future seemed uncertain, then the past might prove more reassuring. In 1942 Carol Reed – fresh from directing H.G. Wells' *Kipps* (1941) for Maurice Ostrer at the Gaumont–British studios in Shepherd's Bush – turned to historical allegory with *The Young Mr Pitt*, starring Robert Donat as the states-

man who defied Napoleon. The parallel between Britain's lone stand in 1940 and her isolation in the Napoleonic wars, and the leadership of Pitt in the past and Churchill in the present, must have seemed seductive at the time, although it bears little historical analysis. As a reviewer in the New Statesman pointed out in July 1942: 'Pitt had neither Mr Churchill's virtues nor his deficiencies. He was by nature a man of peace – indeed he began as an appeaser; and he fought Napoleon chiefly by subsidising foreign armies.'

Some important aspects of Pitt's career were, understandably, glossed over at a time when the Beveridge Report was in preparation and the nation had embarked on fighting a 'total war'. There is no mention of Pitt's role as a hammer of the working class or of the Combination Acts. The only contact Pitt has with anyone outside the charmed circles of aristocratic society and politics is a short chat with boxing champion Daniel Mendoza (Roy Emerton) after he has been rescued by that stalwart from a gang of footpads hired by Charles James Fox (Robert Morley). Mendoza tells Pitt that 'the people' are with him and that a 'game young 'un is better than a game old 'un', whereupon our previously disillusioned hero decides to return to the hurly burly of the House of Commons.

Robert Donat gives a curiously stiff performance as Pitt, although some of the dialogue was calculated to produce a condition near to lockjaw in so sensitive an actor: 'Madam, I was torn between Mr Wilberforce's efforts to abolish slavery and your efforts to abolish boredom', he informs a gushing hostess. Raymond Lovell seizes his chance as George III, clearly already in the

'And always keep a-hold of nurse for fear of finding something worse.' Jean Cadell makes sure that Robert Donat's William Pitt takes his medicine in the historical propaganda piece *The Young Mr Pitt* (1941), directed by Anthony Asquith and scripted by Launder and Gilliat. Other wartime propaganda pageants included Thorold Dickinson's *The Prime Minister* (1941) with John Gielgud as Benjamin Disraeli and Fay Compton as Queen Victoria; Lance Comfort's *Penn of Pennsylvania* (1942); and J. Arthur Rank's ambitious *The Great Mr Handel* (1942), directed by Norman Walker and starring Wilfrid Lawson as the composer.

grip of porphyria and bellowing at Pitt, 'All my life I've tried to make this country manure-minded.' Albert Lieven's German-accented Talleyrand is a virtual stand-in for von Ribbentrop, full of the silky blandishments which the appeasers of the 1930s found so comforting. Pitt's shortlived successor Addington has everything but a 'Man of Munich' placard hung round his neck as he signs the Peace of Amiens. In contrast, the final shot of the film shows the ailing Pitt pushing aside his doctor's proffered medicine and downing a goblet of claret with consciously Churchillian relish.

Frank Launder and Sidney Gilliat have recounted the tremendous battles they had with Reed, Donat and producer Edward Black over the screenplay of *Young Mr Pitt*. Their attempts to make Pitt less of a paragon (including a scene in the Commons in which Pitt, as the Irish say, is not drunk but 'has drink taken') came to nothing. The part of Charles James Fox – whom Launder and Gilliat found far more interesting than Pitt – was reduced to a parade of foppery. They got their own back with some outrageous linking commentary which would have done justice to a Universal B swashbuckler of the 50s: as the camera passes across scenes of Hogarthian abandon, the voice-over intones, 'The country sprawls aimlessly on the multi-coloured quilt of feckless folly.'

In Reed's hands, history becomes a succession of speeches in the Commons, rides in carriages through alternately cheering and booing crowds, and the regular arrival of the news of military disaster carried by breathless messengers in mud-spattered topcoats. The Battle of Trafalgar consists of a couple of model cannons going off like damp Brock's bangers. There is, however, the occasional telling note. When Pitt tells Eleanor Eden (Phyllis Calvert) that 'In peacetime all dreams come true', one can imagine the heartfelt response of the wartime audience.

What About the Workers?

While lessons for the present were sought in the reign of George III, those for the future could be found in the recent past. In 1940 there were still over a million unemployed; large amounts of vital copper were being used for jewellery and curtain rails; and there was no halt to the importation of luxury foods. At the same time the experience of the first wave of evacuation in September 1939 had brought home to many middle class provincial families the extent of urban poverty in Britain. Two timely films of 1940 – John Baxter's *Love on the Dole* and Penrose Tennyson's *The Proud Valley* – dealt with the effects of the Depression on working class communities. *Love on the Dole*, despite a limited budget and Baxter's robust style, is a strikingly angry film. Set in the northern mill town of Hankey Park in 1930, it stars a young Deborah Kerr as Sally Hardcastle, 'an 'eadstrong young lass with a mind of 'er own'. The details of life on the breadline as the Depression begins to bite are captured with unerring accuracy. How to make a boiled egg go three ways at breakfast; the weekly trip to the pawnshop, a mirror image of the first day of the sale at Selfridges as beshawled old crones fight their way in with sagging prams piled high with musty clothing; a cunning middle-aged frump (Marjorie Rhodes) who sells her circle of gossips gin at threepence a tot over sessions of planchette and table tapping. Unemployed apprentices scrabble in the sawdust for the fag-ends of the local billiard-hall sharks. When Sally's younger brother (Geoffrey Hibbert) wins £22 on a racing treble, it seems like a fortune. The whole street turns out to watch as fat bookmaker 'Honest' Sam Grundy pays out. The camera pans slowly across the silent gallery of gaunt faces as Sam slaps the money into Hibbert's hand.

Grundy plays a crucial role in the film's bleak dénouement. Sally is engaged to an idealistic young Labour Party activist (Clifford Evans) who is fatally injured when a strike march is broken up by the police. This sequence has a particular savagery as plunging police horses crash into the crowd and

Mary Merrall and Deborah Kerr admire Geoffrey Hibbert's new hire-purchase suit in John Baxter's clumsy but affecting *Love on the Dole* (1940), a powerful reminder of the mass unemployment of the 30s.

batons move rhythmically up and down: it emphasises not only the repressive nature of the police but also the British horror of violence when 'things get out of hand', in this case the result of union hotheads forcing a change in the route of the march. Grundy 'lends' Sally £5 for her fiancé's funeral and from there it's just a short trip to becoming his housekeeper; 'all fair, square and above board,' he beams. 'I don't like it, we've always been so respectable,' wails Sal's Mum but Marjorie Rhodes takes a more cynical view – 'I'd never turn me nose up at a fat belly, so long as he had a gold watch chain on him.' The film closes with Sally living with Grundy as his 'kept woman', her family dependent on his handouts. She is still in the community but no longer part of it, isolated in her expensive clothes as she glides through the shabby streets in Grundy's big saloon car. Over the closing titles is superimposed a message from A.V. Alexander, a pillar of the Co-operative Movement and First Lord of the Admiralty in Churchill's early wartime government: 'Never again must unemployed men become the forgotten men of the peace.'

The Proud Valley was directed at Ealing studios by Penrose Tennyson, one of the lost leaders of British cinema. The great-grandson of Alfred Lord Tennyson, he left Oxford at the age of 19 in 1932 to go into the film business. He quickly made his mark and two years later he was working as Alfred Hitchcock's assistant on *The Man Who Knew Too Much*. He went to MGM with Michael Balcon, whom he had impressed as an assistant on *The Good Companions* (1933). When Balcon joined Ealing, he recruited Tennyson and gave him a chance to direct his first feature film, *There Ain't No Justice* (1939), a low-budget exposé of the fight game starring that perennial boy-next-door of the 40s, Jimmy Hanley. Encouraged by the Russian emigré producer Sergei Nolbandov, Tennyson then embarked on *The Proud Valley*. Set in a Welsh mining village, the film starred Paul Robeson as a ship's stoker with the evocative name of David Goliath who comes to work at the pit. While Sally Hardcastle finds herself cut off from the community in which she grew up, David Goliath is integrated into a new one, a theme which was to dominate Ealing's output over the years. The process is anticipated early in the film when Robeson arrives for the first time in the village and, off camera, joins the choir practice as the base part is cued by the choirmaster.

There is a serious accident and the pit is

closed down by its owners, remote financiers in London. With the village on the verge of collapse, a march on the capital is organised, the men 'singing as they go' in a manner which recalls the famous Gracie Fields film of that name made at Ealing in 1934. By the time the marchers arrive in London, Britain is at war with Germany and an uneasy truce is reached between the owners and the men to reopen the pit in the national interest. One of the miners in the delegation puts over a succinct message: 'Coal in wartime is as much part of national defence as guns or anything else – so why not let us take our chance down the pit?' In a new accident at the pit David Goliath sacrifices his life to save his fellow miners.

In the first version of *Proud Valley's* script, the workers open the pit themselves and run it as a co-operative. However, events overtook this scenario. Shooting began at the end of August 1939 and Michael Balcon decided that the original ending 'was obviously neither tactful nor helpful propaganda... especially since in real life the miners had given a lead by reacting vigorously to the national call for greater production.' This rather begs the question, for as Charles Barr points out in his brilliant study of Ealing studios, it ignores any consideration of the owners' response to the call for national unity. In *The Proud Valley*, the hostility which the miners feel for the bosses is redirected against Germany, very much in the fashion that the mutinous crew in Lewis Gilbert's *HMS Defiant* (1962) all pull together when the French fleet appears on the horizon.

The Proud Valley makes an interesting comparison with Carol Reed's version of A.J. Cronin's best-seller *The Stars Look Down*,

Paul Robeson as the evocatively named David Goliath and Edward Chapman as Dick Parry in Penrose Tennyson's *The Proud Valley* (1940). Robeson later remarked that it was 'the one film I could be proud of having played in'.

19

Michael Redgrave, Edward Rigby and Nancy Price in Carol Reed's 1939 adaptation of A.J. Cronin's *The Stars Look Down*.

John Clements, Clive Brook and Stewart Granger keep the conversation clipped and the upper lip stiff as the convoy escort *Apollo* closes to 15,000 yards with the German pocket battleship *Deutschland* in Penrose Tennyson's *Convoy* (1940).

released in 1939, in which Michael Redgrave played a miner's son who becomes a crusading MP. Made with Reed's accustomed polish (Graham Greene likened it to Pabst's *Kameradschaft*) it is nevertheless a much cooler film. Many years later Reed underlined this in a revealing remark in an interview: 'I simply took the novel by Cronin; I didn't feel particularly about his subject [the nationalisation of mines]. One could just as easily make a picture on the opposite side.'

Officers and Men

Tennyson's final film at Ealing was *Convoy*, made in co-operation with the MoI. It marks another step forward in the Ealing style, although the playing of Clive Brook as the captain of the convoy escort and John

Clements as the raffish young lieutenant who has had an affair with the captain's wife is still located squarely in the clipped West End drawing-room style of the 1930s. Convention required that Clements set the record straight by sacrificing his life to save the ship in an engagement with a German pocket battleship. Nevertheless, *Convoy* ventures down from the bridge and into the engine room of an antiquated tramp steamer whose captain (Edward Chapman) and mate (Edward Rigby) give sympathetic and slyly observed performances. Much is made of the British habit of understated humour in a crisis: 'Any more for the *Skylark*?' asks a seaman in charge of a lifeboat.

After making *Convoy*, Tennyson, who was a member of the RNVR, went into the Navy and was killed in 1941 in a plane crash while shooting footage for an Admiralty film. Ealing followed *Convoy* with *Saloon Bar*, a comedy-thriller starring Gordon Harker, and four comedies (*Sailors Three*, *Spare a Copper*, *The Ghost of St Michaels* and *Turned Out Nice Again*). Their next war film, *Ships With Wings* directed by Sergei Nolbandov, was released in November 1941. It seems incredible that over two years into the war it was still possible to produce a farrago of Boys Own heroics so out of touch with reality that it makes Biggles' exploits look like gritty, documentary material. Once again John Clements played a ladykiller – Biggles' black-sheep brother – required to make the ultimate sacrifice, this time for the Fleet Air Arm.

Lieutenant Dick Stacey is quite a rip: he says naughty things over the intercom; strums a ukelele in the wardroom of the new carrier *Invincible* whilst singing mildly risqué songs about women with a capital W; and he has a girlfriend, Kay (Ann Todd), who sings in a nightclub. But Dick is smitten by the Admiral's daughter (Jane Baxter): 'I've fallen for Celia Weatherby', he tells Kay at the club, whereupon she gets up and sings 'Santa Sent Me You', while gamely choking back the tears. Celia has a younger brother (Hugh Burden), also on *Invincible* and itching to win his wings. He persuades Stacey to take him up in a prototype which is still being serviced after its trials. The plane starts to break up in mid air, Stacey bales out but Weatherby – the young fool – ignores his orders and stays behind to complete his first and last solo flight in a pile of smouldering wreckage on the carrier's flight deck – 'I flew her, bad landing', he croaks before dying. Stacey is cashiered and next we find him flying for a tinpot Greek airline based on a tiny Mediterranean island. The airline's other pilot is a German (Hugh Williams), suggestively named Wagner. The airline also has two passengers, the yearning Kay and a bluff Lancashire businessman (Frank Pettingell). No sooner has Kay turned up than Wagner tells her that 'in Germany charming women are the relaxation of fighting men.' She has barely had time to suggest 'a massage or a Turkish bath' as an alternative (why not a cold shower and a run?) when he pounces. Stacey strides in to give him a darned good thrashing: 'Get up, you filthy Hun, I want to hit you again.' Before Kay can slip into yet another fetching costume change, war breaks out and the island is taken over by an SS unit summoned up by Pettingell who turns out to be a Nazi agent ('I've lived in England for 20 years and hated every minute of it'). Kay pluckily tries to warn the airborne Stacey and is promptly shot by the beastly Wagner, before she has time to serenade him with 'Hitler Sent Me You'. She dies in Stacey's arms, murmuring gracefully, 'I must look awful, darling.' Wagner rushes off to report to SS General Cecil Parker, and Stacey to make a rendezvous with *Invincible*, which just happens to be cruising by with Admiral Weatherby (Leslie Banks) pacing the bridge. The balloon has gone up, the 8th Army is about to put in a big push and a vital dam must be destroyed. Stacey reveals that there is an Italian minefield waiting for the battle squadron and there's no time to sweep a passage. It's up to the Fleet Air Arm as the big guns fall silent, but the Hun has unsportingly bombed the flight deck. There is only one answer – Stacey must be recalled, there's a job of work to be done. Will the gamble pay awf? It will be a stikeh

John Clements about to rejoin the Fleet Air Arm in somewhat unconventional circumstances in Sergei Nolbandov's *Ships With Wings* (1942). He enjoys some relaxed banter with Michael Rennie before taking off, with a devil-may-care smile playing across his lips, to wipe out the entire Adolf Hitler armoured division.

business without the Navy – will they be theah? Stacey takes off from the blazing deck and heads for the dam. Lacking Barnes Wallis' 'bouncing bomb', he bounces himself and Oberleutnant Wagner's fully-laden Dornier on to the dam which obligingly collapses and washes away the entire Adolf Hitler armoured division.

Ships With Wings did not go down very well with the Navy chiefs, who considered it a poor advertisement for the Fleet Air Arm, and Churchill threatened to cancel its release after seeing a preview. It remains an extraordinary document, presenting a Navy with no ratings and a carrier bursting with hee-hawing overgrown schoolboy officers, with John Clements presiding as head boy. At one point he rebukes Hugh Burden for peddling photographs of Celia to fellow officers Michael Wilding and Michael Rennie, whereupon Burden bends over and presents his backside for chastisement, a gesture that must have occasioned much ribald laughter in cinemas at the time. *Ships With Wings* is inextricably associated with the wealthy and smug élite which nearly destroyed Britain in the 1930s. In endorsing them and their values it echoes that ill-starred and often quoted poster of the early war years:

> Your Courage
> Your Cheerfulness
> Your Resolution
> Will Bring *Us* Victory

Propaganda Strikes Home

By far the best, and most commercially successful, film of 1941 was Michael Powell's *49th Parallel*, which was financed by the MoI. It avoided the traps into which *Ships With Wings* had tumbled with such headlong abandon and allowed Powell and Pressburger to indulge their delight in paradox by placing Germans at the centre of the action. From the moment U-37 surfaces in the Gulf of St Lawrence we see events from the German point of view. This is neatly established as characteristically ruthless and Teutonic in the opening scene when a cameraman is summoned up to the deck to record the death throes of the U-boat's latest victim. A shore party led by Leutnant Hirth (Eric Portman) is

despatched to find much-needed food and fuel. They watch helplessly as U-37 is located and sunk by the Canadian Air Force. The film then follows their flight across Canada, as they attempt to gain the safety of the neutral United States, and their encounters with various representatives of democracy – a French-Canadian fur trapper, a Hutterite community of German immigrants, an effete British anthropologist, and a Canadian soldier who has gone absent without leave.

With one exception, the Germans are presented as brutal fanatics, a treatment which occasionally slides into unintentional caricature – before turning in at night, they snap to attention and give a stiff-armed Nazi salute in their underpants. The risk of the audience identifying with the fugitives is further diverted by ranging against them a succession of stars with their feet pressed firmly down on the sympathy pedal – Laurence Olivier, Glynis Johns, Anton Walbrook and Raymond Massey. The one member of the German party who begins to have doubts is played by another sympathetic performer, Niall MacGinnis. When he decides to remain with the Hutterite community and resume his pre-war trade as a baker, he is shot as a deserter by his comrades.

Eric Portman gives a very strong performance and one that made his name, dismissing the Eskimos as 'racially inferior', ranting about Hitler's New Order to his 'fellow-Germans', the silent and horrified Hutterites, as an electric storm rages outside. In the penultimate episode of the film he encounters Leslie Howard, an English anthropologist whose field trips are conducted from a luxuriously appointed tepee

Effete anthropologist Leslie Howard is tied up in his luxury tepee by Eric Portman's ruthless German submariner in Michael Powell's *49th Parallel*. The film's fine score was by Ralph Vaughan Williams.

A metaphor for the spirit of Munich. Disillusioned journalist Michael Redgrave withdraws to a remote lighthouse on Lake Michigan in the Boultings' *Thunder Rock* (1942).

stocked with original Picassos and Matisses and the works of Thomas Mann. The only impact the war has had on him is to interrupt the supply of good French wine from the local hotel. 'They're rotten to the core,' Portman confides to his remaining companion before eschewing an improvised hot shower for an ideologically sound cold douche. Howard is finally roused to fury when the Germans dump his 'decadent' art and literature on the camp fire. After a chase, Howard corners Portman's companion in a cave and, although suffering from a painful wound, batters him to a pulp ('That's for Matisse...that's for Picasso...and that's for me'). Although this sudden conversion is painfully overdrawn, Documentary News Letter, when reviewing the film, commented '...Whether we like it or not, a picture of the Englishman as soft and decadent has grown up over the past two years, especially in the USA and it is probably good propaganda to take the bull by the horns and put him on the screen.' A comparison can be made with another 1942 feature set in North America, the Boultings' allegorical Thunder Rock, in which a disillusioned journalist (Michael Redgrave) abandons his pre-war crusade against fascism and retreats to a lonely lighthouse on Lake Michigan. There he is persuaded to rejoin the fight by the spirits he summons up of immigrants drowned in a shipwreck near the lighthouse some 90 years before. A measured film, it is notable for a charming performance by Lilli Palmer.

In Which We Serve

49th Parallel was edited by David Lean, who in 1942 graduated to associate director on one of the biggest successes of that year, Noel Coward's In Which We Serve. In the European theatre, 1942 marked a watershed for the British people and the British cinema. The threat of invasion had passed and the Blitz had been weathered. The rigours of rationing and mobilization had thrown people of all classes together in a way which would have been unthinkable in 1939. The Beveridge Report, which outlined the framework for the postwar Welfare State, was published at the end of the year amidst intense public interest: a Gallup poll conducted shortly after its publication discovered that nine out of ten people interviewed believed that its proposals should be adopted. After the United States joined the conflict people looked forward to the postwar world – significantly, Alberto Cavalcanti's Went The Day Well? (released in October 1943) is framed between a prologue

and an epilogue delivered after the war has ended.

This change in mood found an improbable interpreter in Noel Coward, who in 1942 produced and co-directed In Which We Serve, as well as writing its screenplay and composing the score. Behind Coward was the figure of the Italian Filippo del Giudice, another member of that silver-tongued band of emigrés who exercised such an influence on British cinema in the 30s and 40s. His production company, Two Cities (founded in 1937), raised the initial capital for the film and then obtained further finance and a distribution deal with British Lion. The enormous success of In Which We Serve established del Giudice as a powerful figure in the British film business and secured the patronage of J. Arthur Rank.

'This is a story of a ship,' the audience is told at the beginning of In Which We Serve. The film follows the career of the destroyer HMS Torrin, from her commissioning, through action in the North Sea and at Dunkirk, to her sinking during the evacuation of Crete. Her story is told in flashback as a group of shocked survivors cling to a life-raft while they wait for rescue. The focus is on three of the survivors – Captain Kinross (Noel Coward), Chief Petty Officer Hardy (Bernard Miles) and Able Seaman 'Shorty' Blake (John Mills). Coward modelled the Kinross character on that of his friend, Louis Mountbatten, whose destroyer, HMS Kelly – sunk off Crete – suffered the fate celebrated on celluloid by Torrin.

Ships With Wings moved in a world in which the ratings' job was to live and die conveniently off-screen. In Which We Serve

Wally Patch, Kathleen Harrison, John Mills and George Carney in Noel Coward's In Which We Serve (1942).

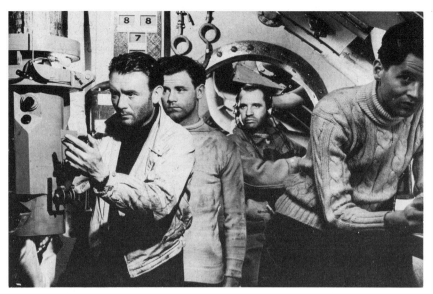

has a vital role to play. This feeling of community, with the captain at its apex, is underlined in a sequence on board *Torrin* at Christmas. During a carol service the camera tracks along the assembled crew as they sing a carol, halting at Coward, who reads a naval prayer. Then, as the ship's company break into 'Good King Wenceslas', the camera tracks back along the ranks of ratings, the simple movement circumscribing the world in which they move.

In the final count, it is *Torrin* herself who dominates all their lives. In an impromptu Christmas dinner speech Celia Johnson refers to the destroyer as an 'implacable enemy', of which she nevertheless remains inexplicably proud. Her sinking leaves an emptiness. In the closing scene the destroyer's crew are paid off. With the studied solicitude which characterizes his actions throughout the film, Coward gives a short speech and then shakes each man by the hand as they file past. As the last man leaves, he wanders away alone, shoulders hunched with emotion.

A fleeting moment in *In Which We Serve* provides a revealing indication of the change in public mood. Crew members of *Torrin* gather round a radio to hear Neville Chamberlain's broadcast on the outbreak of war. They listen silently until the point where Chamberlain tells the nation that it is at war and continues, 'You can imagine what a bitter blow it is for me...' This is interrupted by a minor explosion from John Mills; 'Well it isn't exactly a bank holiday for us!' It seems like an epitaph for all the discredited Men of Munich.

If the point was lost first time around, it was repeated in Coward's *This Happy Breed* (1944), his tribute to the 'ordinary people' of Britain personified by the Gibbons family of 17 Sycamore Road, Clapham. It is election night in 1935 and Frank Gibbons (Robert Newton) and his next-door neighbour Bob Mitchell (Stanley Holloway) are out among the crowds. A van rolls past bearing a big portrait of Stanley Baldwin and the legend, 'I Will Never Stand For A Policy Of Great Armaments'. Holloway beams, 'Ah, there's a face you can trust.' One can almost hear the faint echo of wartime audiences' ironic laughter. It seemed impossible for the wretched Baldwin to wriggle off the hook. In Leslie Howard's *The First of the Few* (1942), Howard's R.J. Mitchell argues with a civil servant for funding for his Spitfire prototype while through the latter's office window one can glimpse a poster urging the voters to 'Trust Baldwin'.

Anthony Asquith's *We Dive at Dawn* (1943), a muted underwater version of *In Which We Serve*, which showed Asquith's uneasiness with the documentary emphasis of the mid-war years. John Mills, Norman Williams, Eric Portman and Derek Bond work up a head of tension as their submarine stalks the German pocket battleship *Brandenburg*. The sequence was written by an uncredited submarine officer and is full of the authentic human touches which the rest of the film lacks.

devotes equal time to officers and men, although it remains very conscious of class distinctions. As the survivors are strafed by enemy bombers, Captain Kinross' thoughts drift back to his Georgian house in Devon, his children and tea on the lawn with his wife, Alix (Celia Johnson). Chief Petty Officer Hardy's mind wanders back to a raucous singalong to 'Roll Out The Barrel' in a wartime music hall. Able Seaman Blake recalls meeting his wife on a crowded blacked-out train, and another train journey, on his honeymoon, when he bumps into the Captain and his wife. This brief episode provides the link between the worlds of family and ship. Coward introduces Mills to his wife as 'one of my shipmates' – part of a community, another family in effect, on board a 'very happy, very efficient ship', where every man

An Englishman's home is his castle. In the cupboard under the stairs of No. 17 Sycamore Road, after their regimental reunion, World War I veterans Stanley Holloway and Robert Newton raise their glasses to Stanley Baldwin and Ramsay MacDonald in Noel Coward's *This Happy Breed* (1944), directed by David Lean.

The Documentary

By 1942, feature films were beginning to address the war with a growing confidence and qualified realism. This ascending curve was crossed at regular intervals by the output of British documentary film makers, whose 'creative interpretation of reality' produced some of the most enduring films of the war.

The 1930s saw the development of a native British documentary movement whose presiding genius was John Grierson, the head of the GPO Film Unit from 1933–7. Grierson made only one film himself, *Drifters*, commissioned by the Empire Marketing Board in 1929, an elegiac account of a trawler's fishing voyage. Grierson's true skill was as organiser and propagandist for a socially derived theory of film. Unconcerned with the aesthetics of cinema he nevertheless grasped the medium's power as a means of mass communication. He wrote, 'It [film] is capable of direct description, simple analysis and commanding conclusion, and may by its tempo'd and imagistic powers be made easily persuasive.' Grierson never offered a thoroughgoing analysis of the ultimate ends to which this persuasion could be put to use. Nor did the bright young men at the GPO Film Unit – leftwingers to a man – bring the documentary to bear on the pressing social problems of the day. As Harry Watt, the director of *Night Mail* (1936), recalled in his autobiography: 'The truth is that if we had indulged in much social criticism to any extent, we would have immediately been without sponsorship and our whole experiment, which artistically was a fine one, would have finished. So we

'They can't take the Spit, Mitch.' Leslie Howard as the dying R.J. Mitchell and David Niven as the composite test pilot figure Geoffrey Crisp in Howard's *The First of the Few* (1942), a romantic account of the development of the Spitfire which concentrated on the inter-war years.

A real pilot. Harry Watt's *Target for Tonight* (1941), the first documentary feature to show Britain on the offensive. Its inspiring message was a little disingenuous as Bomber Command still lacked the resources and the technology to mount an effective bombing campaign against specific targets in Germany.

Briefing for the crew of a Sunderland flying boat, and mascot, in the Crown Film Unit's *Coastal Command* (1942), directed by Jack Holmes.

Bagpipes at war in *Desert Victory* (1943).

compromised.' The result was a series of finely crafted and uncritical hymns to the beauty of work. Occasionally direct social criticism was mounted within the sponsorship system. Edgar Anstey's exemplary *Housing Problems* (1935) was made for the gas industry, which had a vested interest in highlighting slum conditions as rehousing programmes would incorporate its appliances.

What was important in 1939 was that the documentary movement had given a number of talented young film makers the opportunity to learn their craft, indulge in formal experiments and make films about specifically British institutions. The experience had taught them how to improvise films in difficult conditions, on tight schedules and even tighter budgets, and this was to prove invaluable when war came.

Initially, the MoI was at a loss as to what to do with the film makers at its disposal. Harry Watt summed up the mood of indecision: 'Nothing happened for six weeks. We sat on our backsides looking out of the windows, watching the tarts in Savile Row.' The initiative came from Alberto Cavalcanti, the Brazilian film maker who had succeeded Grierson as head of the GPO Film Unit in 1937, and the result was *The First Days*.

The GPO Film Unit followed *The First Days* with Harry Watt's *Squadron 992*, an account of the training of a barrage balloon unit which climaxed with a German bombing raid on the Forth Bridge. *Squadron 992* continued the dramatised documentary style which Watt had first used in *The Saving of Bill*

Blewitt (1937) and also applied a truly 'creative' interpretation of reality. The German bombers were RAF Blenheims with swastikas painted on their fuselages. Two students were kitted out in Luftwaffe uniform to play downed German pilots, but before the cameras could start rolling they were arrested by an over-zealous naval officer. Despite some splendid photography by Jonah Jones, *Squadron 992* remains a 'Phoney War' film and its effect was further muted by a delayed release. When it was shown in the summer of 1940, the balloon had well and truly gone up.

Squadron 992 also revealed a problem which was to frustrate documentary film makers during the first 18 months of the war. Britain was on the defensive and as a result their films of the period necessarily adopted a 'we can take it' attitude, the cumulative effect of which was likely to lower rather than raise morale. David Macdonald's *Men of the Lightship* (1940) dealt with an attack on an unarmed lightship. Harry Watt's *Dover Frontline* (1940) looked at life in the port under long-range bombardment from the other side of the Channel. Humphrey Jennings' *London Can Take It* (co-directed with Watt in 1940) recorded the first big raid of the Blitz. Its opening sequence has an almost science fiction quality as the sirens wail, huddled queues move quietly into shelters and the blackout is suddenly shattered by searchlight beams and the anti-aircraft barrage. In order to secure widespread screening in America, the film had a hectoring commentary by Quentin Reynolds, a Runyonesque war correspondent who apparently spent most of the Blitz propped up at the bar of the Savoy Grill.

In July 1940, the Documentary News Letter agonized '...A nation fighting desperately to defend the present lacks the inspiration which springs from a vision of the future. Now, more than ever, it is necessary to repair past errors and fortify national morale with an articulation of democratic citizenship as a constructive force which can mould the future.' Help was at hand. August 1940 saw the establishment of the Crown Film Unit, into which the GPO Film Unit was absorbed. Under the Crown Film Unit's umbrella a wide range of independent and sponsored documentary teams operated as part of a co-ordinated policy. The three services also set up their own film teams. By 1943 the Army Film and Photographic Service, based in Pinewood, could deploy 80 cameramen and eight directors in the European and Far Eastern theatres of war.

By the end of the war hardly a subject remained untouched by the documentary. Information and inspiration played their parts in films ranging from a short flash on how to enjoy a Woolton Pie (Len Lye's 1941 *When The Pie Was Opened*) to Carol Reed's magisterial collaboration with Garson Kanin, *The True Glory* (1945), which was edited down from some 5½ million feet of film shot by 500 cameramen.

Serious messages were often put across by well-known screen actors. 'Yes, Mrs Wilson, you are right, it is one of those propaganda pictures,' Robert Morley's judge tells Irene Handl, who has knowingly received black market meat from her butcher. John Betjeman, for a time the script editor at the MoI's Film Division, commissioned a number of delightful short documentaries, including *Mr Proudfoot Shows a Light* (1941) in which a chink of light in garrulous Sydney Howard's blackout precautions serves as a beacon to some wandering German bombers. Leslie Howard appeared as a 'passer-by' in *From the Four Corners* (1941) in which he describes Britain's cultural heritage, and her licensing laws, to some soldiers from the Commonwealth. This 15-minute short contains a memorable exchange when Howard inquires, 'How do you like the weather over here?' The reply comes back, 'Too Pygmalion cold.' To get these and other messages across, the MoI employed over 150 travelling film units, putting on shows in schools and village halls all over Britain.

Target for Tonight

Harry Watt's *Target for Tonight* (1941) was the first documentary to show Britain 'hitting back'. Modelled on the pattern established by *Drifters* and Watt's own *North Sea* (1938), it followed a Wellington bomber, 'F for Freddie', and its crew during the planning and execution of a raid on Germany. All the parts were taken by real technicians and servicemen; the pilot of 'F for Freddie' was played by 24-year-old Freddie Pickard, who was Cedric Hardwicke's brother-in-law. The use of non-professionals anchored the film in the documentary tradition but in many respects *Target for Tonight* moved into areas occupied by the feature film. Most of the exteriors were shot at Mildenhall aerodrome where 149 Squadron was based, but the interiors were all reconstructed in the studio. An enormous replica of Bomber Command's HQ was built in Denham, incorporating an impressive tally of operational squadrons on the walls which was twice the actual number.

Model shots were used in the bombing raid and British soldiers stood in for German anti-aircraft batteries. A brand-new Wellington fuselage was provided for the aircraft interior shots, despite Watt's request for something a little more beaten-up. (A mysterious black box next to the pilot's seat turned out to be a top-secret anti-radar device which no-one had thought to remove.) Although the performances are a little stiff, there are some splendid unforced moments. As the damaged 'F for Freddie' limps home through a fog-shrouded southern England, the airfield's CO emerges from the ops room into the surrounding gloom, snorting, 'Hell's bells, just look at this muck.' During the debriefing after the raid, Freddie Pickard, pipe in mouth, remarks, 'I'm afraid I didn't see much, I was rather busy at the time.'

Tailor-made Documentary

In America *Target for Tonight* was seen by over 50 million people and prompted a number of documentaries constructed along similar lines: Jack Holmes' *Coastal Command* (1942); Jack Lee's *Close Quarters* (1943), which followed a submarine on active service; and Pat Jackson's *Western Approaches* (1944), set on the convoy routes of the North Atlantic. *Western Approaches* opens with a shot from a lifeboat of a mountainous Atlantic swell as the crew of a torpedoed merchantman, *Jason*, drift towards Ireland. Shadowing them is a U-boat whose captain anticipates that the lifeboat will act as a perfect decoy,

Wylie Watson's quiet game of billiards is brought to an abrupt conclusion by a German bomb in the delightful MoI short *Mr Proudfoot Shows a Light* (1941), directed by Herbert Mason and scripted by Sidney Gilliat. This humorous warning against the danger of ignoring the blackout regulations was commissioned by John Betjeman, who was for a brief period script editor at the MoI's film division.

The final moments of the doomed U-boat in Pat Jackson's *Western Approaches* (1944), which skirted the narrow dividing line between dramatized documentary and the feature film. The film's remarkable colour photography was by Jack Cardiff.

luring a rescue ship to within range of his one remaining torpedo. The lifeboat is spotted by the merchantman *Leander*, a convoy straggler, and the U-boat moves in for the kill. The frantically semaphored messages of warning from the lifeboat are ignored on *Leander*'s bridge and she is struck by the torpedo. The *Leander*'s crew abandon ship but the first officer and the stoker are left behind. When the U-boat surfaces to finish off *Leander* with gunfire she falls victim to the merchantman's gun in a savage fire-fight. Brilliantly shot in colour in the Atlantic by Jack Cardiff, and using sets at Pinewood designed by Edward Carrick, *Western Approaches* is a feature film in everything but name. Although crammed with salty characters and building up to a genuinely tense climax, it lacks the immediacy and rawness of the documentaries of the early war years. It is too obviously a tailored article.

A degree of tailoring was also applied to the mass of battlefront footage which was assembled by the Service Film Units into a number of compilation films, the first of which was *Wavell's 30,000* (1942), describing the North African campaign against the Italians. The Army and the RAF joined forces in the 1943 *Desert Victory*, directed by John Boulting and produced by David Macdonald, who had enjoyed considerable pre-war success as the director of *This Man is News* (1938), starring Barry K. Barnes and Alastair Sim. (Paradoxically, while documentary-trained film makers like Watt and Jackson developed a fictionalized approach to their wartime subjects, commercial directors like Macdonald and Boulting threw themselves into direct reportage of the war.) But even *Desert Victory*

resorted to reconstruction: a striking sequence in which infantry wait to advance at El Alamein, their faces fitfully illuminated by the colossal artillery barrage, was filmed in the studios at Pinewood. Some of the more dramatic battle scenes were also staged after the event. Nevertheless, *Desert Victory* remains an impressive document, retailing a mass of logistics and events in calm and lucid style and pausing on the way to salute the war workers at home. It collected an Oscar and its success in the United States prompted an enterprising entrepreneur, B.J. Goldernburg, to market a 'Monty beret' which appeared perched on the head of an attractive model on the cover of *Life* magazine.

Desert Victory was followed by *Tunisian Victory* (1943) and *Burma Victory* (1945), the latter chronicling the campaign in the Far East. The last year of the war also saw the compilation by Carol Reed and Garson Kanin of *The True Glory*, a stunning record of the war in Europe from D-Day to the fall of Berlin. It succeeded in capturing the sweep of these titanic events while at the same time retaining the human figure of the individual soldier in the foreground.

Humphrey Jennings

A unique place in wartime documentary was occupied by a graduate of the GPO Film Unit, Humphrey Jennings, whose first film of the war, *Spring Offensive* (1939), showed him moving towards the lyrical style which characterized his later films. The prosaic but vital work of the War Agricultural Committees, charged with putting pasture under the plough, is given a romantic gloss with glowing shots of horse-drawn ploughs on misty mornings and loaded hay wains at harvest time. The reclamation of a bramble-infested farm by a giant traction engine takes on a heroic quality as the metal monster churns up the earth. A homely touch is inserted when a farmer's wife worries about the expected evacuee: 'I do hope they send us a nice clean child.'

Jennings' mature style blended sound and visual images in an almost seamless garment of pictures evoking British life and culture. In the process Jennings' own commitment to defending British values against the barbarism of the Nazis was translated into a general statement about the nation in its darkest hour. A trilogy of films – *Heart of Britain*, *Words for Battle* (both 1941) and *Listen to Britain* (1942) progressively refined this approach. *Listen to*

Two films by Humphrey Jennings. *Fires Were Started* (1943), a poetic tribute to the work of the Auxiliary Fire Service during the London Blitz.

Britain is the most powerful, taking wing after a tedious opening commentary by a Canadian worthy, in a succession of exquisitely balanced pictures of Britain at war. Spitfires swooping over cornfields; an endless tide of dancers swirling round a ballroom; a Wellington taxiing to take-off at dusk, its tail light winking in the gathering gloom. A voice barks, 'Workers' Playtime!' as a train races across a viaduct, pulling us into an effortless tracking shot of an industrial landscape. A canteen concert given by Flanagan and Allen gives way smoothly to a lunchtime recital by Dame Myra Hess in the National Gallery with the Queen in the front row. As the redoubtable Dame Myra pounds away, the camera moves down a line of faces, all furrowed brows and rapt attention, cutting away humorously to a line of mops propped against a sandbagged wall. The music sweeps us out of the National Gallery into Trafalgar Square, down to the docks, and is finally lost in the clangour of a tank factory. The final image is of a dreaming English landscape with a soundtrack of 'Rule Britannia'. When watching this little masterpiece today, it is still difficult to avoid feeling strong surges of emotion, a tribute to its continuing power as a crystallization of how the British chose to see themselves during the war. It is not an accurate picture of how things actually were, but rather an unfolding of all the wartime semi-myths – unity, quiet determination and resilience – which enabled the British to believe that, against all the odds, they would survive and win the war.

Jennings owed much to his editor, Stewart McAllister, who collaborated with him on the feature-length *Fires Were Started* (1943), a

tribute to London's Auxiliary Fire Service in the Blitz. *Fires Were Started* begins with the arrival of a new volunteer fireman, Barrett (played by the novelist William Sansom) at substation 14–Y. His integration into the team operating the 'heavy unit' is brilliantly accomplished as night draws on and the men wait for a raid to begin. Barrett begins to play the piano and the camera moves out of the station into the docks, gliding alongside a munitions ship preparing to sail on the morning tide and squinting up at the silent warehouses. Then we return to the station where Barrett is playing 'One Man Went To Mow', the number increasing as each member of the unit comes through the door. They pause at the start of a fresh round and we hear the sirens fading in underneath the singing. Bombs begin to fall and Barrett finishes the

The moment before mass execution in *The Silent Village* (1943), Jennings' reconstruction of the Lidice massacre which he set in a similar community, the Welsh mining village of Cwngredd. The men sing 'Land of my Fathers'. As Ian Dalrymple recalled, 'no work recalls the atmosphere and feeling of the time more poignantly than Humphrey's films'. Jennings' post-war work failed to capture that elusive lyricism; he died in a bathing accident in Greece in 1950.

29

Bill Blewitt and Mary Hallet in Charles Crichton's drama-documentary of canal life, *Painted Boats* (1945), an Ealing exploration of the clash between the traditional horse-drawn barge and its new motor-powered successors. The needs of the wartime economy – and marriage – unite the two families on opposite sides of the argument, but with peace obsolescence cannot be far away. This measured film, beautifully photographed by Douglas Slocombe, hints at themes taken up in Alexander Mackendrick's *The Maggie* (1954) and Charles Crichton's *The Titfield Thunderbolt* (1953) and can be seen as an early metaphor of Ealing itself.

sing-song on 'Eight Men Went To Mow', the eighth man being himself, now part of the group. We exchange the cosy and relaxed atmosphere of the fire station for a blaze at a warehouse next to the munitions ship. The dirt and danger of the work, and the battle with the blaze, are shot through with striking images: a terrified cart-horse careering down the street; a cascade of water from a rogue hose-pipe running down a wall and glistening in the searchlights. Dawn breaks: the men – wet, grime-caked and exhausted – have put out the fire and saved the ship. One of them has lost his life. The film closes with his funeral followed by a triumphant shot of the munitions ship nosing its way out of harbour and into the open sea.

Jennings' handling of what he saw as traditional British virtues became less certain when he turned his attention to what might lie ahead in the post-war world. *Diary for Timothy* (1945) opens in June 1944 with a baby being delivered in a comfortable Oxfordshire nursing home. As the war draws to a close, the first six months of his life are contrasted with those of a wounded fighter pilot, an engine driver, a farmer and a miner. The film's commentary, which Raymond Durgnat has aptly described as 'nannyish', was written by E.M. Forster and delivered by Michael Redgrave. The point of view is that of a liberal-minded academic, alarmed by the accident rate in the mines (described as 'pretty shocking') but rather muddled as to what to do about it all. After the film's release Forster expressed some of his reservations to the film's producer, Basil Wright. He felt that the film 'suggested that Britain ought to be kept right for one class of baby and not got right

for babies in general.'

While Jennings offered no solutions, fellow-documentarist Paul Rotha strode confidently into the future with *World of Plenty* (1943), which received its first screening at the Hot Springs Conference on World Food. A mixture of compilation and specially-shot 'argument', *World of Plenty* was skilfully edited to shock audiences into grasping that while whole areas of the pre-war world were in the grip of starvation, the developed world, and particularly North America, was accumulating enormous surpluses. Its trenchant argument is in sharp contrast to the muzzled documentaries of the 30s. Today, watching a farmer telling us, 'Do you know they actually poured away, down the drain, a lot of my milk so as I could get a decent price for what was left', produces a strong, and depressing, sense of *déjà vu*.

The Influence of Documentaries

The extent to which wartime documentaries influenced feature films remains the subject of fierce debate. Paul Rotha suggested that his *Night Shift* (1943) provided the inspiration for Launder and Gilliat's first film as co-directors, *Millions Like Us* (1943). Its direct origins, however, lay in a proposal from Roger Burford, John Betjeman's successor at the MoI, that a film should be made covering the whole panorama of home front life. When this proved too unwieldy, the front was eventually narrowed down to the role of 'mobile women' in industry.

Shopgirl Patricia Roc receives her call-up papers but her dreams of joining the WAAF are shattered when she is drafted on to a factory production line. Instead of wiping down the cockpit canopies of dashing young fighter pilots she finds herself turning out bracing tube sockets for Whitley bombers. Along with miner's daughter Megs Jenkins, and languid debutante Anne Crawford, she learns that she can help her country just as much in overalls as in a more glamorous uniform. After a tender, gawky romance, she marries a young sergeant gunner (Gordon Jackson) from the local air base but after a few weeks of happiness he is shot down and killed over Germany.

Millions Like Us closes with a heart-wrenching scene executed with complete conviction and confidence. The night shift are having their dinner and are being entertained in the vast canteen by a singer and a band. The camera moves in a long, expressive boom shot over a sea of quiet, upturned

Women at war.
'Mobile women' Patricia Roc and Megs Jenkins in Launder and Gilliat's populist epic *Millions Like Us* (1943), one of the most moving evocations of wartime sacrifice and solidarity leavened with characteristically idiosyncratic humour. At one point the irrepressible Charters and Caldicott make a brief appearance laying mines on a beach. Unable to agree on whether they have laid 86 or 87 mines, Charters remarks, 'We must remember not to bathe here after the war.' Wartime privation is neatly conveyed in a subtitle in the opening moments which explains that an orange is 'a spherical pulpish fruit of reddish-brown colour'.

Czech refugee Lilli Palmer reads Joyce Howard's palm in Leslie Howard's *The Gentle Sex* (1943), which followed the progress of seven yong women through the ATS.

Renée Houston and Phyllis Calvert face up to a pair of Nazi robots in Frank Launder's comedy-thriller *2000 Women* (1944), which was set in an internment camp at a former spa hotel in occupied France. Flora Robson is seated on the extreme right. The women hide three RAF airmen (Reginald Purdell, James McKechnie and Bob Arden) and engineer their escape during a camp concert while they sing 'There'll Always be an England'.

31

The spud-bashing detail for a mixed bunch of recruits in Carol Reed's *The Way Ahead* (1945). From left to right, Leslie Dwyer, Jimmy Hanley, Raymond Huntley, James Donald and John Laurie. This unpromising material is licked into shape by William Hartnell's sergeant, survive the torpedoing of their troopship and finally move into action, through a smoke screen, against a German mortar battery in the Western desert. The excellent screenplay was by Eric Ambler and Peter Ustinov.

faces before settling on Megs Jenkins and Patricia Roc. The singer launches into the old favourite 'Waiting at the Church', and Roc's eyes begin to glisten with tears. Megs Jenkins takes her hand and coaxes her into singing along. Behind them we can see Anne Crawford, also singing and now fully part of the group. Over Roc's face is superimposed a flight of bombers as the end titles come up. I find this sequence, and particularly the opening moments, inexpressibly moving – a summoning-up of the great British wartime experiment of socialism without tears. The film itself underlines the possible fragility of this sense of wartime unity. Anne Crawford has an affair with brusque north country foreman Eric Portman. Up on the moors overlooking the town they discuss marriage and Portman puts his feelings this way: 'The world's roughly made up of two types of people – you're one sort and I'm the other. Oh, we're together now there's a war on – we need to be. What's going to happen when it's over? Shall we go on like this or shall we slide back...I'm not marrying you, Jennifer, till I'm sure.'

One the most mature films of the war, Carol Reed's *The Way Ahead* (1944), grew directly out of a documentary project. Its germ was an Army Film Service short, *The New Lot* (1943), commissioned to show how civilians adjusted to service life. The Adjutant General, Sir Ronald Adam, was so impressed with the result that he suggested it might serve as the basis for the Army's answer to *In Which We Serve*. The resulting feature, scripted by Peter Ustinov and Eric Ambler, was released at the time of the Normandy landings. It followed the progress of a mixed bunch of seven conscripts – ranging from a stoker in the House of Commons boiler room to a department store floorwalker — as they are welded into fighting men under the stern eye of Sergeant Major William Hartnell. David Niven played the lieutenant in charge of their platoon. A garage mechanic and pre-war Territorial, he was typical of the young officers in Britain's wartime army, no longer looked down on as 'temporary gentlemen' as they had been by the snobbish regulars in World War I.

Ealing Goes To War

The documentary movement had a direct impact on Ealing in the persons of Alberto Cavalcanti and Harry Watt, who joined the studio in 1940 and 1941 respectively, as part of a deliberate policy of 'cross-fertilisation', initiated by Michael Balcon. Both directors played important roles in Ealing's films of the next two years, which can be seen as a conscious attempt to exorcise the ghost of *Ships With Wings*.

In Charles Frend's *The Foreman Went to France*, released in April 1942, we can see the process under way. Based on the real-life exploits of Melbourne Johns it starred Clifford Evans as a factory foreman who undertakes a personal expedition to France to rescue some vital war machinery from under the noses of the advancing Germans. With the help of a courageous American girl (Constance Cummings) and two Tommies (Gordon Jackson and Tommy Trinder, driving an appropriately named 'Albion' truck) the machinery is located and ferried though aerial bombardment and refugee-clogged roads to a small port on the west coast of France. A German pincer movement is closing in and the last boat, a small fishing vessel captained by Francis L. Sullivan, is about to leave. The refugees aboard vote to throw their possessions overboard to accommodate the machinery, a celebration of democracy and the *entente cordiale*.

Clifford Evans' foreman is a working-class man who is not there merely to provide comic relief (though, alas, there is rather too much of it from Trinder). The machinery is saved by his determination – at the beginning of the film his superiors at the factory patronise him when he begs to be allowed to go to France and smugly assume that, since the French government has given them 'assurances', nothing can be amiss. The 'officer class' is portrayed throughout as either hopelessly inept or positively traitorous. A French

Clifford Evans and Tommy Trinder find the vital machinery that must be spirited back to England in Charles Frend's *The Foreman Went to France* (1942).

mayor (Robert Morley) turns out to be a Fascist and fifth columnist ('Everything is under ze control', he reassures Evans with oily relish as he attempts to lay his hands on the machinery). A pukkah British officer (John Williams) is revealed as a German agent. Evans' little band of helpers consists of a Cockney, a Scot and an American, encompassing along with himself (a Welshman) the regions of mainland Britain and our allies across the Atlantic.

Harry Watt's first feature at Ealing, *Nine Men* (1943), provided a mirror image of *Ships With Wings*. Instead of a war without men, we have a war without officers. A patrol in North Africa lose their officer and under the leadership of a tough Scottish sergeant (Jack Lambert) hold out in a deserted tomb against a series of fierce Axis attacks. The focus is on a small group of men getting on with the job. The Germans are a respected enemy, not the caricatured figures of earlier films; at one point a soldier remarks of some Italians, 'There might even be a Jerry among them, they're fighting so well.'

The dynamics of a small group operating against superior odds was a favourite Ealing theme. Basil Dearden's *The Bells Go Down* (1943), released three months after *Nine Men*, moved from a North African patrol to an auxiliary fire unit at the height of the Blitz. A mixed bunch of volunteer firemen forge a mutual loyalty and respect in the face of adversity. Their relaxed solidarity is underlined by their cheerful tolerance of petty crook Mervyn Johns' occasional theft of a barrel of Guinness and the careful measures they take to protect him from the police. At the height of a raid he saves the life of the

policeman who has been pursuing him throughout the film. The 1930s are placed in context by the presence of William Hartnell, a seasoned fireman who is a veteran of the International Brigade. Wise-cracking greyhound fancier Tommy Trinder conducts a running battle with senior fireman Finlay Currie (the film's equivalent of Jack Lambert) who is constantly catching Trinder smoking on duty. Currie is trapped in a blazing hospital wing and Trinder goes into the flames to rescue his 'auld enemy'. Their way out is blocked as walls and floors begin to cave in all round them. 'Well, I reckon that puts us off duty,' says Trinder, offering Currie a cigarette moments before they are fatally engulfed by falling masonry.

The Bells Go Down ends with a christening in a bombed-out church. The father is one of

Post-war Britain anticipated in miniature: Philip Frend's middle class newly-wed, Tommy Trinder's working class greyhound fancier, Mervyn Johns' 'basically decent' petty crook and William Hartnell's veteran of the International Brigade in Basil Dearden's *The Bells Go Down* (1943).

The changing mood was reflected in the quiet heroism of Charles Frend's *San Demetrio, London* (1943). Robert Beatty's cynical American is on the extreme right. Next to him, radiating working-class integrity, is Frederick Piper's bos'un.

Trinder's comrades and the child is to be named after him. As the vicar sprinkles the water the camera pulls back out of the church and cranes over the bustling street market outside. We move from the individuals in the church to the larger community of the city and then, with the arrival of the wartime Ealing symbol of the Union Jack over the end titles, we make the final link with the nation.

Despite some jarring notes struck by Trinder's hoarse and ingratiating clowning, *The Bells Go Down* is an impressive film, full of humour and warm observation. Buried in its structure are some small harbingers of Ealing films to come. The memory of Mervyn Johns' basically 'decent' petty criminal will be evoked at the beginning of Basil Dearden's *Blue Lamp* (1950). The bustling market scene which opens and closes the film and the prologue – 'London isn't a town. It's a group of villages...This is the story of one of those villages, a community bounded by a few streets...' – anticipates the embattled fragment of Burgundy in Henry Cornelius' *Passport to Pimlico* (1949).

The Ealing cycle closed in December 1943, with the release of Charles Frend's *San Demetrio, London*. The ship of the title is an oil tanker whose convoy is attacked by a German pocket battleship. *San Demetrio* is badly damaged and abandoned by her crew. After drifting for several days, one of the ship's lifeboats encounters her, smouldering dangerously and still afloat. As in *The Foreman*

Went to France, a vote is taken about what to do next. The men decide to board and, later, vote to sail her on to the Clyde rather than take the safer option of returning to the United States. The tanker's engines are repaired, the fires put out and she sails under her own power back to Britain, where the men receive £14,000 in salvage money.

San Demetrio, London pulls together all the positive wartime themes which Ealing had been developing since *The Proud Valley*. The devil-may-care gallantry of the officer class in *Ships With Wings* is found to be wanting as the convoy escort steams straight for the pocket battleship and is blown out of the water. There is only one officer (Ralph Michael) among the ship's rescuers and he exercises his authority within the democratic decision-making of the crew. The latter comprise a range of strongly-drawn regional working-class types, whose understated courage represents, as Charles Barr has suggested, an adaptation of *Pimpernel Smith*'s more attractive qualities to the demands of a 'people's war'. There is the statutory American (Robert Beatty), whose initial brashness is mellowed as he becomes part of the team effort. Even the reward the men receive at the end of the film is placed in the context of their communal effort. As Ralph Michael puts it when they are offered a tow, 'We've come more than a thousand miles on our own. I think we can manage the rest.' Nothing is farther from their minds than the reward.

8927 C

Careless talk costs lives. Raymond Huntley's German agent has the drop on Alastair Sim's bungling Sergeant Bingham as, along with Phyllis Calvert, they thunder through the night in *Inspector Hornleigh Goes to It* (1940). The Inspector Hornleigh stories, adapted from Leo Grex's novels, were originally broadcast on the Monday Night at Seven radio programme. There were three low-budget spin-offs, the first two being *Inspector Hornleigh* (1939) and *Inspector Hornleigh on Holiday* (1939), starring Gordon Harker as the eponymous detective who solved crimes through a single mistake by the criminal.

The Fifth Column

It is one of the ironies of the war that, although Germany failed almost totally to establish an espionage network and fifth column in Britain, the one phrase that everyone remembers from the conflict is the stern warning, 'Careless Talk Costs Lives'. Lack of real spies did little to stem the flow of thrillers with an espionage background, most of them little more than escapist entertainment of varying quality. In *Inspector Hornleigh Goes To It* (1940) policemen Gordon Harker and Alastair Sim found an investigation into the pilfering of strawberry jam at an army camp developing into a spy hunt. John Mills played an enemy agent masquerading as an RAF officer in Anthony Asquith's *Cottage To Let* (1942). In *They Met in the Dark* (1943) James Mason was a disgraced naval officer who joins forces with Joyce Howard to expose a spy ring run from Tom Walls' theatrical agency.

Two films, both from Ealing, provided a more serious warning against the dangers of complacency and lack of vigilance: Thorold Dickinson's *Next of Kin* (1942) and Alberto Cavalcanti's *Went The Day Well?* (1943).

Thorold Dickinson, who was not one of the regular Ealing team, was initially drafted into the studio to make a training short aimed at tightening up military security. At Michael Balcon's suggestion, the original storyline was built up by Dickinson and scriptwriters John Dighton and Angus MacPhail into a feature-length film.

A commando raid is being planned on German submarine pens in a port in occupied

France. A security officer (David Hutcheson) is given the task of keeping the operation 'hush hush'. Ominously, he remarks on arriving in the training area, 'I've always thought if I wanted a nice cushy job, I'd come to England as a German spy.' Certainly there seems to be no shortage of them at large – Stephen Murray, running an antiquarian bookshop, blowzy stripper Phyllis Stanley and her dresser-cum-minder Mary Clare, and soft-spoken Mervyn Johns, posing as a bombed-out Welsh businessman. A rising tide of casual indiscretions enables the German agents to piece together the details of the raid. Some aerial reconnaissance 'mosaics' of the port are stolen by Mervyn Johns, with horrifying ease, from an RAF intelligence

Eric Portman tries on his RAF uniform in *Squadron Leader X* (1942), directed by Lance Comfort. Portman played a Luftwaffe pilot sent to bomb Ghent, bale out and spread the news that the British were bombing civilians (this was before the strategic bombing offensive got underway). He is rescued by patriots who insist on smuggling him back to England. Eventually he escapes by stealing a Spitfire but is shot down over the Channel by a flight of Me109s.

Reporter Richard Greene is hot on the trail of a Nazi spy ring masquerading as a peace organisation in Harold French's *Unpublished Story* (1942).

An Ealing film which warned against complacency and lax security. Phyllis Stanley's cut-rate Mata Hari is brought to heel by her controller Mary Clare in Thorold Dickinson's *Next of Kin* (1942).

The tense Tommies surrounding Muriel George's village postmistress in the church hall are in fact German paratroops, the advance guard of an invasion, in Alberto Cavalcanti's *Went the Day Well?* (1943). John Slater is the squaddie in close attendance.

officer's briefcase and taken to Germany by an Irish sailor (Charles Victor), who turns out to be an IRA man. When the attack goes in, the Germans are waiting for the commandos and, although the objective is achieved, the casualties are heavy. The raid, shot in the Cornish village of Mevagissey, is vividly conveyed, much of it being given a grainy documentary quality. The film closes with a short scene in a train in which the familiar figures of Basil Radford and Naunton Wayne are casually discussing their postings while Mervyn Johns sits listening in the corner of the compartment.

Like *Ships With Wings*, *Next of Kin* provoked Winston Churchill's displeasure, although the reasons were more immediate. By sheer coincidence Churchill was given a screening of the film two weeks before the raid on St Nazaire (28 March 1942). He noted with alarm that at one point in *Next of Kin* an officer points to a spot on the map of northwest France not far from St Nazaire itself. He ordered the film to be withdrawn until after the raid had been carried out and insisted that when it was released fewer British casualties should be shown.

Went the Day Well? belongs to a later stage of the war. A sleepy village deep in the green heart of England is unexpectedly visited by a company of army engineers on a 'secret' exercise. The men are billeted on the villagers and the two officers (Basil Sydney and David Farrar) stay at the big house with the lady of the manor (Marie Lohr). A series of small clues reveals to the audience and to the vicar's daughter (Valerie Taylor) that the engineers are in fact German infiltrators, parachuted in to establish a sabotage unit ahead of Hitler's invasion. The Germans take over the village, locking most of its inhabitants in the church. When the elderly vicar attempts to ring the bells to announce the invasion, he is shot dead. The local Home Guard, out on manoeuvres, ignore the warning and are mown down in an ambush as they cycle home down a leafy lane. Frantic efforts to contact the outside world are frustrated, principally by the presence among the villagers in the church of a fifth columnist – the local squire (Leslie Banks). Eventually aid is summoned by an elderly poacher (Edward Rigby) and a scruffy little evacuee (Harry Fowler). As the Army closes in, the villagers barricade themselves in the manor house and fight off the last desperate attack by the German parachutists. The squire remains at large almost to the end, as the deferential villagers are unable to grasp that his suspicious behaviour marks him out as an enemy agent. Finally, he is shot by the vicar's daughter as he sets about dismantling an undefended barricade in the villagers' redoubt.

Went the Day Well? is the starkest of all the wartime warnings against complacency. It was given greater resonance by casting Leslie Banks and Basil Sydney – the stuffed-shirt officers of *Ships With Wings* – as agents of the enemy. When Banks is shot by Valerie Taylor he falls at her feet in slow motion, a device which brilliantly conveys the trauma of the act. One of the most striking aspects of the film is the brutal contrast made between the idyllic rural setting and the violence that is set in train by the arrival of the Germans. In her cosy kitchen the middle-aged postmistress (Muriel George) throws pepper into the face of her guard and then buries an axe in his head, but before she can complete her hysterical progress to the telephone switchboard, she is bayoneted by another German. At the film's climax the Germans lurking in the ornamental shrubbery are picked off by the excited villagers like rabbits at a shoot.

This catharsis anticipates, in very British fashion, the orgies of destruction which were to conclude so many of the science fiction features of the 50s in which aliens take over the bodies of human beings. It is almost as if *Went the Day Well?* is a wartime version of Don Siegel's *Invasion of the Body Snatchers*. Indeed, as the film progresses, the behaviour of the Germans becomes increasingly harsh and zombie-like as they go about their grim business.

Blimps and Censorship

Went the Day Well? questioned the automatic habit of deference to one's 'betters' which initially paralyses the beleaguered villagers. One of the most famous representatives of that blinkered and reactionary élite was David Low's cartoon character, Colonel Blimp, a portly relic of Britain's colonial wars, speaking out on behalf of the 'wealthy classes' from the bowels of his club's Turkish bath. In *The Life and Death of Colonel Blimp* (1943) Powell and Pressburger placed this symbol of obsolescence at the heart of a long and densely-layered 'national epic' which survives as one of the great films of the war period.

In Powell and Pressburger's hands, Blimp became Major-General Clive Wynne Candy VC, whose career is traced from his days as a headstrong young subaltern to old age in World War II, when he throws his

Roger Livesey's Major-General Clive Wynne Candy makes sure that the Royal Bathers Club is ready to repel the beastly Hun in Michael Powell's *The Life and Death of Colonel Blimp* (1943). Vincent Holman is the attentive club porter and Home Guard stalwart.

considerable weight behind the Home Guard. Using an elegant flashback device, the film locates Wynne Candy in three periods – 1902, 1918 and 1942. In each period his life intertwines with those of a German, Theo Kretschmar-Schuldorff (Anton Walbrook) and an 'ideal woman' (played in each of the three periods by Deborah Kerr) with whom Wynne Candy falls in love.

Originally, Michael Powell had wanted Laurence Olivier (then a serving officer in the Fleet Air Arm) to play the title role but the MoI, having read the script, refused permission to release him for the film. He was replaced by Roger Livesey and, instead of a 'slashing, cruel and merciless' Blimp, we have 'a dear old bumbler'. Livesey's is a brilliant portrait – warmhearted, hidebound, philistine and tinged with that rigidly suppressed romanticism which often lurks deep beneath the bluff surface of professional military men. Returning on leave from the Boer War, he impulsively undertakes a personal mission to Germany to defend his country's honour against stories of 'concentration camps' in South Africa. He contrives to insult the entire German officer corps and as a result has to fight a duel with a young Uhlan, Theo Kretschmar-Schuldorff, in one of the great set pieces of British cinema. Their subsequent friendship throws Wynne Candy's antiquated notions into sharp relief against Kretschmar-Schuldorff's more astringent view of the world. At the end of World War I, Kretschmar-Schuldorff dines with Wynne Candy and his friends on his way back to Germany from a POW camp in Derbyshire. These stouthearted pillars of the establishment tell him not to worry as they

will 'soon have Germany back on its feet again'. Later he reflects that 'They are children, boys playing cricket. They have taken the shirts from our backs and now want to return them because the game is over.'

At the start of World War II the old friends are reunited – Kretschmar-Shuldorff is now a refugee from Nazism. Vainly, he tries to alert Wynne Candy to the true nature of the threat which Britain faces – 'It isn't good enough to be a gentleman and sportsman. If you lose, there won't be a return match next year.' The lesson is then rubbed home in humiliating fashion during a Home Guard exercise. An eager-beaver young officer – with his mind on Pearl Harbor – takes the major-general prisoner in a pre-emptive strike on the steam room of the Royal Bathers Club several hours before the manoeuvres are supposed to begin. 'But war begins at midnight!' splutters the old tusker. This scene, which occurs at the beginning of the film, identifies Wynne Candy as Blimp sitting like an old bull walrus, towel-clad and with glistening bald pate, amid the rising steam of the Turkish bath. It also provides the film's framing device. In a surge of rage Wynne Candy wrestles the young officer into a swimming pool and, as they both disappear under the water, we plunge with them back into Blimp's personal history and, by implication, back into the history of Britain.

The film ends with Wynne Candy deciding to ask the bumptious young officer to dinner, just as a similar offer was made to him by a crusty War Office official when he returned from his duelling exploits in Germany. A military band passes by playing 'The British Grenadiers' and the old soldier snaps vigorously to the salute, superannuated but surviving.

Powell's Blimp is painted with great affection and there is more than a merely coincidental parallel between the Englishman and the German in the film and its High Tory director and emigré screenwriter. The occasional pathos of Blimp's blinkered view of the world is caught with great delicacy and humour. Wynne Candy takes Kretschmar-Schuldorff down to his den to show him a portrait of his wife, which occupies pride of place among a massive array of stuffed rhinoceros and water buffalo heads. He can't understand his German friend's (and our) amusement at his decision to hang the picture in these surroundings. When Wynne Candy tells Kretschmar-Schuldorff that his wife died in the West Indies, the German reflects, 'It must be a terrible blow to lose someone you

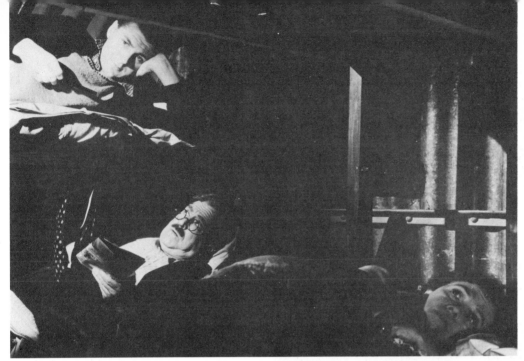

The home front.
Mr Bunting (Edward Rigby) spends an apprehensive night in the Anderson shelter with son Eric Micklewood and wife Mabel Constanduros in Maurice Elvey's *Salute John Citizen* (1942), a modest family saga which anticipated Noel Coward's more ambitious *This Happy Breed* (1944).

Truculent and worldly-wise evacuee George Cole endures the well-meaning flutterings of Muriel Aked and Jeanne de Cassalis (radio's Mrs Feather) in Anthony Asquith's *Cottage to Let* (1941). A walking Sherlock Holmes encyclopedia, Cole helps to prevent inventor Leslie Banks' revolutionary new bombsight from falling into the hands of John Mills' Nazi agent. The film reaches a bravura climax as Mills, posing as an RAF fighter ace, is unmasked and shot in a bazaar tent full of distorting mirrors.

Eliot Makeham and wife Amy Veness in Jiri Weiss's *John Smith Wakes Up* (1941), in which Makeham gets a knock on the head and wakes up in an occupied Britain.

love in a foreign country.' 'It wasn't a foreign country, it was Jamaica,' grunts Candy, without looking up.

Two years earlier, in *49th Parallel*, Powell and Pressburger had successfully met the propaganda requirements implicit in that film's theme of the 'defence of democracy'. Indeed, they very nearly overdid it – one begins to feel almost sorry for Leutnant Hirth as he steels himself for yet another lecture on freedom from one of his antagonists. However, *Colonel Blimp*, an intensely personal statement, ran foul both of critics on the left in the documentary movement and officials in the MoI, who felt that the film might even encourage defeatism.

The Documentary News Letter tore into *Colonel Blimp*: 'If you think back over the film, not one single ordinary person, such as you may meet in the street or on a bus in England, has anything more than a walking-on part in the film.' Broadsides were also aimed from the other end of the political spectrum. In a lengthy minute to Churchill, the Secretary of State for War pointed out that *Colonel Blimp* 'focuses attention on an imaginary type of Army officer which has become an object of ridicule'. Furthermore it completely ignored the 'thug element' in the German soldier and suggested that if we adopted their 'realistic' approach to war we might be better soldiers. Churchill – many of whose own attitudes were decidedly Blimpish – sent a memo on 10 September 1942 to his crony Brendan Bracken, then Minister of Information: 'Pray propose to me the measures necessary to stop this foolish production before it gets any further. I am not prepared to allow propaganda detrimental to the morale of the Army...who are the people behind it?'

The dispute rumbled on throughout 1943, with Churchill keeping up a stream of memos badgering the MoI to find a way of preventing the film's export. When news of this leaked out, it provided *Colonel Blimp* with a great deal of excellent free publicity. In September 1943 the bureaucrats caved in and the export ban – which the Ministry privately admitted was illegal – was lifted. The long-drawn-out episode throws a tantalisingly isolated beam of light on the limits of 'acceptable' wartime propaganda, apparently determined in a characteristically British atmosphere of general muddle and self-censorship. The belated lifting of the ban, and the film's commercial success, enables us to raise two and a half cheers for the democracy which *49th Parallel* set out to defend.

A Descent into Whimsy

For Michael Powell, *Colonel Blimp* was located at the heart of a living tradition. For his critics, the film seemed to confirm reactionaries in the belief that, as they had always thought, they were the salt of the earth. More acceptable than Powell's calculated ambivalences were the reassuring stereotypes of Anthony Asquith's *The Demi-Paradise* (1943) which, as Richard Winnington observed, showed 'us poor juvenile-minded cinemagoers that the England of Mrs Miniver and Mr Punch lives for ever'.

Written and produced by the Russian Anatole de Grunwald for Two Cities, this deeply narcissistic film set out to celebrate Britain's alliance with the Soviet Union. In truth, it provided little more than a national ego massage which had absolutely nothing to do with the Soviet Union at all.

A young Russian marine engineer Ivan Kuznetsov (Laurence Olivier) arrives in England in 1939 to supervise the construction of a revolutionary propellor for a Russian icebreaker being built in the yards of the sleepy old shipbuilding town of Barchester. A Stakhanovite son of the Revolution, he finds the British very puzzling. They seem more interested in the close-of-play cricket scores than in the deepening crisis in Europe. The elderly chairman of the shipyard, Runelow (Felix Aylmer), is obsessed with the minutiae of Bradshaw and absentmindedly offers pinches of snuff to the deferential workers. 'We are in the midst of cataclysmic events,' he tells the bewildered Ivan, referring not to the disintegrating international situation but to the annual historical pageant directed by the redoubtable Miss Rowena Ventnor (Margaret Rutherford).

A misfiring romance with Runelow's daughter, and an undignified scuffle with a hearty young shipyard executive during the pageant, send Kuznetsov back to Russia a disillusioned man. When he returns to take delivery of the icebreaker the skies over Barchester are flecked with the vapour trails of dogfighting Spitfires and Messerschmitts. He receives the friendliest of welcomes – the film tactfully omits any mention of the Nazi–Soviet pact – and is amazed to learn that, in the midst of war, the yard's engineers are still struggling with the casting of his propellor. The problems seem insuperable, but the greatest of all British institutions comes to the rescue when Ivan finds the answer as he stares lugubriously into the sluggish swirl of a cup

The imperious Miss Rowena Ventnor (Margaret Rutherford) takes charge of the Roman episode in the annual Barchester pageant in Anthony Asquith's *The Demi-Paradise* (1943).

of tea in a railway station buffet. With only a week to go before the launching, Runelow tosses aside the Bradshaw, rolls up his sleeves and works all night on Kuznetsov's plans. Now that Hitler has obligingly invaded Russia, the workers pitch in to help their new ally, working round the clock to finish the job. The icebreaker slides down the ramp complete with new propellor after a speech by Kuznetsov – now a true-blue Stakhanovite – which singles out the special quality of the British – you've guessed it, their 'sense of humour'. As in *Millions Like Us*, the central romance is delicately fudged over. Ivan returns to Russia without Runelow's daughter, but imbued with a lifelong love of Britain which, no doubt, will carry him laughing all the way to the nearest gulag.

Herbert Wilcox's *I Live in Grosvenor Square* (1945) achieved for the upper classes what *Demi-Paradise* achieved for shipbuilders. American sergeant Dean Jagger finds himself over here and out of his depth when he falls for shapely WAAF Anna Neagle, who just happens to be a duke's granddaughter. As she is also being chased by Major Rex Harrison the entire 'special relationship' is under threat. Jagger goes off and conveniently gets himself killed but not before sampling the delights of aristocratic life.

Dottiness about animals has always been considered an endearing British trait – in *Demi-Paradise* the BBC come down to Barchester during an air raid to record the nightingales in Runelow's garden. In Bernard Miles' *Tawny Pipit* (1944) a pair of rare South African migrant birds nest in an English field and the preservation of their eggs becomes an overriding national obsession. Ploughing

schedules are disrupted; army manoeuvres are diverted; the nation heaves a collective sigh of relief when the eggs are finally hatched out. The film remains a pleasant conceit but is shot through with smugness and a cliché-ridden view of country life – thatched cottages lovingly caught in sepia, winding lanes, placid streams and, as C.L. Lejeune suggested, 'the slim, selected figure of a land girl, leading a gee-gee, with the future mirrored in her brave, steady eyes'.

A land girl of less heroic stature was played by Sheila Sim in Michael Powell's *A Canterbury Tale* (1944). She falls victim to the bizarre activities of the local JP (Eric Portman) whose mystical infatuation with his native Kent leads him to pour glue on the heads of the local beauties in the blackout when they display distressing signs of interest

Our gallant allies. Sergeant John Patterson of the USAAF (Dean Jagger) takes tea with the Duke of Exmoor (Robert Morley) in Herbert Wilcox's *I Live in Grosvenor Square* (1945).

41

A Russian sniper (Lucy Mannheim) addresses the villagers in Bernard Miles' *Tawny Pipit* (1944). Miles is lurking under several inches of moustache and make-up as the crusty Colonel Barton-Barrington.

Ealing's *Johnny Frenchman* (1945), directed by Charles Frend. Françoise Rosay provides some refreshment for exhausted Tommies as the German blitzkrieg sweeps through France in June 1940. Alfie Bass is sitting next to her.

in the local soldiery. The activities of the 'glueman' provided the unpromising foundation for a modern pilgrimage to Canterbury which also included a young American soldier (John Sweet), and a cynical British private (Dennis Price) who rediscovers his gifts as a musician in the organ loft of the cathedral.

Gainsborough's War Effort

The mid-war years of 1942 and 1943 saw public interest in war subjects rise to a peak and then fall away. Ironically, by the time the British had real victories to celebrate, the popularity of war films had diminished. In January 1944, a Bristol woman wrote to her local newspaper, 'I've just seen the Bette Davis film *Now Voyager* and what enjoyment and what relief – no war'.

This mood was tapped with enormous success by Gainsborough studios in Leslie Arliss' *The Man in Grey* (1943), an outrageous costume melodrama starring Margaret Lockwood, Phyllis Calvert, James Mason and Stewart Granger. The film provided the studio with a formula which it busily reworked until the late 40s, employing an unchanging battery of stars and melodramatic plotlines whose familiarity bred contempt among the critics but exerted a strong and abiding appeal to their predominantly female audiences.

At the beginning of *The Man in Grey* the contents of Lot 227 at the wartime auction of the Rohan estate provide the clues to a tale of seduction, betrayal and murder set in Regency England. The snarling, brutal Marquis of Rohan (James Mason) is married to sweethearted, passive Clarissa (Phyllis Calvert) but lusts after his wife's old schoolfriend Hester (Margaret Lockwood), now her companion. Hester is a woman in whom Rohan recognizes a spirit as ruthless as his own. Clarissa falls for Rokeby (Stewart Granger), a dispossessed plantation owner, who has been installed by the scheming Hester as the family librarian in an attempt to destroy the marriage and claim Rohan for herself. But the low-born Hester has failed to think through the subtle ramifications of the class system. She poisons Clarissa as she lies ill with a fever, but her crime is observed by Clarissa's little black servant, Toby, who informs Rohan. Curling his lip in a savage sneer the enraged aristocrat asserts the family motto – 'Who Dishonours Us Dies' – by horsewhipping Hester to death.

Gainsborough glamour. End of the line for Margaret Lockwood's scheming Hester as James Mason's vengeful Rohan works himself up into a frenzy before whipping her to death in Leslie Arliss's *The Man in Grey* (1943). This robust costumer was the first in a cycle of melodramas which carried Gainsborough profitably through the late war years and into the austerity which came with peace.

The film's Regency background licensed Arliss and screenwriter Margaret Kennedy to release a torrent of powerful sexuality – both male and female – which would have been impossible in a contemporary setting. The aristocratic Clarissa is almost masochistically passive; the rootless Hester is ambitious and sexually active. Rohan's 'cruel good looks' are emphasised by a powerful brand of misogyny. We first see him at a ball, fresh from spitting young Lord Coxley in a duel of honour. When his mother tells him that she has 'half the young women in London' waiting for him, he hisses, 'They'll keep'. Marriage for the upper classes is shown to be a pretty cynical affair. On her wedding night, Clarissa enquires of the maid, 'Marriage is an agreeable state, is it not?' while downstairs her husband busies himself with more important affairs – his fighting bull terriers. Later he expresses no objection to their living separate lives – when he discovers his wife's affair with Rokeby his rage is prompted solely by the fact that her lover is a lackey.

In Anthony Asquith's *Fanny by Gaslight* (1944) we are taken on another journey into this nineteenth-century mirror world. Fanny Hopwood (Phyllis Calvert) is the illegitimate daughter of Cabinet Minister Clive Seymour (Stuart Lindsell) and is fostered by the owner of a high-class brothel (John Laurie). Hopwood is pushed under a cab by the drunken Lord Manderstoke (James Mason) and Fanny is taken in as a maid by her real father. The emotional convolutions involved in this arrangement – and the fact that his bitchy wife (Margaretta Scott) is having an affair with the licentious Manderstoke – drive the poor man to suicide. Fanny spends an idyllic

period living in the Jolly Bargee, a pub run by an old family friend (Wilfrid Lawson), where she is courted by Seymour's former private secretary, Harry Somerford (Stewart Granger). When she is warned off by Granger's embittered, snobbish sister she does the decent thing and goes off to work in a laundry, and with a childhood friend (Jean Kent) takes her place in 'the pen' at Evans' club, a kind of paddock from which members of the quality select the woman of their choice. Here she is saved from the reptilian embrace of the ubiquitous Manderstoke by the passing Somerford who lays him out with a neat left hook. Reunited, the couple run off to Paris for a final showdown with Manderstoke. In a duel, Manderstoke is killed and Somerford gravely wounded. Battling against the ministrations of French doctors

Anthony Asquith's *Fanny by Gaslight* (1944). Phyllis Calvert's Fanny Hopwood, toasted among rich Victorian clutter, is still blithely unaware that her father (John Laurie) keeps a high-class brothel in the basement. Her mother (Nora Swinburne) is on the left; Wilfrid Lawson's memorable Chunks grins away behind her while threatening to burst out of his loud tweed suit. The film's superb art direction was by John Bryan, achieved as always at Gainsborough on a tight budget subject to all the wartime restrictions and the cramped conditions of the Shepherd's Bush studio.

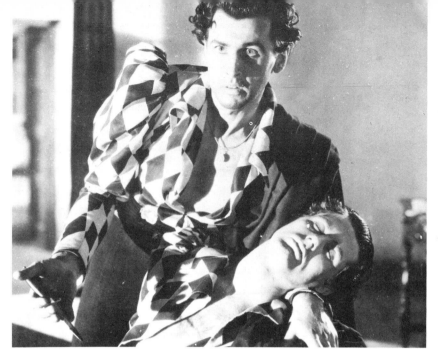

Wild-eyed Florentine cut-throat Stewart Granger discovers his younger brother, Peter Glenville, stabbed to death by Phyllis Calvert's schizophrenic *Madonna of the Seven Moons* (1944), a glorious piece of melodramatic tushery directed by former cameraman Arthur Crabtree. The stylized, picturesque sets were designed by Andrew Mazzei.

and Somerford's venomous sister, Fanny rallies Harry with promises of a married life together.

Fanny by Gaslight is a fluidly handled film, which despite its overheated storyline is executed with Asquith's customary cool sense of style. In contrast, former cameraman Arthur Crabtree's *Madonna of the Seven Moons* (1944) plunged boldly into a world of unrestrained melodrama. Although it has a twentieth-century setting, its picaresque background effectively turns it into a costume hybrid. Adapted from a novel by Margery Lawrence, it gave Phyllis Calvert the opportunity to combine the active/passive female roles of *The Man in Grey* in one person. She played a schizophrenic who divides her time between being a banker's dutiful wife and the tempestuous gypsy moll of Florentine cut-throat

Stewart Granger. This impossible duality is resolved when she sacrifices her life to save her daughter (Patricia Roc) from being raped by Granger's degenerate playboy brother (Peter Glenville). Her body is laid out bearing the twin symbols of her divided self – the crucifix which represents her repressed bourgeois life and the wild rose of her gypsy existence.

The Gainsborough films had much in common – unbelievable plots full of amazing coincidences, swaggering villains, generous amounts of cleavage, and Stewart Granger. He made his first bit impression in *The Man in Grey* and C.L. Lejeune caught his style perfectly in a review in the *Observer*: 'This is his first film of any size. His screen technique is entirely undisciplined. He throws away, with prodigal nonchalance, the sort of moments veterans have taken years to achieve. As a star performer, he is still quite brilliantly bad.' He remained so. It mattered not whether Granger was a gypsy bandit, a Waterloo Road spiv or the violin virtuoso Paganini. The same ready grin, strangled devil-may-care laugh and flexed shoulders were trundled out for each performance. With every new film, 'real acting' was earnestly promised by the studio, but of 'acting' came there none. Instead Stewart Granger remained serenely centre-screen while waves of passion from Margaret Lockwood, Patricia Roc and Anne Crawford crashed all around him, as immobile as the Eddystone lighthouse, his flashing teeth and rather close-set eyes providing beacons of a 40s glamour which have long since grown dim.

In *Love Story* (1944), one of the most

Margaret Lockwood and Stewart Granger in Leslie Arliss's cleverly crafted piece of Gainsborough fluff, *Love Story* (1944). Concert pianist Lockwood has just taken three minutes to compose a 'Warsaw Concerto' sound-alike, the 'Cornish Rhapsody'.

popular films of the period, Granger and Margaret Lockwood play a contemporary wartime couple. He is an RAF pilot and former mining engineer who is going blind after being shot up by the Hun; she is a brilliant concert pianist who is dying of a heart disease. They meet in a Cornish hotel and fall in love. But although they spend a great deal of time together riding around in donkey carts and clambering over studio cliffs, they do not reveal to each other their Awful Secrets. In a short break between donkey cart rides Lockwood dashes off the 'Cornish Rhapsody' on the hotel piano and when Granger makes mild noises of approval, tells him, 'It's funny in an engineer, this feeling for beauty.' There is a spot of feminine rivalry in the form of Granger's childhood sweetheart, Patricia Roc, who wears dungarees, directs outdoor theatre plays and gives one of the most sustained displays of chain-smoking seen before the arrival on our cinema screens of Jean-Paul Belmondo. However, everything is sorted out by kindly Northern businessman, Tom Walls, who has been quietly stealing most of the scenes in the film. Granger saves a team of engineers when a cave-in traps them in the local tin mine, gets his eyes fixed and dashes off to London, where he is on hand to catch Lockwood in his arms as she collapses after pounding out the 'Cornish Rhapsody' at her farewell concert in the Albert Hall. They decide to grasp the happiness of the moment and get married. Cut to a final shot of Lockwood standing alone on a Cornish clifftop waving goodbye to a squadron of bombers and looking, if anything, rather fitter than Stewart Granger.

In another Gainsborough melodrama of 1944, *They Were Sisters*, James Mason exchanged Regency ruffles for a double-breasted business suit. He played a sadistic domestic tyrant who drives his wife (Dulcie Gray) first to drink and then to suicide. Such behaviour may seem excusable if you are the Marquis of Rohan but is less acceptable if you are the director of a firm of insurance brokers. He is given his comeuppance at his wife's inquest by his sister-in-law, Phyllis Calvert.

The response of the critics to these costume melodramas and 'women's pictures' was, in the main, hostile. Asquith's *Fanny by Gaslight* received predictably respectful treatment but *Madonna of the Seven Moons* was given a terrible mauling. The *New Statesman* was of the opinion that 'with *Madonna of the Seven Moons* we slip back almost as far as it is possible to slip'. Generally, the critics were unable to take these films on their own terms,

understandable perhaps at a time when there was so much emphasis placed on 'quality', national prestige and documentary realism. Nevertheless, in their own hyperbolic fashion the Gainsborough films dealt with the questions of female roles and sexuality which many other more 'serious' features shied away from confronting. It was all too easy to see them as exotic, escapist pabulum for the dungaree-clad 'mobile women' exhausted by their shifts on factory production lines. In fact the war and its attendant social upheavals gave many women a taste of a sexual freedom which they had not experienced before. They could see some of this reflected in the broad brush strokes of the Gainsborough output.

Social Realism

Gainsborough's head, Maurice Ostrer, was the keenest supporter of the cycle of costume melodramas. He had been less enthusiastic about Launder and Gilliat's populist *Millions Like Us* and he put every available obstacle in the way of Sidney Gilliat's next project, *Waterloo Road* (1944). Disagreements over the film eventually led to the resignation of its producer, the blunt Yorkshireman Edward Black, who had been responsible for many of Gainsborough's biggest successes.

With *Waterloo Road* we return to the late war period of social realism, concentrating on the lives of a number of working-class Londoners with the war pushed into the background. Private Jim Colter (John Mills) goes AWOL when he learns that his young wife Tillie (Joy Shelton) has taken up with local amusement arcade spiv and black marketeer Ted Purvis (Stewart Granger). He spends a

John Mills beats the living daylights out of amusement arcade spiv Stewart Granger while the Blitz rages overhead in *Waterloo Road* (1944), written and directed by Sidney Gilliat. Of Granger's performance, Gilliat remarked, 'at least (his) phoneyness as an actor in the film suited the intentional phoneyness of the character'.

Two allegorical films from Ealing – both adapted from West End plays – which attempted to set out the hopes and fears of the British people about the post-war world. Mervyn Johns and Glynis Johns as the ghostly landlord and his daughter in Basil Dearden's *Halfway House* (1944), from Dennis Ogden's play *The Peaceful Inn*.

Mabel Terry Lewis as Lady Loxfield and Frances Rowe as her daughter in Dearden's lumbering version of J.B. Priestley's *They Came to a City* (1944). Nine civilians, a cross-section of British society, are magically transported to a dream city, a kind of Utopia, and are presented with the choice of embracing or rejecting its welfare state values. Both films were invincibly stagey, and despite their topicality were commercial failures.

frantic day dodging the military police and tracking down Purvis and his wife in the pubs and dance halls of the Waterloo Road. He finds them in a flat above Purvis' amusement arcade just as a big air raid is beginning. After a prolonged and realistic fight he reclaims his wife, who has already realized what a ridiculous phoney Ted Purvis really is.

Waterloo Road provides a cautious kind of realism. It is studio-bound, melodramatic at times and hampered by John Mills' laboured efforts to portray a working-class type (he was always better at officers). It is, however, crammed with moments of telling social observation. Hot on Purvis' trail, Colter pumps hairdresser Jean Kent for his whereabouts. 'I'd like to help you,' she tells him, 'but I've got to get down the tube shelter, or

someone will take my place.' Then she relents and suggests where Purvis might be found, summing him up in a single sentence: 'He might be at the pictures picking up a few hints from Victor Mature, or he might be at the Alcazar jitterbugging – that about sums up his war effort.'

The only substantial middle-class figure in the film is Alastair Sim's 'penny doctor', wandering the markets of Waterloo Road, dispensing friendly advice and orchestrating events like an eccentric *deus ex machina*. It is not too difficult to see him as a portent of the Labour government of 1945 – austere in the fashion of Stafford Cripps but caring none the less, not without humour and knowing in paternalistic fashion what's best for the workers.

The underlying rhythms of the war, and the way in which they interpenetrated people's lives, were treated in more romantic style in Anthony Asquith's *The Way to the Stars* (1945). The war has already passed on as the film opens, with the camera taking a nostalgic tour of a deserted airfield, ranging through empty rooms, picking up a notice, a torn photograph, a telephone number scribbled on a wall, a signature scrawled across a misthrow at darts. Each detail anticipates a moment in the unfolding story of a bomber base which is occupied first by the RAF and then by the US 8th Air Corps. It is 1940 and Peter (John Mills), a young pilot who has just finished training, arrives at an RAF bomber base in the Midlands, where he shares a room with David (Michael Redgrave). David marries Toddy (Rosamund John), the manageress of a local hotel, the Golden Lion, but is killed in action when their son, Johnny,

Michael Redgrave, Basil Radford and David Tomlinson in Asquith's *The Way to the Stars* (1945), a mature masterpiece which caught perfectly the atmosphere and underlying rhythms of war as they affected the airmen on a Midlands bomber base and the local people who enter their lives.

John Laurie, Roger Livesey and Wendy Hiller in Powell and Pressburger's idiosyncratic response to the beckoning post-war world, an exploration of Celtic mysticism and High Tory anti-materialism in *I Know Where I'm Going* (1945).

is only five months old. When Peter goes through David's effects he finds a poem, 'For Johnny', (written for the film by John Pudney) and his reading of it remains one of the most touching moments in wartime cinema. After David's death, Peter decides against marrying his intended bride Iris (Renee Asherson). The RAF move on and the Americans move in. Toddy is courted by, and gently resists, a married pilot, Johnny (Douglass Montgomery). Iris steps out with the rumbustious Joe (Bonar Colleano) but when she meets Peter again they make up their minds to marry. Johnny sacrifices his life making a crash landing on the airfield.

Richard Winnington aptly described *The Way to the Stars* as 'a war film without slogans and brilliant heroics'. It distilled the British experience of five years of war, their own brand of emotional restraint, the differences they have with their American allies and the things they have in common. The two central characters – David and Johnny – never meet but both love the same woman. The strategic bombing grinds on, off-screen – a counterpoint to the exploration of the lives of individuals on the ground who must learn to live with the demands of war.

The Comedy War

Wartime comedy films provided a welcome boost to morale and also a direct link with the traditions established in the 1930s by George Formby, Will Hay and Gracie Fields. Fields left Britain at the beginning of the war, with her Italian-born husband Monty Banks, when the internment of aliens was announced. Her

Old Mother Riley Joins Up (1939), gets tied up and has to get the wind up to avoid Nazi agent Garry Marsh's intended fry-up. Arthur Lucan's fellow-prisoners are stage daughter (and real-life wife) Kitty McShane and a young Bruce Seton. In their music-hall act Lucan's jabbering old washerwoman dominated McShane, but in their married life the roles were reversed with a vengeance.

George Formby and Phyllis Calvert don angelic wings in a dream sequence from *Let George Do It* (1940), directed by Marcel Varnel. The sequence reaches a satisfying climax in which George shoots off German agent Garry Marsh's trousers to reveal a sagging pair of underpants stitched with swastikas.

last film in Britain was *Shipyard Sally* (1939), whose theme song, 'Wish Me Luck As You Wave Me Goodbye', was taken up by the troops of the British Expeditionary Force on their way to France.

The first comedy feature of the war was *Old Mother Riley Joins Up* (1939), starring Arthur Lucan and Kitty McShane. Lucan's demented Irish washerwoman, a non-stop whirlwind of grimaces and flailing arms, rampaged through a string of knockabout wartime quickies, including *Old Mother Riley in Business* (1940), *Old Mother Riley Detective* (1943) and *Old Mother Riley Overseas* (1944). In her first venture, as a distinctly unlikely district nurse, she rounds up a gang of Nazi spies with the help of the local fire brigade and a troop of Boy Scouts. Handsome Lieutenant Bruce Seton was on hand to provide the romantic interest for daughter Kitty.

Fifth columnists, mistaken identities and mysterious European *femmes fatales* rapidly became the staples of wartime comedy. In his first Ealing film of the war, *Let George Do It* (1940) directed by Marcel Varnel, George Formby was a member of a concert party, the Dinkie Doos, who stumbles aboard a ship bound for Bergen and tumbles into a spy intrigue. Arriving in Norway (the film was made before the German invasion), he is mistaken for a British agent sent by intelligence to infiltrate a big band led by Nazi spy Mark Mendez (Garry Marsh). 'I'm not intelligent, I'm a Dinkie Doo', he protests to bewildered British agent Phyllis Calvert. In the usual Formby style, there are regular pauses for ukelele-bashing and bouts of slapstick humour. A chase for a vital roll of film ends in a bakery with Formby thrashing around in vats of dough, sliding along conveyor belts and disappearing in snowstorms of flour. The spy ring stands no chance against Formby's ferocious band of gormlessness; trapped on board a U-boat, George escapes by being fired from one of the torpedo tubes into the waiting arms of Phyllis Calvert aboard a handy British warship.

In *Spare a Copper* (1940), directed by John Paddy Carstairs, Formby came closer to home, playing a special constable on Merseyside whose persistence unmasks a band of saboteurs led by a blustering theatre owner and a shipyard executive. The notion that apparent pillars of the community could be revealed as traitors was to be taken up subsequently in three of the best Ealing films of the war – *The Foreman Went to France*, *Went the Day Well?* and *Next of Kin*.

Marcel Varnel, a polished director of comedy, handled the first Will Hay film for Ealing, *The Ghost of St Michael's* (1941). Hay lost Moore Marriott and Graham Moffatt when he left Gainsborough, but he gained a superb foil at Ealing in Claude Hulbert, prince of 'silly asses', and continued an association with Charles Hawtrey as a hideous know-all schoolboy which had begun in the 1939 film *Where's That Fire?* For *The Ghost of St Michael's*, Hay brought his invincibly shabby and ignorant schoolmaster out of retirement to teach for victory in an isolated Scottish castle which houses an evacuated school. It also conceals a gang of German spies who are signalling to U-boats on the supposedly 'phantom bagpipes' which the crazed porter John Laurie insists are part of an ancient curse. The film contains some vintage Hay routines. His attempts to teach the law of gravity to a sceptical class leave him stranded on the top of a swaying mountain of chairs which are supposed to represent the Leaning Tower of Pisa. Hay's capacity for brilliantly muddled logic is displayed in an inquest scene held in a farmyard barn, in which he takes the stand with a pig under his arm and blithely sets about incriminating himself while under the impression that he is demonstrating his skill as a sleuth.

Mistaken identity provided the plot-line for Hay's next film, *The Black Sheep of Whitehall* (1941). Once again he was a down-at-heel, bogus academic, this time running a correspondence college with only one pupil, a miscast John Mills. He is mistaken for a distinguished economist by fifth columnists Basil Sydney and Felix Aylmer, who kidnap him as part of a plan to sabotage Anglo-South American trade. Confusion runs riot when Hay is interviewed by the BBC's Leslie Mitchell and embarks on a bluffer's guide to international trade which, it seems, is based on nuts from Brazil and port from Portugal. *The Goose Steps Out* (1942), which Hay co-directed with Basil Dearden, continued in the same vein. This time a captured German spy turns out to be the double of Hay's seedy pedagogue, whereupon he is despatched by British Intelligence to Germany. Here he takes over his *Doppelgänger*'s role as a teacher in a school for spies, adolescent brownshirts learning British customs. In no time at all Hay has his pupils – who include Peter Ustinov, Barry Morse and Charles Hawtrey – producing a rude version of Churchill's V-for-Victory in front of a portrait of the Führer.

Other unorthodox spycatchers included

Will Hay's shabby pedagogue William Potts – masquerading as the German spymaster Professor Muller – in *The Goose Steps Out* (1942), directed by Basil Dearden. Peter Ustinov is the bespectacled adolescent stormtrooper on the extreme left. Seated in the centre are, left to right, Barry Morse, Charles Hawtrey and Peter Croft.

Left
Richard 'Stinker' Murdoch and Arthur Askey get the jitters in *The Ghost Train* (1941), an updated version of Arnold Ridley's minor comedy classic directed by the reliable Walter Forde, who also directed the 1931 version starring Jack Hulbert.

Arthur Askey and Richard 'Stinker' Murdoch. They starred in a revamped version of Arnold Ridley's *The Ghost Train* (1942) in which the smugglers of the original became German spies. In *Back Room Boy* (1942) big-hearted Arthur had his work cut out guarding the BBC's 'six pips' time signal and hunting down a spy ring in an isolated lighthouse. Robertson Hare and Alfred Drayton lost their uniforms on Home Guard manoeuvres in Laurence Huntington's *Women Aren't Angels* (1942). Undeterred, they borrow their wives' ATS outfits and sally forth to round up the local fifth column. In *Crooks' Tour* (1940) Basil Radford and Naunton Wayne (alias Charters and Caldicott) find themselves stranded in the middle of an Arabian desert on an ill-advised holiday with Spindles Tours. Over the sandy wastes rides the local sheikh

Charters and Caldicott, alias Basil Radford and Naunton Wayne, find themselves the prisoners of Nazi super-agent K-7 (Cyril Gardiner), and are summoned to dinner by his butler in John Baxter's *Crooks' Tour* (1940). The script was lifted without acknowledgement from the Launder and Gilliat radio series featuring the cricket-mad diehards.

Centre
My Learned Friend (1943), directed by Basil Dearden. Beefeaters Claude Hulbert and Will Hay are trapped behind the clock face of Big Ben by cheerful psychopath Mervyn Johns, whose time-bomb is primed to blow up the Houses of Parliament when the nation's timepiece strikes the hour.

Below
The Crazy Gang made only one wartime film together, *Gasbags* (1940), directed by Marcel Varnel. Having secured their barrage balloon to a handy fish and chip stall, they are blown by a gale to the Western Front where they are captured and briefly imprisoned in a concentration camp (sic). They make their way home in the secret weapon of Moore Marriott's crazed inventor, an underground submarine. From left to right, Teddy Knox, Bud Flanagan, Jimmy Nervo, Jimmy Gold, Chesney Allen and Charlie Naughton.

who immediately recognizes Charters' old school tie and declares himself to be an old Marlburian, too. They are invited back to his encampment ('But we haven't got dinner jackets,' protests Charters) where the sheikh's musicians provide a rousing version of the old school song as his guests toy with the sheeps' eyes. Hurrying back to the final Test, our intrepid pair blunder into a Baghdad cabaret where they are mistaken for German agents and are handed a gramophone record which, unknown to them, contains vital information about sabotage plans on the Gulf oil supplies. They escape elaborate assassination attempts in Istanbul and Budapest, where they finally run into a far greater peril than the German secret service – Charters' sister Edith (Noel Hood), who also happens to be Caldicott's fiancée. Surprising Caldicott in his hotel room with a shapely double agent, night club singer La Palermo (Greta Gynt), she hisses, 'I always suspected there was a shoddy streak in your character.' With Edith on her way back to London, Charters and Caldicott make the ultimate sacrifice: they will stay in Budapest and get to the bottom of the mystery, *even if it means missing the final Test*. Greta Gynt instructs them to hand over the record to a man they believe to be a British agent – no less a figure than E.J.K. Spanswick, the former Gloucestershire all-rounder. In fact he is K-7, head of the German spy ring, who imprisons them in his remote Hungarian Schloss. Being an officer and a gentleman, K-7 waits until the port has gone round after dinner before telling Charters and Caldicott that they will be shot at dawn. Freed by Greta Gynt, they head for England – and the Test Match – in K-7's limousine.

Some of the best comedies of the period eschewed a wartime setting. Will Hay's last, and best, film for Ealing was *My Learned Friend* (1943). Playing Britain's seediest solicitor, he forms an unlikely partnership with her most incompetent barrister, Claude Hulbert. Before they can subvert the entire legal system, their lives are threatened by one of Hay's former clients, a splendidly deranged Mervyn Johns, who is busily murdering his way through all those responsible for sending him down. Hay is the last on the list, and the unavailing chase to warn each of the victims leads to a succession of splendid set pieces – a Limehouse dive, a lunatic asylum and a provincial theatre. The humour has a very black edge to it; in the asylum the hapless superintendent is accidentally impaled in a gruesome trap devised by one of the inmates out to catch an imaginary tiger. 'This place is becoming like a madhouse', sighs inmate Ernest Thesiger as Hay and Hulbert make good their escape. In a Limehouse back room 'Safety' Wilson (so named because of his fondness for impromptu plastic surgery with the aid of a razor) is disposed of with his own weapon – a knobkerry with a razor attachment. *My Learned Friend* provides a number of hints of Ealing films to come and underlines the increasingly organic nature of its output, the result of the tightly-knit team assembled by Michael Balcon. Mervyn Johns' murderous progress prefigures Dennis Price's short cut to the peerage in Robert Hamer's *Kind Hearts and Coronets* (1949), and Ealing scriptwriter John Dighton had a hand in both films. The climax of *My Learned Friend* takes place on the face of Big Ben with Johns, Hay and Hulbert alternately yawing

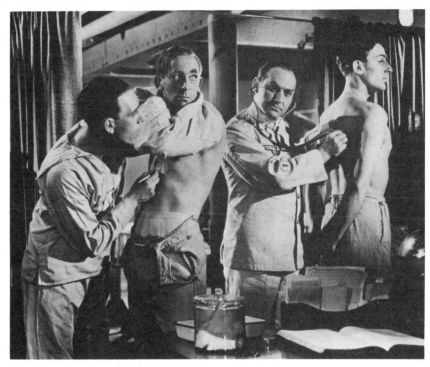

Above
Tommy Trinder made a number of popular wartime comedies at Ealing. In Walter Forde's *Sailors Three* (1940) he played a British matelot who, along with shipmates Claude Hulbert and Michael Wilding, is stranded in a fog-bound South American port and mistakenly boards the German pocket battleship *Ludenlord*.

Below
Alberto Cavalcanti's *Champagne Charlie* (1944) was a comedy-drama set in the world of the Victorian music hall with Trinder playing the entertainer George Laybourne, and Stanley Holloway as his rival, The Great Vance. The chorus girl in the centre is Jean Kent, soon to become a Gainsborough star.

Robbie Vincent's Enoch provided the gormless foil to Harry Korris's down-at-heel impresario in *Happidrome* (1943), the film version of the popular radio series directed by Phil Brandon. Cecil Frederick's wide boy Ramsbottom completed *Happidrome*'s comic trio.

Below
In his element at the camp concert: slack-jawed comic Frank Randle stole the show in the 1940 film *Somewhere in England*, a knockabout army comedy whose slapstick formula Randle repeated in a series of low-budget farces, including *Somewhere in Camp* (1942) and *Somewhere in Civvies* (1943). Randle was still stumbling through the same 'awkward squad' routines in the early 50s in *It's A Grand Life* (1953), which looked as if it was made for about 1/9d, although it did boast the busty charms of the young Diana Dors.

Tommy Handley as the Mayor of Foaming-at-the-Mouth is propositioned by the ubiquitous Ali Oop (Horace Percival) in *It's That Man Again* (1943).

wildly out into space clutching the giant hour-hand – rather like Herbert Lom's exit from *The Ladykillers* (1955), as he clings to an iron railway ladder on his backwards plunge into a goods wagon.

In Marcel Varnel's *Turned Out Nice Again* (1941), George Formby works for an old-fashioned women's underwear manufacturer whose 'reinforced' woolly combinations are threatened by a rival company's exotic Los Angeles all-elastic playsuits. He is hood-winked into buying the rights to an apparently worthless reel of experimental yarn which in fact turns out to be a revolutionary new material. There is more than a passing similarity here to Alexander Mackendrick's *The Man in the White Suit* (1951) – a frantic battle of wits between the two rival companies over the rights to Formby's new wonder cloth is almost exactly paralleled in the later film.

Radio Fun

Throughout the 1940s radio enjoyed a golden age that was to be brought abruptly to an end in the next decade by television. The immensely popular 'Band Wagon', starring Arthur Askey and Richard Murdoch was transferred to the screen by Gainsborough in 1940. Another popular show of the time, though virtually forgotten now, was 'Happi-drome', with Harry Korris, Robby Vincent and Cecil Frederick. The 1943 film version cast Korris as J. Sheridan Lovejoy, a penniless but grandiloquent impresario auditioning in

the provinces for 'a London season'. In Archie Rice style he raises money for his show by giving a local bigwig's daughter a part in his revue. *Happidrome* is a remarkable mixture of terrible one-liners, pratfalls and thunderous dance routines, with everyone hoofing away as if their lives depended on it. In his dressing room on the opening night Korris encapsulates the whole world of fifth rate provincial hams as he runs over the lines for his cod historical drama 'Nero': gazing blearily at the mirror, he observes, 'Voice a bit bloodshot tonight, old boy'. The efforts of his overenthusiastic troupe quite literally bring the house down, but in the manner of Peter O'Toole's infamous *Macbeth*, the show becomes a huge hit in London – it's so bad, it's good. *Happidrome*'s extended finale closes with a string of 40s favourites, including singer/pianist Hutch warbling 'You Are My Love Song' in front of an extraordinary surrealist backcloth, a desert landscape populated with dead cellos.

The surreal humour of the most popular wartime comedy show, 'It's That Man Again', starring Tommy Handley, failed to survive its transfer to the screen in 1943. Seeing so many of its famous characters in the flesh was inevitably disappointing, although Handley was superb as the crooked, fast-talking Mayor of Foaming-at-the-Mouth, sinking the entire council budget in a bombed London theatre. It's hard to resist a comic who can effortlessly get away with such awful one-liners as 'I kissed my mother-in-law on the mouth, with a lighted cigar.'

Rex Harrison and Constance Cummings tangle with the ghost of Harrison's first wife, Kay Hammond, in David Lean's smooth adaptation of Noel Coward's elegant supernatural divertissement *Blithe Spirit* (1945), brilliantly photographed in Technicolor by Ronald Neame. This was the first Rank film to be shown at the huge Winter Gardens Theatre in New York.

Joseph Arthur Rank had a very good war. By 1945 he had become the most powerful figure in the British film industry, and in the opinion of many, not least his own, the arbiter of its future. Yet the Yorkshire tycoon remained an enigmatic figure. As one observer remarked in 1946: 'The state of the [film] industry is at the moment largely dependent on the state of J. Arthur Rank, and the state of J. Arthur Rank is more or less anyone's guess.'

The heir to a flour-milling fortune, Rank went into films in the early 1930s as a result of his strong Methodist convictions. He recalled

with characteristic bluntness: 'I was warned that I would meet people who would try to pull me down to their level. I rejected this advice, as I felt called to this work.' This brand of missionary zeal, combined with considerable shrewdness, was characteristic of Rank and led one of his early partners, Lady Yule, the eccentric jute millionairess, to remark that he was a believer in 'Christianity with five per cent'.

Rank's brief association with Lady Yule at British National produced his first major feature film, *The Turn of the Tide* (1936), starring Wilfrid Lawson, Moore Marriott

and Geraldine Fitzgerald. It taught Rank the basic principle of the film industry, that no matter how good your product is, it is of no value without a guarantee of widespread distribution. *The Turn of the Tide* was well received at the Venice Film Festival but failed to get a circuit release and did not recoup its costs. Having absorbed the lesson, Rank set about creating an empire. An important move was his decision in 1935 to back C.M. Woolf, who had resigned from Gaumont–British to set up General Film Distributors. It was General Film Distributors which acquired for Rank a 25 per cent stake in Universal, a reversal of the one-way process of American production companies buying substantial interests in the British film industry.

While Rank set about expanding, most of his competitors, hit by the economic slump of the mid-1930s, were contracting. Rank was thus able to become a powerful figure by absorbing other people's white elephants. In 1936 he took over the Gaumont–British film-making interests (including Gainsborough Films) transferring them to the newly built studios at Pinewood. By 1938 Alexander Korda's fortunes had foundered on the rocks of his own extravagance and Rank and the Prudential Insurance Company moved in to assume a controlling interest in Denham studios. A new company, D & P Studios, was formed to run them both, with the Prudential as a major backer. In 1939 Rank acquired a third studio, outbidding John Maxwell of the Associated British Picture Corporation (ABPC) for the Anglo Amalgamated set-up at Elstree. At the same time Rank acquired a major share in Oscar Deutsch's Odeon cinema chain.

Rank's rapid acquistion of studio space might have proved an embarrassment but for the war. The studios at Pinewood and Elstree were requisitioned by the government at a healthy return on capital. Rank's position was further strengthened in 1940 by the death of his chief rival John Maxwell and the departure to Hollywood of Alexander Korda, and in 1944 Rank bought out the Prudential interest in Denham. Cinemas were next on the shopping list. In 1941 Rank succeeded the ailing Oscar Deutsch as chairman of the Odeon circuit. Soon afterwards Deutsch died and Rank acquired Deutsch's interests and control of Odeon's 306 theatres. During this hectic period he also became chairman of Gaumont–British on the retirement of Isidore Ostrer. Having bought out the MGM interests in Gaumont–British and brought in

Twentieth Century-Fox's chairman, Spyros Skouras, as a board member, Rank could count 619 cinemas in his exhibition empire (ABPC had 442), accounting for more than one-third of the total seating in the country and most of the prime sites. The Board of Trade stepped in at this point to prevent Rank from gobbling up any more of the film industry. Nevertheless, for an outlay of approximately £1,700,000 Rank had acquired assets which the wartime cinema boom revealed to be in the region of about £50,000,000. In addition, the battle lines of the post-war British cinema had been drawn up, marking a duopoly in which Rank, with his two independently run circuits, faced ABPC, a quarter of whose shares were owned by Warner Brothers.

The Palache Report

The Beveridge Report was just one, albeit the most important, of the proliferation of wartime reports which anticipated the end of the conflict and the Brave New Wold which lay beyond. In 1944 the Palache Report cast a critical eye over the British film industry. It had been set up at the urging of Michael Balcon and other members of the Film Council, who sought some measure of government control over the burgeoning Rank empire. The title of the report was 'Tendencies to Monopoly in the Cinematograph Film Industry', the biggest tendency being incarnated in the imposing form of J. Arthur Rank.

Four years of war had radically altered the government's attitude towards the cinema. Palache began with a resounding assertion: 'A cinematograph film represents something more than a mere commodity to be bartered against others. Already the screen has great influence, both politically and culturally, over the minds of the people. Its potentialities are vast as a vehicle for expression of national life, ideals and tradition, as a dramatic and artistic medium and as an instrument for propaganda.' The Palache Report reached the conclusion that the prospects for an 'independent and unfettered' film industry were threatened by the Rank/ABPC duopoly and also by the possibility that the heads of these organizations might ultimately be guided by American interests. In addition, it criticized the tendency of the big groups to tie up the available studio space with prestige blockbusters. Its members felt that independent film-makers were being squeezed out, and recommended a future programme which would incorporate a greater number of medium-length features, second features and documentaries to provide forcing grounds for new talent. Palache met the fate of so many subsequent reports: its findings were noted and, with a number of significant exceptions, politely ignored. Nevertheless, it correctly identified some of the important areas of weakness in the film industry which, superficially, had emerged from the war in a strong position. There was no embarrassed talk of 'quota quickies' in 1945, rather a feeling that with films like *In Which We Serve*, *The Way to the Stars* and *Henry V* (1945), British cinema had come of age. Audiences were at an all-time high, climbing in 1946 to 1,365 million admissions, despite the fact that at least 230 theatres remained closed because of bomb damage. Once again there was talk, not heard since the early 1930s, of taking on the Americans in their own market.

America, America

In the vanguard of this crusade was J. Arthur Rank. Like Korda before him, he was convinced that he could establish a foothold in the United States and make films that would rival Hollywood in finish and spectacle. To achieve his object he was prepared to spend a great deal of money, and most of his public statements of the period contain the words 'no matter what the cost'. This was music to the ears of big spenders like Gabriel Pascal whose adaptation of Shaw's *Caesar and Cleopatra* began shooting in June 1944. Eighteen months and £1,278,000 later the ponderous epic proved a disastrous artistic and financial flop both at home and in the United States. Its swashbuckling producer ended up in hospital with, appropriately, a camel bite sustained on location. *Caesar and Cleopatra* was too much even for Rank and he severed his connections with Pascal, in the process having to write off another £30,000 which had already been spent on Pascal's next Shaw project, *Saint Joan*. Del Giudice's budget on Laurence Olivier's *Henry V* ran to £475,000, although this turned out to be money well spent, and the film played to packed houses in the United States. An oddly jarring note was struck by our own *Daily Mirror* critic, who wrote: 'The highbrows and the longhairs, both sincere and phoney, are wild about the film. But we peasants are puzzled and disturbed.'

More disturbing was Rank's determination to take on the Americans at their own game, an endeavour which prompted some succinct advice from Nicholas Schenck, head of Loew's Inc. which controlled MGM – 'You're a flour miller, you haven't got a chance'. Undaunted, Rank brought over Hollywood veteran Wesley Ruggles to direct *London Town*, Britain's first Technicolor musical, starring comedian Sid Field. Ruggles had directed the amiable 1938 Bing Crosby vehicle *Sing You Sinners*, but his faltering touch was torpedoed by the traditional British inability to produce a home-grown musical with the vulgar self-confidence which animated even the most banal MGM or Fox entertainments of the period. Sid Field, Claude Hulbert, Sonnie Hale, the London Town Dozen and One Girls, Mr Ruggles and £800,000 sank without trace. In sharp contrast was Sydney Box's international success of 1946, *The Seventh Veil* – not a Rank film – which was made in six weeks at the Riverside Studios, Hammersmith, at a cost of only £67,000.

London Town represented only one element in Rank's ambitious post-war expansion programme. Abroad, he acquired cinema chains in Canada, Australia, New Zealand, South Africa and Italy. He bought the Winter Gardens in New York as a showcase for his new releases. At home he set about consolidating his vertically-integrated organisation on Hollywood lines, something of an irony at a time when the great American cinema empires were about to be broken up.

Expansion at Home

In an attempt to capture a share of the market dominated by *The March of Time*, Rank set up a regular new feature magazine, *This Modern Age*, providing his cinemas with a monthly 20-minute two-reeler. At a cost of £500,000, an animation division was established at Cookham under the control of David Hand, who had learned his craft with Disney. A children's film unit, headed by Mary Field, was given the job of providing the weekly Saturday programme with some of the moral uplift dear to Rank's heart. A bold experiment was initiated under the direction of production designer David Rawnsley. His Independent Frame system was devised to cut down on studio shooting time by making provision for detailed advanced planning, and the application of industrial methods to set design. This boiled down to a great deal of back projection, process work and pre-planned shooting. The concept was simple enough, but to put it into effect required the installation of much expensive and elaborate

Laurence Olivier's *Henry V* (1944), a commercial and critical success for Rank. The sweeping battle scenes at Agincourt, reminiscent of *Alexander Nevsky*, were filmed in Ireland. Among a distinguished cast, Robert Newton was outstanding as the blustering braggart Ancient Pistol. *Henry V* was photographed in Technicolor by Robert Krasker with music by William Walton.

The price of prestige: Stewart Granger as Apollodorus and Flora Robson as Ftatateetah in Gabriel Pascal's extravagant production of George Bernard Shaw's *Caesar and Cleopatra* (1945).

Olivier's *Hamlet* (1948) was a bravura but rather hollow technical display: Desmond Dickinson's camera roamed obsessively through Roger Furse's sets and the battlements of Elsinore castle, capturing the players in stunning deep focus. Jean Simmons was a touching Ophelia and Stanley Holloway a wry gravedigger. Sadly, the ghost of Hamlet's father, wreathed in mist, came over as a cross between Darth Vader and a big garden gnome. *Hamlet* won four of the 1948 Academy Awards.

equipment at Pinewood – ceiling tracks, hydraulic elevators and adjustable floor rostra. Inevitably, Independent Frame was not popular with directors, who liked to explore their options when they got on the set. As Frank Launder remarked, 'Independent Frame was an art director's dream and a director's nightmare.' The first Independent Frame film was *Warning to Wantons* (1949), directed by Donald Wilson, but the system was shortlived and was eventually abandoned at a cost of about £600,000. Although a failure in its time, it anticipated many of the methods which are now standard procedure in television studios.

One of the Palache recommendations of which Rank took heed resulted in the establishment of the Rank Company of Youth. Rapidly dubbed 'The Rank Charm School' by an unkind hack, the name still strikes a nostalgic echo today. The aim of the school was to groom young actors for stardom, in the time-honoured Hollywood fashion, by blooding them in B features made at Rank's small, two-stage Highbury Studios. In a converted church hall next to the studios young hopefuls such as Diana Dors, Pete Murray, Susan Shaw, Christopher Lee and Barbara Murray underwent an eccentric assault course in film acting conducted by a fearsome Gorgon named Molly Terraine. As we shall see, the Charm School was axed, along with much else, during the financial crisis which hit Rank in the late 1940s.

The Charm School may have provided the opportunity for many a jibe at Rank's expense, but his wide umbrella also sheltered some of the most prestigious teams in British cinema. Under the loose overall organisation of Independent Producers were grouped Cineguild (David Lean, Ronald Neame and Anthony Havelock-Allan), the Archers (Powell and Pressburger), Individual Pictures (Frank Launder and Sidney Gilliat) and Wessex (Ian Dalrymple). Also sucked into the Rank orbit was Ealing Studios. Michael Balcon had long been one of Rank's fiercest critics, but the need to secure reliable distribution for Ealing films led to a deal with Rank which guaranteed circuit release in return for a 50 per cent stake (later raised to 75 per cent) in Ealing. With a seat on the Rank board and the retention of complete artistic autonomy, Michael Balcon was quick to acknowledge that the agreement verged on the side of generosity towards Ealing.

Brief Encounter

Cineguild was perhaps the most 'finished' team in the Rank stable, and 1946 was topped and tailed by two David Lean films, *Brief Encounter* and *Great Expectations*. *Brief Encounter*, developed from a segment of the pre-war entertainment 'Tonight at 8.30', was Lean's last collaboration with Noel Coward and the first film in which his distinctive style emerged. It is strange to reflect that when *Brief Encounter* was released some critics drew comparisons with French cinema, so utterly English is its portrayal of a doomed love affair stifled by the conventions of its middle class setting.

Celia Johnson was Laura Jessop, a suburban housewife who comes into the provincial town of Milford once a week to change her library books and go to a cinema matinée. Trevor Howard played Alec Harvey, a doctor who comes in every week on the same day for surgery at the local hospital. He catches the 5.40 down, she catches the 5.43 up. A speck of grit in Laura's eye is the small incident which leads to the blossoming of a doomed love affair amid the Virol advertisements, rock-hard Banbury cakes and steamy fug of the station buffet.

Classically constructed, *Brief Encounter* begins with the couple's final moments together in the buffet. Before they can say their farewells, they are pounced upon by a gushing neighbour of Laura's. The story then unfolds in flashback, with Celia Johnson's voice over, as back at home she silently rehearses the confession that she knows she will never make to her dull husband (Cyril Raymond). The use of Rachmaninov's lush Second Piano Concerto and the painstakingly artificial world in which the story is played out provide effective counterpoints to Laura

A speck of dirt in the eye leads to a doomed romance in David Lean's *Brief Encounter* (1946). Celia Johnson's discomfort is observed by Stanley Holloway's porter and Joyce Carey's splendidly 'refained' old trollop, guardian of Milford Junction buffet's rock-hard Banbury cake mountain.

Jessop's agonized commentary as a trip to the pictures, a drive in the country and an outing on a boating lake propel her into an affair which can only be barren.

Brief Encounter's throttled emotions are forced through that very middle-class phenomenon, the interchange of constant apology. 'I'm so sorry for boring you with long medical words,' Alec tells Laura over lunch at the Kardomah. She replies, 'I'm so sorry for being so dull and stupid in not understanding them.' The reining-in of feelings ('I must control myself', 'We must be sensible') leads to a curious infantilism. Alec describes his liking for Bath Buns as 'one of my earliest passions – I've never outgrown it'. When he starts to talk about his special field, preventive medicine, Laura exclaims that his enthusiasm makes him seem like 'a little boy'. At the height of the affair, Laura travels back on the 5.43 to Ketchworth feeling like a 'romantic schoolgirl'. She pictures herself in a series of romantic clichés straight out of the B–features that she and Alec watch every Thursday afternoon, but the palm trees of her South Seas fantasy fade into the knobbly shapes of pollarded willows as the train chugs into Ketchworth station.

Finally, the full weight of suburban inanity is unleashed on the hapless couple as the prattling Dolly Messiter (Evelyn Gregg) descends on them: 'I've been shopping till I'm dropping,' she trills. Alec can only gently squeeze Laura's shoulder as he leaves her for a new start with his family in South Africa. A non-stop express is approaching Milford Junction. In a despairing gesture of suicide Laura rushes to the very edge of the platform as the train flashes past, her hair tangled sadly over her disappointed little face. Then a slow trudge back to Dolly Messiter and the dull certainties of her married life. 'I don't know where you've been, darling,' says husband Cyril Raymond as she emerges from her reverie, 'but thank you for coming back.' He never will know, poor fool.

What the Dickens?

This melancholy little suburban interlude was followed by Lean's masterly adaptation of *Great Expectations*, which remains one of the greatest of all British films, an object lesson in compression, definition and narrative drive. The landscape itself is integrated into the onward thrust of the story, as Young Pip wanders over the windswept Medway Saltings, past gibbets silhouetted against lowering skies, to his rendezvous with

Above
Great Expectations (1946), David Lean's masterpiece and the definitive film interpretation of Dickens. Martita Hunt was Miss Havisham and Anthony Wager, Young Pip.

Left
With eyes at full roll, Robert Newton's Bill Sykes joins Alec Guinness's Fagin at the window of the thieves' rookery in David Lean's *Oliver Twist* (1948).

Below
Derek Bond as the eponymous hero of Alberto Cavalcanti's disappointing *Nicholas Nickleby* (1947).

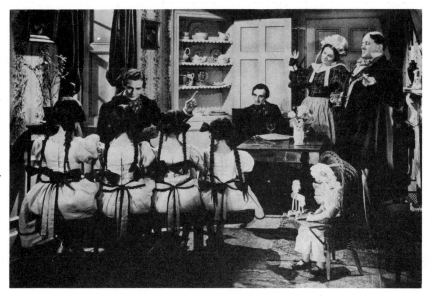

Magwitch. The casting of *Great Expectations* is well-nigh faultless. Finlay Currie as Magwitch, erupting from the marly graveyard like a force of Nature, and providing the audience with as big a shock as did Anthony Wager's Young Pip; Martita Hunt's Miss Havisham, brooding magisterially over the cobweb-clogged remains of her wedding feast in a set of baroque decay, created by John Bryan and eloquently shot by Lean in deep focus. John Mills was the grown-up Pip, moving from gaucherie to snobbery with the aid of the money supplied by his unknown benefactor. Alec Guinness's Herbert Pocket (his first screen appearance) was a whimsically charming companion. The film's only disappointment comes when Pip meets Estella on her return from Europe. The coquettish, sexy and cruel little girl, played with instinctive pertness by the young Jean Simmons, has grown up to become the glacial and stiff Valerie Hobson.

Lean followed *Great Expectations* with another Dickens film, *Oliver Twist* (1948). The assurance and sweep were there, but as Richard Winnington observed, there were already indications that Lean was becoming the prisoner of his own technical virtuosity. Moreover, while the characters in *Great Expectations* remained true to their originals, there was some unhappy tampering with Dickens in *Oliver Twist*. The savagery which courses through the novel has been muffled, particularly in Francis L. Sullivan's Bumble, who is transformed from a figure of loathing to a study bordering on the comic-pathetic (the process was completed by Harry Secombe in Carol Reed's 1968 *Oliver!*). Lurking under several inches of make-up is Alec Guinness, whose portrayal of Fagin aroused such fury among Jewish groups in the United States that *Oliver Twist* was not shown in America until January 1951, and then only in a heavily cut version.

The other major adaptation of Dickens in the 1940s came from Ealing. Alberto Cavalcanti's *Nicholas Nickleby* (1947) is a gallant failure overwhelmed by the novel's half a million words and endless gallery of grotesques, and undermined by a notably wet performance by Derek Bond in the title role. The pruning was savage: we are offered only a fleeting glimpse of the Mantalinis (Cyril Fletcher and Fay Compton); and there is an all-too-brief sojourn with the Crummles and their picaresque entourage, complete with the Infant Phenomenon. Nevertheless, Stanley Holloway seizes his chance to give a delightful thumbnail sketch of Vincent Crummles, that grandiloquent and indomitable man of the theatre. Alfred Drayton and Sybil Thorndike are suitably villainous as Wackford and Mrs Squeers – with his eye patch Drayton looks curiously like John Wayne in *True Grit* – terrorising the tiny inmates of a rather cramped Dotheboys Hall. Sadly, the great set piece in which Squeers is thrashed with his own cane by the outraged Nickleby is hopelessly botched, and the feeling of fearsome retribution is lost in a thicket of flailing arms and legs. The casting of Cedric Hardwicke as Ralph Nickleby (surely the original monetarist?) was an imaginative move, but the veteran actor gave a muted performance, overshadowed by the gin-tippling, knuckle-cracking Newman Noggs of Bernard Miles. For some inexplicable reason John Dighton's screenplay transfers the sordid marriage of Madeline Bray (Jill Balcon) and Mr Gride (Laurence Hanray) to Ralph Nickleby himself.

The Wicked Lady and her Successors

In the immediate postwar period Gainsborough's output was severely cut back by Maurice Ostrer. Nevertheless, the release in 1945 of *The Wicked Lady* saw the studio reach a peak in the style which retrospectively has acquired the description of 'Gainsborough Gothic'. Given *The Wicked Lady*'s Restoration setting, perhaps 'Gainsborough Baroque' might have been more appropriate, although the film's *mise en scène* was about as historically faithful as a medieval banquet served up for American tourists.

Margaret Lockwood was the eponymous villain, Barbara Worth, a bold adventuress who 'never could resist anything that belongs to someone else'. True to her word, she acts on a whim to steal Patricia Roc's betrothed (Griffith Jones) on the eve of their wedding. Installed as Lady Skelton, she soon finds life in the manor house beginning to pall. In an attempt to recoup the disastrous loss of her mother's diamond brooch at the gaming table, Milady takes to highway robbery and falls in with the experienced highwayman Captain Terry Jackson (James Mason). Repairing to the local thieves' roost, the Leaping Stag Inn – a kind of Carolingian road house complete with tasteful bowls of daffodils and gateleg tables – the gallant captain insists that he 'drives a *hard* bargain' before their partnership is sealed in a smouldering clinch.

Milady proves herself a dab hand with the pistol – 'I'd rather shoot a man than a horse', she tells Jackson before plugging young Ned, the son of one of her husband's tenants, in a bullion hold-up. When the aged Major Domo at Skelton Hall (Felix Aylmer) stumbles on her secret, she tricks him into silence and then slowly poisons him. She ensures that he takes her secret with him to the grave, smothering him with a pillow when he makes a feeble attempt at a deathbed exposure of his mistress's wicked ways. Like her forbear Hester in *The Man in Grey*, Barbara Worth is a woman who swings between calculation and impulse. When she finds Jackson in the arms of a gipsy moll (Jean Kent) she immediately betrays him to the authorities. But his hanging at Tyburn is botched and he is cut down by his friends as a riot breaks out. He returns to Skelton Hall to exact his revenge – throttling Barbara into submission and then raping her.

Jackson's reprieve is shortlived; Milady does not hesitate to shoot him in the back when he threatens to warn Sir Ralph Skelton of her latest plan to kill her husband in a hold-up and marry the dashing Kit Locksby (Michael Rennie). Sir Ralph's coach lumbers round the bend but the Wicked Lady loses her nerve when she is confronted by her lover Locksby, who promptly shoots and mortally wounds the mysterious masked 'highwayman'. Milady regains the safety of her bedchamber, but the bloodspattered sheets and a treasure-crammed trunk reveal her secret life. She dies alone, abandoned by her husband and rejected by Locksby, the only man she has ever loved. 'If I'd met you sooner, I'd never done these things,' she tells him, but Locksby, like the audience, remains unconvinced.

At a time when the frozen sexuality of *Brief Encounter* represented an acceptable norm, *The Wicked Lady* embarked on a playful celebration of sexual image and innuendo. Margaret Lockwood's androgynous highwayman's get-up, the 'secret passage' which admits Mason to her bedroom, their knowing exchanges and candid passions provided a seductive glimpse of illicit and pleasurable sexuality. As Lockwood and Mason lift gold bars from the bullion coach she insists that they take 'just one more'. 'I've heard you say that in different circumstances,' Mason replies roguishly. As this was at a time long before the Pill liberated women from the automatic association of sex with marriage, Gainsborough's sexually active females always remain lonely and isolated. They either kill the thing they love (Mason can easily be seen as a male sex object) or, as in the climax of *The Wicked Lady*,' are them-

selves killed by another sex object (Michael Rennie).

James Mason's intense sensual presence and rich, deep voice were essential to sustain the illusion of this inviting world. Resplendent in her highwayman's outfit, Margaret Lockwood seemed more like a wayward principal boy than the incarnation of female ruthlessness, capable enough of turning heads at a suburban cocktail party but lacking the power generated by American 40s *femmes fatales* of the calibre of Rita Hayworth and Barbara Stanwyck.

Mason's dominating and sadistic screen personality were put to effective use in Compton Bennett's *The Seventh Veil* (1945), a big box office success in Britain and America produced by Sydney Box's independent Ortus company at the Riverside Studios,

Beauty with cruelty. James Mason discovers that highwayperson Margaret Lockwood provides a provocative 'skirt in the saddle' in Leslie Arliss' *The Wicked Lady* (1945). Ignore all remakes.

Gypsy temptress Jean Kent emerges from the shadows to vamp Stewart Granger in *Caravan* (1946), directed by Arthur Crabtree. John Bryan provided the splendid sets, Dennis Price the smoothest of villains.

'If you won't play for me, then you won't play for anyone else!' James Mason all set to bring his stick crashing down on Ann Todd's knuckles in Sydney Box's *The Seventh Veil* (1945), directed by Compton Bennett. Todd's nervous, ethereal beauty made her the perfect ice maiden of post-war British cinema, *noli me tangere* stamped all over her sensitive features.

Hammersmith. He played the tyrannical, lame guardian of concert pianist Francesca (Ann Todd), whose pathological obsession with her hands is rooted in a childhood caning administered on the day of her musical scholarship exams. With her mind in turmoil and her fingers blistered and raw, she cannot play and fails the exam. Her father dies and she goes to live in the vast and gloomy town house of her cousin Nicholas (James Mason) – 'a bachelor establishment,' he tells her. 'I don't like women around the place.'

Realizing her gifts as a musician, Nicholas employs the techniques of a slavedriver to turn the gawky young girl into a brilliant pianist. His control over her life is total. He snuffs out a romance with easygoing American bandleader Peter Gray (Hugh McDermott) by taking his charge away to Paris to complete her studies. The obsession with her hands remains: at her first concert she imagines that her fingers are swelling as she plays. When she attains her majority, Nicholas magnanimously tells her that she is completely free to do as she pleases, then without more ado reels off a seemingly endless and minutely detailed itinerary, finishing by handing her a small bunch of roses. 'No autographs tonight, but you might toss these from a car,' he brusquely tells her.

Her attempts to create some kind of life for herself lead to a romance with a society portrait painter, Maxwell Leyden (Albert Lieven). When she tells Nicholas that she is going to live with him in Italy, his reaction

provides one of the enduring images of the British cinema of the 1940s. Nicholas advances on her as she plays the Moonlight Sonata. Rigid with impotent fury, he brings his stick crashing down on her knuckles, hissing 'If you won't play for me, then you won't play for anyone else!' She flees into the night with Leyden, but his car crashes and she wakes in hospital with burned and bandaged hands. The trauma destroys her ability to play and it is left to psychiatrist Dr Larsen (Herbert Lom) to strip away the 'seventh veil' of her subconscious and remove the block. At the foot of the vast staircase in Nicholas's house stand Peter Gray, Maxwell Leyden and Dr Larsen. To the strains of a half-remembered waltz to which Francesca and Gray used to dance, the 'new Francesca' walks slowly down towards them. Which one will she choose? The bandleader, the artist, perhaps the psychiatrist? Unwaveringly, she makes for the study and the brooding embrace of her true Svengali, 'Uncle' Nicholas, and a lifetime of tossing frigid little bunches of roses to her public from the antiseptic interiors of hired limousines.

Sydney Box succeeded Maurice Ostrer at Gainsborough in the autumn of 1946. Pledged to stepping up the studio's output, he continued the policy of costume melodramas, but by now the cycle was on the wane. Box had brought with him an ambitious project, *The Man Within* (1946), adapted by his wife Muriel from Graham Greene's metaphysical adventure story. *The Man Within* is a cinematic curiosity – an unconscious British reply to the Hollywood vogue for 'psychological' Westerns in the form of a 'psychological' eighteenth-century smuggling yarn. Richard Attenborough, in his first starring role, spends the greater part of the film in a state of near or total hysteria, having betrayed his guardian and hero Carlyon's smuggling gang to the Gaugers. As the smuggler baron is Michael Redgrave, dreamily quoting the Song of Solomon and tootling away on a recorder, this is no run-of-the-mill swashbuckler. Wrestling with his conscience, Attenborough flees through the damps and mists of the Sussex countryside, the distant notes of Carlyon's music ringing in his ears. Bouncing like a shuttlecock between cottager Joan Greenwood and scarlet woman Jean Kent, he finally redeems himself after both he and Carlyon are taken prisoner as they stand over the body of one of Carlyon's men (killed by Carlyon as the man was about to rape Joan Greenwood). Confronted with a red-hot branding iron wielded by interrogator Torin Thatcher, Atten-borough makes a gallant attempt to protect his mentor. He is freed and walks away to a new life while the condemned Carlyon watches him from his cell. Floggings, torture and a compulsively cowardly central figure give the film a weird quality, heightened by Geoffrey Unsworth's lush photography and Andrew Mazzei's elaborate, stylized sets, which seem like projections of Atten-borough's fevered imagination.

Gainsborough were on firmer ground with formula productions like *Caravan* (1946), starring Stewart Granger as a penniless young writer who undertakes to courier some valuable jewels from France to Spain. He is ambushed and left for dead by the minions of the degenerate Sir Francis (Dennis Price), his rival for the hand of the lovely Oriana (Anne Crawford). He wakes up in a mountain cave without his memory and with gypsy wildcat Rosal (Jean Kent) leaning over him in a cling-ing blouse. While Stewart and Jean lead a perfectly laundered life in the middle of the wilderness, things go from bad to worse at home. Oriana has married the dastardly Sir Francis, who seems to be showing more interest in the chambermaids. 'A little healthy competition keeps a woman up to scratch,' he tells her when she catches him fondling the tweeny.

In order to leave the field clear for the star-crossed lovers, Jean Kent makes the ultimate sacrifice, stopping a bullet intended for Granger. Sir Francis dies horribly, whim-pering as he is sucked down in a quagmire, his face livid with the scars from Granger's whip. His memory restored, Granger falls into the prim arms of Oriana. *Caravan*'s deliriously idiotic convolutions are dominated by Dennis Price's performance as the evil baronet, rehearsing his villainy with juicy self-confidence: 'Serve the wine downwind or, so help me, I'll lay my cane across your shoulders,' he sneers at a malodorous Spanish waiter. He is ably abetted by Robert Help-mann as his creepily camp henchman Wycroft. Detailed to tail Granger on the sea voyage to Spain, Helpmann spends much of his time skipping round the poop deck sur-reptitiously nipping our hero's rippling biceps as he works out with the dumbbells.

In *The Magic Bow* (1946) Stewart Granger sawed away prettily at a Stradivarius to Yehudi Menuhin's soundtrack in a lavishly mounted but highly implausible biopic of the violin virtuoso Paganini. There is a lovely moment at the beginning of the film when the young Paganini sets off to seek fame and

fortune, gaily cramming his violin into an overnight bag as if it was a stagecoach time-table. Granger contrives to gamble away his Strad on one occasion, but little else is made of Paganini's legendary mania for the tables. (The one film of the period which captured brilliantly the psychopathology of gambling was Thorold Dickinson's 1949 *Queen of Spades*, adapted from a Pushkin story, in which Anton Walbrook becomes obsessed with learning the secret of winning at cards from Edith Evans' ancient countess.)

Bernard Knowles' *Jassy* (1947), taken from a novel by Norah Lofts, was a glossy Techni-color attempt to reproduce the *Wicked Lady* formula. Margaret Lockwood took the title role and the familiar Granger/Mason parts were none too successfully filled by Dermot

Scenes from a musician's life in *The Magic Bow* (1946), directed by Bernard Knowles. Jean Kent and Cecil Parker comfort Stewart Granger's Paganini after the dashing violin virtuoso has been pronged by Dennis Price's French officer in a duel over Phyllis Calvert.

Dennis Price looked the part as the hero of David Macdonald's *The Bad Lord Byron* (1949), but the film fell flat. Raymond Lovell's John Cam Hobhouse observes Byron's hypnotic way with society ladies.

Maxwell Reed, Patricia Roc and Will Fyffe in David Macdonald's *The Brothers* (1947). Sydney Box's predilection for risqué violence was fully realised in this adaptation of L.A.G. Strong's gloomy tale of Hebridean folk. The arrival of pert mainlander Roc drives the men of the island's two warring clans wild, and leads to a rowing race to the death, which polishes off patriarch Finlay Currie. Reed loses his thumb to a hungry conger eel and is finally tricked into killing Roc by his jealous brother Duncan Macrae. After Reed's suicide Macrae receives the islanders' traditional punishment – he is tied up and lashed to cork floats which leave his bobbing head, complete with attached fish, as live bait for the skull-crushing beaks of the local sea eagles. And they all look so happy in the picture!

End of the cycle: the outrageous whip fight from Maurice Ostrer and R.J. Minney's independent Premier Films production, *Idol of Paris* (1948), set in the Paris of Napoleon III. Courtesan Countess Paiva (Beryl Baxter) parries a thrust from her arch-rival, queen of the *demi-monde* and Napoleonic mistress Cora Pearl (Christine Norden). The considerable erotic charge generated by the fight is gleefully defused when the vanquished Norden is left clutching the sagging remains of her severed whip like the detumescing imperial phallus.

Walsh and Basil Sydney. Flogging, violence and mayhem are the order of the day, and the ground is deliciously laid in an exchange between Lockwood and wicked squire Basil Sydney. 'Jassy Woodroffe? Woodroffe? I seem to know that name,' he muses as he escorts her into dinner. 'You are thinking of my father. You shot him dead outside that door,' is the understandably cool reply.

As the Gainsborough cycle drew to a close, the studio abandoned zesty trash for two painstaking attempts to produce quality historical dramas, *Christopher Columbus* (1948) and *The Bad Lord Byron* (1949). Entertainment values took a back seat to historical truth and the results were predictably dull. The early Gainsborough costumers succeeded in achieving a lavish look on a limited budget; *The Bad Lord Byron* and *Christopher* *Columbus* contrived to be both boring and expensive. Halfway through the location shooting of *Christopher Columbus* in the West Indies, the 173-ton reconstruction of Columbus's flagship *Santa Maria* caught fire and was destroyed. A model was built in London, and the matching of tank shots with footage shot in the West Indies added £100,000 to the budget. It was imaginative casting to import Fredric March to play the title role, and the Hollywood star gave a strong performance, conveying something of the obsessive personality displayed by all the great explorers. But the plot gets so bogged down in the intrigues of the Spanish court that by the time the little armada sets sail, the film, along with Columbus and his mutinous crew, has lost its way.

Critical reaction to *Christopher Columbus*

The Gainsborough output was by no means confined to swashbucklers and weepies. David Macdonald's *Broken Journey* (1948) was based on a big news story of 1946 in which an American Army Dakota crashed in the Alps and rescue parties battled through the snow to reach the survivors. They were a mixed bunch, anticipating the *Airport*-style group jeopardy cycle of the 70s: Andrew Crawford's boxing champion, Francis L. Sullivan's opera singer, even a man in an iron lung who gives up his battery, and his life, to keep the radio going. Here, David Tomlinson, Sonia Holm, Raymond Huntley and Phyllis Calvert shiver it out.

In Ken Annakin's *Miranda* (1947) young doctor Griffith Jones meets Glynis Johns' mermaid on a Cornish holiday and is persuaded to take her back to London – suitably draped in a wheelchair – to see the sights.

was cool, and *The Bad Lord Byron* fared no better. The film suffers from a cumbersome framing device – a kind of celestial court in which the dying Byron's reputation is held in the balance as various figures from his past (including Lady Caroline Lamb, John Cam Hobhouse and Lady Melbourne) clump in and out of the witness box. Dennis Price as Byron and Joan Greenwood as Lady Caroline Lamb gave performances which echo in minor key Louis Mazzini and the delicious Sibella of their Ealing triumph of the same year, *Kind Hearts and Coronets*.

Launder and Gilliat

The first film made for Rank by Frank Launder and Sidney Gilliat's Individual

Pictures was Gilliat's *The Rake's Progress*, released in November 1945. Rex Harrison played a 30s playboy, Vivian Kenway, the kind of central character who in the wartime years would have sent the editors of the Documentary News Letter lurching angrily towards their typewriters. Sent down from Oxford for climbing the Martyrs Memorial and leaving a chamber pot as a memento of his visit, he is packed off to a coffee plantation in South America. He loses his job when he rebels against the endless round of cricket and bridge and the burning of the coffee crop to keep up prices. From this point Kenway pursues a downward spiral, seducing his best friend's wife (Jean Kent), enjoying brief fame as a racing driver and then marrying a young Jewish girl (Lilli Palmer) in Vienna, to save her from the Nazis, and trying to cheat her on

Top
Rex Harrison and Lilli Palmer in *The Rake's Progress* (1945) directed by Sidney Gilliat and the first film from Launder and Gilliat's Individual Pictures. Sidney Gilliat has remarked, 'This is the film nearest to my heart, it keeps coming into period and then going out again. Untidy and uneven, but it improves as it goes.'

Above
Deborah Kerr finds herself sitting next to Katie Johnson in Frank Launder's comedy-thriller *I See a Dark Stranger* (1946). Launder got the idea for the film after a trip to Belfast while making a wartime documentary, *Soldier, Sailor* (1944).

the price of the transaction. He kills his father (Godfrey Tearle) in a drunken driving smash and drifts through a series of dead-end sales jobs before ending up as a professional dancing partner. The war saves him from complete disintegration and enables him to channel his erratic energies in an appropriately destructive direction. He dies heroically, driving a tank over a mined bridge. Far from being out of character, the rake's end is pointed with characteristic Launder/Gilliat irony. Kenway dies expressing the sentiment that it was 'a good year'. A senior officer is impressed with this gung-ho approach until a colleague who knows Kenway better remarks that he was probably referring to the champagne he was drinking.

Frank Launder directed the next Individual film, *I See a Dark Stranger* (1946), which marked a return to the pair's stylish thriller work of the 1930s. Deborah Kerr played a

young Irish girl, brought up to hate the British, who falls in love with British officer Trevor Howard. Garry Marsh and Tom Macaulay replaced Basil Radford and Naunton Wayne of *Night Train to Munich* as two highly unintelligent intelligence officers, the names being changed to Goodhusband and Spanswick. In Sidney Gilliat's *Green for Danger* (1946), Alastair Sim played Inspector Cockrill, investigating a murder in a London hospital at the height of the doodlebug raids. An affectionate pastiche of the detective genre, *Green for Danger* ran into bizarre censorship problems. Initially, the British film censor refused a release on the grounds that any wounded serviceman who might see the film would lose all confidence in his nurses. It transpired that the censor had confused the film with the Christianne Brand novel on which it was based, which indeed was set in a military hospital. The misunderstanding was settled over a lavish black market lunch in Soho.

In 1947 Frank Launder returned to Ireland to make *Captain Boycott*, in which Cecil Parker played the nineteenth-century Anglo-Irish landlord whose name has passed into the language. Stewart Granger was the young firebrand who leads the peasantry into a strike against the depredations of absentee landlords. It was, perhaps, ironic that at a time when the Labour government was laying the foundations of the Welfare State, Launder was shying away from making films which directly tackled the unanswered question posed by Eric Portman in *Millions Like Us*. A kind of retrospective social criticism was being buried underneath frock coats and stovepipe hats. It was all right to biff the capitalists and rack renters, provided they were insulated from audiences by a good 100 years. Brian Desmond Hurst's *Hungry Hill*, adapted from Daphne du Maurier's bestseller, explored the same Irish territory as *Captain Boycott*, though with a touch more melodrama. *Esther Waters* (1948) gave Dirk Bogarde his first screen role as the ne'er do well footman William Latch of George Moore's novel. He gets Kathleen Ryan pregnant, abandons and then marries her, loses all their money on the horses and then dies of consumption. Bogarde has described how in *Esther Waters* he received a discouraging introduction to film acting at the hands of director Peter Proud: 'I walked around with hundreds of pounds worth of costume on my back in a daze. When I asked the director how I should play a scene, he told me, "You're the actor, you should know".'

A Woman's Place

At Rank there was a straightforward policy, recalled by Muriel Box: 'We were not under contract...to make films with overt statements on social problems or those with strong propaganda themes.' When tentative attempts were made to tackle contemporary themes – the role of women, for example – the results were muffled and implausible. In Compton Bennett's *The Years Between* (1946) Tory MP Michael Redgrave is reported missing during the war. His wife (Valerie Hobson), left with their small son, takes her husband's place in Parliament – naturally, there is a nanny to look after the child. She then takes up with a local farmer, only to be confronted by her husband who returns from the dead to announce that all along he has been on a top secret mission and that she has 'usurped' his seat in the Commons.

Gainsborough's *The Root of All Evil* (1947), directed by Brock Williams, also tackled in ambivalent fashion the notion of a woman adopting a traditionally masculine role. Phyllis Calvert played Jackie Farnish, the daughter of a daydreaming and improvident farmer (Brefni O'Rorke). When the bank forecloses and he is forced to sell his rundown property, right down to the sheep dog, his daughter decides that there is only one unforgivable sin – poverty. Rejected by her callow fiancé Albert, the son of the market town's leading grocer George Grice (Arthur Young), she sues him for breach of promise. With a settlement of £1,500 she opens an upmarket provision store opposite Grice's dusty, cluttered emporium.

The blustering, bullying old paterfamilias is rapidly broken, driven out of business, and succumbs to what in earlier times would have been diagnosed as a fit of apoplexy. Having by an effort of will turned herself into an ersatz man, becoming as 'ruthless' as her competitors, Jackie now falls head over heels for suave mining engineer Charles Mortimer (Michael Rennie), who has discovered a rather improbable oil lake on a local farm. Can life be all accounts and tins of corned beef? The mask slips and in kittenish mood Jackie snaps off a rose in the garden for his buttonhole. With the profits from her store, she buys a big house for them both. Mortimer isn't too pleased about this as he has omitted to tell her that he is already married. Hell hath no fury like a businesswoman scorned, and in no time he is frozen out of the oilfield. While Jackie broods in the empty

house, Mortimer and her childhood sweetheart Joe Bartle (John McCallum) find a rough form of male camaraderie, sharing a cigarette after a scrap in a country lane over their mutual inamorata.

As our melancholy litle rich girl contemplates a solitary world tour, crazed farmer Scholes (Moore Marriott), who has been finagled out of his land by the oil company, sets fire to the refinery. The plant goes up in a spectacular blaze while Jackie watches its destruction alone, ignored by the milling crowds of firemen and morbid sightseers. A wayward spark sets light to the thatched roof of Scholes' farmhouse and Jackie rushes in to save his trapped children, closely followed by old flame Joe Bartle. 'Get out of my life and stay out,' he bellows as he tosses her out of an upstairs window, along with the children,

Businesswoman Phyllis Calvert abandons the accounts for a brief fling with the cherry brandy and old boyfriend John McCallum in *The Root of All Evil* (1947), directed by Brock Williams.

Policeman Torin Thatcher tells Patricia Roc that her husband is a bigamist in Lawrence Huntington's *When the Bough Breaks* (1947), one of the few films of the 40s which attempted to deal with the common wartime problems faced by unmarried mothers, and from the point of view of a young working-class woman. It was produced by Betty Box.

Dowdy Dulcie Gray is relegated to the back seat by her tyrannical husband James Mason while her sister Phyllis Calvert displays a well-tailored concern in Arthur Crabtree's *They Were Sisters* (1944).

into an outspread blanket below. No chance. The film ends back at the old Farnish spread, now in Joe's capable hands and with Jackie all set to resume a suitably subordinate role as his wife. The message is clearly written in the farmhouse's freshly whitewashed walls and neat garden – Joe brings harmony and order, Jackie's aberrational activities are a denial of her femininity and bring death, disorder and destruction.

Post-war Problems

At Associated British, Harold French's *My Brother Jonathan* (1948), adapted from Francis Brett Young's novel, posed some questions about the new National Health Service. Set in the days immediately before and after World War I, it starred Michael Denison as a young doctor with his eyes on Harley Street. His dreams are shattered when his poetry-spouting, improvident father (James Robertson Justice) is brought into his hospital after an accident. The death certificate reveals that the bibulous man of letters is in fact a 'corset salesman', a terrible jolt for the priggish Denison. Further shocks are in store. Father has died a bankrupt and Denison has to settle for a 'working class' practice in a grimy mining town, in order to send his bright younger brother to Cambridge. The film charts with considerable skill the young doctor's disillusionment with the inequalities of the medical system, embodied in the private hospital of slimy consultant Stephen Murray, the son-in-law of the local coal magnate. Steadily paced and full of pleasing detail, *My Brother Jonathan* accomplishes in two hours what would now take an eternity

of episodes in an overdressed television series. There is an understated feel for the old-fashioned, improvised style of medicine and the acceptance of pain. While performing a tracheotomy on a boy with diphtheria, Denison tells the frantic mother, 'Count the lights you can see from the window – I'll be finished before you reach 100.'

Another milestone of the Beveridge years was the Education Act of 1944, which provided a limited number of scholarships to Britain's public schools for grammar school boys. In Roy Boulting's *The Guinea Pig* (1948) the 26-year-old Richard Attenborough sheds a dozen years to play a bright boy from Walthamstow who crashes the world of the toffs. He is persuaded by kindly crippled master Stephen Murray to take the knocks and accept the system, and no doubt is now in the Labour shadow cabinet.

One post-war social problem which proved irresistible to film makers was the so-called 'crime wave' which apparently swept Britain in the years following the war. It seemed that the very fabric of society was being shredded by an army of spivs, razor gangs and cosh boys. In *The Boys in Brown* (1949) scripted and directed by Montgomery Tully, Richard Attenborough was allowed to creep into adolescence as a Borstal Boy with a conscience as queasy as that of the novice smuggler he played in *The Man Within*. Understandably, he loses his bearings in a sea of baggy shorts and knobbly knees belonging to a set of inmates, many of whom seem older than the warders. Quite what Jimmy Hanley, aged 31 and looking older, is doing in a Borstal is anybody's guess. Dirk Bogarde, at 26, runs Hanley a close second. He also has

Uncertain voyager in the post-war world. Richard Attenborough receives the attentions of the appropriately named Cecil Trouncer's public school master in John Boulting's *The Guinea Pig* (1948).

the knobbliest knees. Presiding over these elderly delinquents is stern but fair governor Jack Warner. Hanley is his star inmate, coming up for release and determined to go straight this time. Warner tries to smooth the illegitimate Hanley's path, and save him from the 'bad environment' of his foster family, by tracking down his real mother. In the film's most telling moment, he confronts the woman (Elspeth March) in the chintzy living room of her smart suburban home. As a small girl in a spotless white dress plays on a swing in the garden, she tells him, 'I have no son.' Hanley fails to hold down a job and soon he is back inside planning a mass break-out with his pals Bogarde, Andrew Crawford, Alfie Bass, Michael Medwin, John Blythe and the feebly wobbling Attenborough (shades of *The Man Within*). The escape is planned for the night of the Borstal concert (an anticipation of all those POW films of the 50s), but things begin to fall apart after the panicky Attenborough seriously injures a prison officer while trying to filch some of his clothes. On recapture, the escapers display emotions ranging from remorse (Attenborough) through open defiance (Glasgow 'hard-man' Crawford) to derangement (pathological liar Bogarde). Warner concludes by asking us the rhetorical question: 'I wonder how Eton and Harrow would get on if their intake was limited to the failures and no-goods?' Put that in your cosh and swing it.

Jean Kent came to no good in the 1947 *Good Time Girl*, which was loosely based on a sensational news story of the time dubbed 'The Cleft Chin Murders'. The film opens with

Post-war crime wave. Youth runs wild as Andrew Crawford gets heavy with wobbling Richard Attenborough in *The Boys in Brown* (1949), adapted from Reginald Beckwith's play by Montgomery Tully. The other knobbly knees, and elderly Borstal inmates, are provided by (left to right) Michael Medwin, John Blythe, Alfie Bass, Dirk Bogarde and Robert Desmond.

Good Time Girl (1947), directed by David Macdonald. Gwen Rawlings (Jean Kent) falls in with super-spiv Jimmy Rosso (Peter Glenville), the only man who Brylcreems his moustache, and begins a headlong descent into the world of vice rings and protection rackets which ends with a fifteen-year sentence for murder.

magistrate Flora Robson telling truculent young juvenile offender Diana Dors the cautionary tale of Gwen Rawlings (Jean Kent), sentenced to 15 years for murder. Gwen leaves home at 16, having been given a beating by her drunken father. She drifts into that evocative and possibly mythical Soho of the 1940s, peopled with sinister continentals and colourful spivs wearing double-breasted suits with stripes as wide as tram lines. She gets a job at Herbert Lom's nightclub despite the warnings of genteel pianist Red Farrell (Dennis Price) that she is walking into a spider's web. The nearest spider is Jimmy Rosso (Peter Glenville), a nasty piece of work who carves up Lom's face with his flick knife and fits Gwen up for receiving 'hot' jewellery. Gwen gets three years in Borstal, a veritable academy of crime presided over by

Laurence Harvey and a sexy young Joan Collins in the dock in Ealing's *I Believe In You* (1952), directed by Basil Dearden. It attempted to do for the probation service what *The Blue Lamp* did for the police, using the familiar 'introduction of new recruit/mosaic of individual stories' format. It is symptomatic of the Ealing approach that the 'new boy' probation officer was a middle-aged military man played by Cecil Parker.

Right
He fell among thieves. The cosh descends on Richard Attenborough in John Paddy Carstairs' *Dancing with Crime* (1947).

Old lag Jack Warner saws through the handcuffs which bind him to callow George Cole in *My Brother's Keeper* (1948), directed by Alfred Roome. Hovering over them with the tea tray is Jane Hylton. Warner's freedom is shortlived – he is blown up as he picks his way across a minefield – '...now was it 86 or 87 mines we laid?'.

big bad Roberta (Jill Balcon). Gwen escapes during a riot in the dining room worthy of *Each Dawn I Die*, and then falls among thieves. She becomes Brighton mobster Griffith Jones' moll and runs over and kills a policeman on a drunken drive up to London. Dumped and beaten up by Jones, and pursued by the police, she falls in with a pair of GIs (Bonar Colleano and Hugh McDermott) who run a nice line in mugging. By the wildest of coincidences their last victim is Red Farrell, dragged from his car and shot dead when it becomes clear that Gwen knows him. The distraught Good Time Girl is led away to the slammer and we cut back to Diana Dors – suitably impressed by this sordid tale – who assures Flora Robson 'I won't 'alf cop it from Dad if he finds out I'm late.'

Soho also provided the background for *Appointment with Crime* (1946), and *Dancing with Crime* (1946), in which Richard Attenborough played an ex-commando who gets caught up in the underworld. Former commandos featured in *Nightbeat* (1946) in which Ronald Howard and Hector Ross join the police and fall foul of Maxwell Reed's black-market gang. The following year Trevor Howard plunged into the black market to recapture the excitement of his war career in Cavalcanti's *They Made Me a Fugitive* (1947).

In all these films there were engagingly British attempts to emulate the Hollywood thick-ear stuff which even the grainiest Monogram B managed without difficulty. Manhunts, a staple of the American thriller, were a good model, and in *My Brother's Keeper* (1948) old lag Jack Warner and callow youth George Cole make a jailbreak handcuffed together. In the Twentieth Century-Fox British *Escape* (1948) American expertise was on hand in the form of director Joseph Mankiewicz, as detective William Hartnell pursued convict Rex Harrison over fog-shrouded Dartmoor. During the late 1940s Edward Dmytryk spent some time in England after the HUAC had made him *persona non grata* in Hollywood. His *Obsession* (1948) was a moody *film noir* in which Robert Newton played a doctor who imprisons his wife's American lover in a bomb-site basement with the intention of dissolving his body in acid. *Obsession* is dominated by Newton's glowering, gravel-voiced presence. In a macabre touch he carries the acid on his nightly trips to the basement concealed in that most homely of devices, a hot water bottle. In a Britain sunk deep in austerity and shortages, it was no coincidence that

Played-out criminal Wylie Watson is edged towards the rickety bannisters by Richard Attenborough's Pinkie in the Boultings' *Brighton Rock* (1947). William Hartnell looks on, wearing one of the most spectacularly tasteless suits in film history.

Googie Withers in Robert Hamer's minor classic of 40s social realism, *It Always Rains on Sunday* (1947). Patricia Plunkett was her daughter. John McCallum, playing her old lover, escaped convict Tommy Swann, skulks behind the kitchen door.

Newton's prisoner was a young American. In his club, the elderly members provide a constant background chorus, grizzling about American economic imperialism like elderly senators querulously peeping over the battlements of Byzantium to view the approaching Turkish hordes.

Running through the thrillers of the 40s was the hysterical presence of baby-faced Richard Attenborough. In John Boulting's *Brighton Rock* (1947) he played Pinkie, the teenage psychopath of Graham Greene's novel, running a shoddy little razor gang in the sleazy rookeries of the Brighton Lanes. Moving through a world of race-track gangs and protection rackets, his baleful stare makes him seem like a horrible marionette. Lying on his bed, he idly pulls the hair off a china doll, its blank face mocking his own as he gives orders to his confederates Nigel Stock, Wylie Watson and William Hartnell. *Brighton Rock* is full of ripe performances. Hermione Baddeley as the blowsy old bar fly obstinately groping towards the truth behind the death of former gang member, Alan Wheatley; Harcourt Williams as the bent lawyer Prewett, ironically referring to the 'last of the old crusted' as he tugs a bottle of cheap sherry from a dust-caked box marked 'the Prideaux Estate'. The weak casting link is Carol Marsh as the young waitress Pinkie marries to conceal the evidence of Wheatley's murder. Try as she might, Marsh cannot prevent the cut-glass vowels of haute suburbia from breaking through her carefully rehearsed 'working class' accent.

Brighton Rock is further undermined by the Boultings' dilution of Greene's bleak Catholic imagery, although there are some carefully placed hints of Pinkie's tortured, life-hating Catholicism. A recording booth in a store provides a form of instant confessional as Pinkie pours out his feelings of contempt for his child bride. This only serves to establish the film's final scene, a lamentable copout, in which Carol Marsh finally places the disc on a gramophone and it instantly sticks on the phrase 'I love you' as — naiveté and virginity intact — she walks into the sunset.

In 1948 Attenborough was back as a youthful killer in Sidney Gilliat's adaptation of Norman Collins' best-selling novel set in a pre-war boarding house, 10 Dulcimer Street, in South London. *London Belongs to Me* was crammed with a small army of character actors (including Alastair Sim, Joyce Carey, Gladys Henson, Hugh Griffith, Maurice Denham and Wylie Watson) and turned turtle under the weight of its sub-plots. An interesting footnote to the film was that a treatment of the script was provided by Lord Goodman, then a movie-struck young solicitor, but was not used.

Ealing provided an equally rich slice of life in Robert Hamer's *It Always Rains on Sunday*, which was released in November 1947. Set in Bethnal Green, in London's East End, it starred Googie Withers as Rose Sandigate, a wilful, passionate woman trapped in a suffocating marriage to a portly, beer-swilling working man of the old school, Edward Chapman. The hardening crust of ration cards, washing days and dirty dishes is shattered by the escape from prison of her former lover, gangster Tommy Swann (John McCallum). Swann finds his way to Rose's house, where she hides him, first in the Anderson shelter in the garden and then upstairs in her bedroom. Downstairs, life has to go on as usual — Sunday lunch must be prepared for George, shuffling back from darts at the pub, and her two stepdaughters (Patricia Plunkett and Susan Shaw). Rose is gripped by a mounting hysteria as the hopeless contradictions in her life — one locked in the bedroom, the other munching away at the roast beef in the kitchen — begin to overwhelm her. In a moment of explosive passion she literally tears the dress from the back of her sluttish stepdaughter Vi (Susan Shaw).

Eventually, a local journalist (Michael Howard) makes the connection between Rose and Swann, and stumbles on his hiding place. Swann makes a break for it and is tracked down and taken in a railway marshalling yard. Rose tries to commit suicide by putting her head in the gas oven. Like Laura Jessop's dash to the edge of the platform in

The magnificent Googie Withers, as the murderess Pearl Bond in Robert Hamer's *Pink String and Sealing Wax* (1945), slowly poisoning her alcoholic publican husband, Garry Marsh.

Brief Encounter, the bid fails. The film closes with Rose in hospital, being comforted by her husband. Despite its tender conclusion the film suggests that Rose is glumly resigned to her lot rather than positively integrated into the busy life of Bethnal Green – from now on life will be an eternity of rainy Sundays, with the *News of the World* and 'haddock for breakfast'.

Hamer's attempt to establish the detailed social background of Rose's life, faithfully following the tangled sub-plots of Arthur La Berns' novel, almost succeeds in throwing the film off balance and this is ironically exacerbated by the energy and high definition of some of the cameo performances. John Slater was the widest of wide boys, with a little niterie 'up West' and always on the look-out for new hostesses. Sidney Tafler was his brother, a back-street Don Juan presiding over a tatty music shop plastered with posters advertising his band – 'Lou Hyams, the man with sax appeal'. Jack Warner played a deceptively slow-moving detective sergeant in charge of the man hunt. He dispenses a relaxed and homely line of backchat as he conducts his enquiries, foreshadowing the mood of Basil Dearden's *The Blue Lamp*. 'There's such a thing as libel, Mr. Fothergill,' threatens a slightly less than honest tea stall owner. 'And there's such a thing as ham, but not in this sandwich,' replies Warner, reproachfully leaving the offending article on the counter.

From the opening shot – rain gently spattering on the greasy metal top of a kerbside rubbish bin – *It Always Rains on Sunday* establishes a consistent if somewhat stylized picture of post-war austerity: knots of men huddled in the rain outside the pub, waiting for opening time; the petty intricacies of the cheese ration; the crumbling Anderson shelter in the garden of 26 Coronet Grove. In a back-street mugging the victim's false teeth shoot out and come to rest in a dirty puddle. Never far away are the screeching whistles of goods trains on the nearby sidings, one of the great call signs of British cinema of the 1940s.

Googie Withers

It Always Rains on Sunday was Googie Withers' last film at Ealing, and her best. She stands out among the anaemic leading ladies of the time as one of the very few with the presence to match her Hollywood rivals. Rose Sandigate was the third Ealing role in which she had played a strong-willed woman, too big almost for the films which confine her. In Robert Hamer's *Pink String and Sealing Wax* (1945) she was Pearl Bond, a publican's wife who slowly poisons her corpulent and alcoholic husband (Garry Marsh) and then attempts to pin the blame on an infatuated young admirer (Gordon Jackson). In Charles Frend's *The Loves of Joanna Godden* (1947) she was a determined young woman who inherits a run-down sheep farm on the Romney Marshes and decides to run it herself. 'Not worth a hatful of shrimps,' her childhood sweetheart (John McCallum) tells her – it's Joe Bartle time again. Grizzled old Walter Gabriel types mutter about ''er needin' a man', but Googie has other ideas. 'I'd like to meet the man who wouldn't take orders from me,' she barks, eyes blazing and arms akimbo. She hires a new stockman (Chips Rafferty) to put in hand a bold experi-

73

ment in cross-breeding (a notion, as we know, dear to Michael Balcon's heart) and for a while it seems as if we are in for an Ealing version of *Cattle Queen of Montana*, with Googie giving Barbara Stanwyck a good run for her money. Disaster strikes and most of the lambs die. Undeterred, she breaks up her pasture for fodder and is engaged to wimpish Derek Bond, the squire's son, who is conveniently swept away to a watery grave while skinny-dipping at Dungeness. Meanwhile the disconsolate McCallum has taken up with Googie's flighty young sister (Jean Kent) who is just back from finishing school. They marry and she leads the plodding farmer a merry dance for a year, but when foot and mouth overwhelms his herd, she skips off with the squire (Henry Mollison), and ''im old enough to be 'er grandfather'. We leave

Googie and McCallum clasping hands, staring into each other's eyes and into a future which one hopes will be less littered with the piles of dead livestock to which the audience have been subjected for the preceding 89 minutes.

The Portmanteau Film

As British as the Romney Marshes, so lovingly photographed in *The Loves of Joanna Godden* by cameraman Douglas Slocombe, was the portmanteau film, in which a number of characters are thrown together on a train journey or in a boxing hall or at a race meeting, their stories being told in sequence. In part a legacy of the wartime years in which people from very different backgrounds come together in the factories and forces, it enabled screenwriters to provide audiences with an entertaining cross-section of society, usually portrayed as class stereotypes.

The first and best-remembered portmanteau film of the period was Ealing's *Dead of Night* (1945), a collection of ghost stories bound together with a cunningly circular narrative. Architect Mervyn Johns arrives at a country house where from the moment of his arrival he is struck by an overwhelming sense of déjà vu. It increases as each of the people assembled there tells him a tale of the supernatural. The first, directed by Alberto Cavalcanti, is a Victorian ghost story. The second, directed by Basil Dearden, is a tale of premonition in which a man in hospital foresees and avoids his own death. The third, directed by Robert Hamer, is woven around a haunted mirror. There is a brief comic interlude, a shaggy ghost story in which golfers Basil

Two ghost stories. Gainsborough's *A Place of One's Own* (1945) directed by Bernard Knowles from Osbert Sitwell's novel. An elderly couple (James Mason and Barbara Mullen) find their companion (Margaret Lockwood) possessed by the spirit of a girl murdered in their house forty years before. Rex Whistler had a hand in the film's elegant design.

Michael Redgrave's ventriloquist Maxwell Frere is possessed by his dummy in Ealing's supernatural portmanteau film *Dead of Night* (1945). The face at the door is that of Frederick Valk, familiar in a host of 40s films as a mid-European psychiatrist or Nazi heavy. The *Dead of Night* formula was imitated in the low-budget *House of Darkness* (1948) and successfully adapted in the 60s by producer Milton Subotsky. His Amicus company made a number of diverting horror assemblages, including *Dr Terror's House of Horrors* (1964), *The Torture Garden* (1967) and *Tales from the Crypt* (1971).

Radford and Naunton Wayne fall out over pretty Peggy Bryan. The final segment, directed by Alberto Cavalcanti, follows the possession of ventriloquist Michael Redgrave by his sinister dummy. With the completion of the final story the film builds up to a nightmarish climax which finds a sweating Johns waking up in his own bed. His wife tells him that he has an appointment that day, in the country. We leave him approaching the same house and greeting the same host of his dream.

Despite the enduring memory of Michael Redgrave's invasion by his little wooden friend, the most significant episode is 'The Haunted Mirror', a key moment in post-war British cinema. Googie Withers and Ralph Michael played a handsome and self-satisfied engaged couple, the type that would now adorn an advertisement for after-dinner mint chocolates. She presents him with a Victorian mirror. Gradually, the mirror drives her fiancé towards a breakdown, reflecting not his own bedroom but another, disturbing room in another time and place. The couple marry and for a time the glimpses into the mirror world fade away. But soon they return, plunging Michael into frenzies of sexual jealousy. Googie Withers discovers from the dealer that the mirror had been shut away after it 'witnessed' the disintegration of its owner, a masterful and energetic man confined to bed after a riding accident. He found the confinement unendurable, killed his wife and then committed suicide. The frustrated drive and sexuality of the long-dead man are being channelled through Michael, forcing him to become the mirror image of his normally repressed self. Before his wife can tell him of her discovery he attacks her and tries to strangle her in front of the mirror, and for the first time she, too, sees the other room, with its four-poster bed and blazing fire. She breaks free, smashes the mirror and the spell is broken. Once more they are the bloodless, smart young couple – 'lobotomized' in Charles Barr's memorable phrase – the forces of sensuality and violence subdued. We will have to wait until the mid-50s and the accelerating Hammer cycle of horror films before these forces are released and once more the genie flies free of the bottle.

It was four years before Ealing produced another portmanteau film, Train of Events (1949). The 3.45 express from Euston to Liverpool, driven by Jack Warner, pulls out from the ominously appropriate platform 13, heading for a crash at high speed. The film then goes into flashback, following the

stories of three sets of people on board the train. An unbalanced actor (Peter Finch) who has murdered his wife and stuffed her body in his theatrical trunk; a young woman (Joan Dowling) shielding an escaped German POW who has never given himself up (Laurence Payne); and an amorous orchestra conductor (John Clements) anticipating an adulterous affair with a tempestuous pianist (Irina Baranova).

The flashback enables the audience to agonise over who will survive the crash as the passengers converge on the station. For the record, Finch is crushed by a falling coach as he flees the scene of the accident; Joan Dowling dies on a stretcher, her German lover running off into the darkness, the roaring of the Nuremberg rallies filling his ears; John Clements and Irina Baranova survive to give their concert, swathed in bandages, under the watchful eye of Clements' wife, Valerie Hobson; and Jack Warner returns to a nice cup of tea with his wife, Gladys Henson, and a new job as an inspector. Warner was married to Henson in Ealing's The Captive Heart (1946) and he was to be married to her again in The Blue Lamp (1951). The combination of these comfy working class backgrounds with his role as Detective Sergeant Fothergill in It Always Rains on Sunday were to produce the home life of George Dixon, the fatherly police constable at the heart of The Blue Lamp.

In Dance Hall (1950) Diana Dors, Jane Hylton, Natasha Parry and Petula Clark played factory girls finding excitement and romance at their local palais de danse. Dors is marvellous throughout, continually squealing, 'I'm through with men', before falling

Peter Finch tells his unfaithful wife Mary Morris that his wartime experiences have made him used to 'sudden death' before going on to strangle her in Ealing's Train of Events (1949), whose segments were directed by Sidney Cole, Charles Crichton and Basil Dearden.

After *Train of Events*, Ealing pushed their portmanteau films into a more integrated form in the hands of a single director. Diana Dors toys with a Coke and her hulking partner James Carney in Charles Crichton's *Dance Hall* (1950).

Robert Beatty's punched-out boxing champ meets an old girlfriend, Kay Kendall, in Basil Dearden's *The Square Ring* (1953).

Earl Cameron and Bonar Colleano in *Pool of London* (1951), directed by Basil Dearden, an accomplished film which followed the stories of a group of merchant seamen on weekend shore leave. Petty smuggler Colleano gets involved in a botched jewel robbery and finally gives himself up to the police. Cameron strikes up a tentative friendship with Susan Shaw and experiences some unpleasant racial discrimination. *Pool of London* is full of excellent documentary-style location shooting and, as an historical footnote, was one of the last British films to feature a London tram ride.

for inarticulate hulk James Carney. Pubescent Petula and her partner (Douglas Barr) stumble their way into the finals of the amateur ballroom dancing championship but remain rooted to the spot while a flash pair from Cricklewood scissor their way round the floor. Natasha Parry has a brief fling with lounge lizard Bonar Colleano but eventually settles for pudgy motor mechanic Donald Houston. The latter is an Othello worthy of ration-bound Britain. What drives him to fury is not a handkerchief but a crate of kippers from Colleano's black market hoard. Gainsborough's *Marry Me* (1949), directed by Terence Fisher, adopted the same scheme as *Dance Hall*, following the fortunes of eight people who meet through a marriage bureau.

The Square Ring (1953) went behind the scenes of a boxing promotion during the course of one hectic night of action. In the dressing room, presided over by Jack Warner, a number of pugilistic clichés go smartly through their paces. Wise-cracking lightweight contender Bill Owen anticipates Muhammad Ali, crooning 'I'm beautiful' to his reflection in the mirror, and adding 'I don't like broken noses, they're so uncouth.' Maxwell Reed's horizontal heavyweight does everything but sell the soles of his boots for advertising space. Bill Travers played a musclebound Joe Palooka type, absorbed in his science fiction comic and its heroine, Sylvia, Queen of the Spaceships. Inevitably there was a shy young novice, Ronald Lewis, up from the Valleys, and a punched out ex-champ, Robert Beatty, trying to claw his way back into the big time. Sidney James was superb as a seedy promoter, storing cigar ends in a tin box and spending most of the evening vainly appealing to the assembled 'sportsmen and gentlemen' for the return of the Boys Brigade collection box.

Ealing did not have a monopoly on the portmanteau format. Gainsborough's successful *Holiday Camp* (1947), directed by Ken Annakin and starring Jack Warner and Kathleen Harrison, led to a spin-off series built around the couple they played in the film, the Huggetts. South London's answer to Ma and Pa Kettle bumbled through a short series of cosily unmemorable films, at one point making a rash overland trip to South Africa (*The Huggetts Abroad*) which inevitably ended back in the dilapidated matiness of austerity Britain. In *Here Come the Huggetts* (1948), busty young relative Diana Dors comes to stay – 'My, you're a big girl now,' breathes Jack Warner, as Swindon's very own Good Time girl sashays into the Huggetts' little

'I think they've over-baked my perm,' Esme Cannon confides to her chalet companion Flora Robson in *Holiday Camp* (1947). A marvellous compendium of British social life in the late 40s, it was directed at a cracking pace by Ken Annakin from an original story by Godfrey Winn. Amid the thunderous exhortations from the camp tannoy, endless cups of tea and massed ballroom dancing reminiscent of Jennings' *Listen to Britain*, the holidaymakers go about their pleasures with characteristic British doggedness. During an early morning callisthenics session Jack Warner's Mr Huggett urges his flagging wife Kathleen Harrison to 'Stick it, mother…we're paying for this, we don't want to waste it.' All human life is contained in a holiday camp, from card sharps to sex murderers, and at the end of the film sad little Esme Cannon's hair is permanently baked by Dennis Price's bogus squadron leader.

Dirk Bogarde's tragically optimistic young pianist and Honor Blackman in 'The Alien Corn', an episode from Gainsborough's *Quartet* (1948), directed by Harold French. *Quartet* was a lavish production based on four Somerset Maugham short stories, adapted by R.C. Sherriff and played by strong casts. The other episodes were 'The Kite' (Arthur Crabtree), 'The Facts of Life' (Ralph Smart), and the charming 'The Colonel's Lady' (Ken Annakin) in which Cecil Parker played a colonel who, mystified when his wife (Nora Swinburne) produces a book of passionately romantic poetry, sets out to find the inspiration.

South London terraced house.

Easy Money (1947), directed by Bernard Knowles, followed the fortunes of a number of football pools winners. The four separate stories are linked by a semi-documentary commentary on the inner workings of the pools firms. The best episode is the one in which nightclub vamp Greta Gynt seduces pools worker Dennis Price into fixing her coupon. Gainsborough also had a considerable success with *Quartet* (1948), a handsomely mounted package of Somerset Maugham stories – The Kite, The Colonel's Lady, The Alien Corn and The Facts of Life. It was followed by futher Maugham adaptations in *Trio* (1950) and *Encore* (1951).

The moment of truth for James Mason's unhinged neuro-surgeon in Lawrence Huntington's *The Upturned Glass* (1947). Fellow doctor Brefni O'Rorke knows there is a body in the back of Mason's car. The critic C.L. Lejeune thought that the film combined 'the delights of an evening spent in the company of Miss Betty Grable and an hour or so in an armchair with Freud'.

The Film Noir

Nothing could be more typical of our home-grown cinema than films about the football pools or the mild antics of the Huggett family. But what of the darker side of human nature, the world of uncertainty and deception explored in that elusive talisman of 40s cinema, the *film noir*? British film makers did not come up with a *Double Indemnity* or an *Out of the Past*, but a number of features gingerly ventured into the shadows cast on the fringes of the genre.

Lawrence Huntington's *The Upturned Glass* (1947), a pet project of its star James Mason, was a psychological thriller in the Hitchcock vein. In a criminology lecture a brilliant neurosurgeon (Mason) outlines a

'perfect crime' committed by 'a perfectly sane man' for the best possible motives. The murder is one he is about to commit himself to avenge the death of the woman he loved (Rosamund John) at the hands of her vixenish sister-in-law (Pamela Kellino). The film is full of macabre touches. The 'perfect murder' degenerates into a clumsy struggle before Kellino is pushed out of a window, leaving Mason locked inside the room. He jemmies his way out and bundles the body into his car, driving off into an almost impenetrable mist. In the murk a face looms up eerily through his window as he is flagged down by a local doctor (Brefni O'Rorke) on an emergency call to a young girl who is dangerously ill. As they crawl towards their destination O'Rorke plies Mason with a flow of cheerfully cynical professional banter, joking about losing any notions of sentimentality 'when you've killed as many patients as I have'. Mason operates on the girl in a lonely farmhouse and saves her life, but O'Rorke, sensing his paranoia, discovers the body in the car. Mason drives off to Beachy Head where he throws himself off the cliffs.

The screenplay of Lance Comfort's *Bedelia* (1946) was written by Vera Caspary, the author of the novel on which *Laura* (1944) was based. There is a fleeting echo of that little masterpiece as *Bedelia* opens, the camera dollying up to a portrait of Margaret Lockwood, the Wicked Lady of the title. There is more than a hint of Barbara Worth in Lockwood's plausible psychopath, who has poisoned two husbands, collected the life insurance and now has designs on her third, Yorkshire businessman Ian Hunter. A twist of *Double Indemnity* is added in the form of

Margaret Lockwood's demure psychopath is cornered over the place settings by feline insurance investigator Barry K. Barnes in *Bedelia* (1946), directed by Lance Comfort. Written by Vera Caspary, *Bedelia* was a well-mannered British cross between *Double Indemnity* and *Laura* by way of *The Wicked Lady*.

Ann Todd is transfixed by Maxwell Reed's baroque hair style in *Daybreak* (1947), directed by Compton Bennett, in which Eric Portman played a barge-owner with a secret life as the public hangman. An anticapital punishment tract, the film was heavily cut by the censor.

feline insurance investigator Barry K. Barnes, posing as an artist and setting a series of intricate traps for his mendacious prey. As everyone is cut off by a blizzard at the climax, we can also toss in a pinch of David Mac-Donald's *Snowbound*. The scales finally fall from the besotted Hunter's eyes when Bedelia tries to rid herself of the troublesome insurance man by lacing his mackerels with arsenic. The family cat Topaz gets there first and dies in convulsions. 'You're mad, I loved a woman who doesn't exist,' Hunter tells Lockwood. 'I'm ill, very ill,' is her reply. 'Yes, I know, incurable.' Whereupon he leaves her in the bedroom with the rest of her poison, the next best thing to the loaded revolver in the library.

The civilized barbarities of British murder were exquisitely retailed in Arthur Crabtree's *Dear Murderer* (1947). Businessman Eric Portman flies back from America to confront his wife's lover, barrister Dennis Price, in his bachelor flat. Recovering from his surprise, Price offers him a drink and the two men settle down to swapping courteous ironies – 'It's not the going out that bothers me,' remarks Portman of Price's friendship with his wife, 'it's the staying in.' At Portman's suggestion, Price begins to write a note calling the whole thing off. Quite suddenly, Portman pulls a gun on him and ties him up. He tells Price with icily controlled anger that he has planned a foolproof murder, informing the hapless barrister of the carefully contrived method by which he will be gassed and his death made to look like suicide (his broken-off farewell letter will, of course, in the process become a suicide note). He even invites his victim to point out any flaws in the plan –

if he can, he will go free. Price fails. 'You were a bit of a failure as a lawyer; I'm glad my life didn't depend on your arguments,' Portman observes reproachfully before going about his grim business. These barbed exchanges remind one irresistibly of Dennis Price's observation, in *Kind Hearts and Coronets*, of the difficulty of disposing of people 'with whom one is not on friendly terms'.

Portman's gloomy, tormented screen persona was put to good use in Compton Bennett's *Daybreak* (1948). In this tortuous melodrama he played a very private man with three lives: as a hairdresser, bargee and public hangman. He marries a rootless waif (Anne Todd), gives away his hairdressing business to assistant Bill Owen and goes to live with Todd on one of his barges. His 'business trips' as a hangman remain a closely guarded secret and a ripe field for irony. When he bids goodbye to Bill Owen, he gives him a present for his son, a yo-yo. 'You always look so washed out when you come back,' Todd tells him

Throughout the 1940s, Eric Portman was haunted by the hangman. In Lawrence Huntington's *Wanted for Murder* (1946) he played a businessman who is driven out of his mind by his grandfather's gruesome reputation as the public hangman. He embarks on a strangling spree which ends in Hyde Park where, surrounded by virtually the entire Metropolitan police force, he conveniently drowns in the Serpentine. Dulcie Gray provided that staple of 1940s cinema, a shopgirl with a Roedean accent.

79

after one trip, 'like you've got a hangover.'

While the hangman is away, one of his barge hands, Olaf (Maxwell Reed), begins to make free with his young wife. At first she resists him but eventually succumbs to his rough embraces – perhaps overcome by the devilishly seductive way Reed slides a comb through his brilliantined locks. Portman returns home unexpectedly – the man on death row has been reprieved – to find them together. There is a fight and Portman disappears over the side, coming to in the morning on the low-tide mud. By going back to work in his hairdressing saloon (Owen knows nothing of his life as a bargee) he maintains the fiction of his death, causing his wife's suicide and Reed's conviction for murder. At the last, however, the rigidly insulated compartments of his life collapse in on each other when he is called in to officiate at Reed's hanging. He breaks down and returns to the hairdressing saloon where he hangs himself.

Perhaps the most remarkable British *film noir* of the 1940s was Michael Powell's *The Small Back Room* (1949). Set in World War II it is full of the darkness of self-doubt in its pitting of a crippled, alcoholic scientist (David Farrar) against a peculiarly nasty German booby-trap bomb, which he must dismantle on the windswept emptiness of Chesil Beach. The sinister little canister mocks his metal foot, containing within itself the infinite blackness which drowns Farrar's life. *The Small Back Room* is a haunting film of mood, marred only by an extraordinary Expressionist dream sequence in which Farrar attempts to clamber up a gigantic whisky bottle, one of those 'lapses of taste' which critics were never slow to point out in Powell's work.

David Niven and Marius Goring's whimsical French aristocrat, Conductor 71, in Powell and Pressburger's *A Matter of Life and Death* (1946). Powell recalled that the film was prompted by a suggestion from the MoI that the Archers make a film about Anglo-American relations 'because they were deteriorating'. Powell added, '...of course, they didn't know we would come up with *A Matter of Life and Death*'.

Powell and Pressburger

The mixture of bafflement and incomprehension which had greeted *The Life and Death of Colonel Blimp* followed Powell and Pressburger throughout the 1940s. Ignoring the notions of 'realism' forged in the wartime cinema, they went their own way, indulging in rich flights of fancy, dabbling in mysticism and employing sheer technical virtuosity to play tricks with time and space.

With *I Know Where I'm Going* (1945), Powell returned to the Scottish Isles, the scene of his first major film, *The Edge of the World* (1937). Brisk young career woman Wendy Hiller goes to the Western Isles to marry a multi-millionaire but is gradually seduced by the pagan enchantments of the Celtic fringe. Her journey is interrupted by a storm and she meets and falls in love with a young laird (Roger Livesey). She abandons her dreams of wealth; he throws off an ancient family curse, entering the forbidden keep of his ancestors to find that the curse is in reality a challenge which he has now fulfilled.

A Matter of Life and Death (1946), in Powell's words 'a hit at the documentary boys', was a remarkable exercise in rearranging time and space, moving with enormous technical panache between reality and hallucination. The film opens with a shot of the universe. The self-confident voice-over ('There goes another solar system; someone's been mucking about with the uranium atom again. Don't worry, it's not ours') provides an ironic dig at the documentary style. The vision narrows down to a raid over Germany and then to a blazing bomber whose pilot Peter Carter (David Niven) is spending the last moments of his life talking on his radio about love and poetry to June (Kim Hunter), an American WAC on a seemingly deserted airfield. He bales out with a parachute and miraculously survives to meet and fall in love with June. The 'miracle' is in fact the result of the bungling of the heavenly Conductor 71 (Marius Goring) who has lost Peter in the fog and failed to collect him. This foppish aristocrat, who met an untimely end in the French Revolution, is despatched from Powell's monochrome Heaven to the Technicolor world of Earth to claim the young airman. The film chronicles Peter's fight to stay on Earth aided by June and eccentric motorbike-riding doctor and brain specialist Dr Reeves (Roger Livesey). As we move towards the film's climax, Powell contrives a 'Chinese box' structure in which actions on one level

are paralleled on another. While Peter undergoes a complicated brain operation on Earth, his appeal is heard in the heavenly High Court filled with every nationality of every history and age. Peter, whose plea is that in his 'borrowed time' he has fallen in love, requests 'an ordinary Englishman' to defend him. His counsel is Dr Reeves, who has died in a motorbike accident while riding through a storm to fetch Peter's ambulance. The prosecutor is Abraham Farlan, the first American to be killed in the American War of Independence. Peter is finally saved when June agrees to take his place in Heaven and steps on to the mighty escalator leading to the other world. The machinery breaks down, demonstrating that, although there might be nothing stronger than the law in the Universe, there is nothing stronger on Earth than love. In the hospital the operation is completed and the surgeon removes his mask to reveal the face of the Judge in the heavenly Court of Appeal. Peter wakes in a private ward to be reunited with June.

For Powell and Pressburger, *A Matter of Life and Death* was 'a marvellous conjuring trick' and the film is a dazzling array of *coups de cinéma*: one of June's tears caught in a red rose; the camera panning back and forth to follow the ball in a game of table tennis; the moment in the operating theatre in which we find ourselves inside Peter's head as a giant pink eyelid closes over the camera lens. Perception, 'ways of seeing', the contrast between the documentary mode (the monochrome, ordered world of Heaven) and the fictional narrative (the 'impossible' Technicolor love story on Earth) are among the film's principal preoccupations. Significantly, Dr Reeves amuses himself by watching the villagers through his *camera obscura*, whose apparatus is lovingly delineated by Powell, prefiguring his 1960 masterpiece, *Peeping Tom*. With its lengthy courtroom battle between the embittered American Abraham Farlan and the patriarchal figure of Reeves, *A Matter of Life and Death* can be seen in part as a discourse on Anglo-American relations. It can also be viewed as a critique of the Welfare State; the black and white Heaven – a bureaucratic and directed Utopia – is the child of socialism, the wartime projection of which lay primarily in the hands of left-wing documentary film makers.

A Matter of Life and Death displays Powell's complete mastery of the studio. His next project, *Black Narcissus* (1947), an adaptation of a Rumer Godden novel, was a melodrama set in the Himalayas. It was filmed almost

entirely at Pinewood studios. A community of nuns, led by Deborah Kerr, arrive in a remote Nepalese kingdom to establish a mission in an abandoned palace which was once the home of the concubines of the kingdom's rulers. From the moment of their arrival, it is clear that the 'House of Women' will remain obstinately at odds with its new female intake, as the camera moves slowly over the fading erotic murals in its draught-whipped, deserted halls. The nuns find themselves in a limbo, caught between the lush, chaotic little statelet and the forbidding figure of the holy man who keeps his silent vigil on the boundary of their retreat. Perched over a dizzying drop into the valley below, the limitless views and crystal-clear air bring doubts and uncertainties crowding in. Deborah Kerr recalls her engagement to a young man in Ireland. Flora Robson, the gardener, forsakes the vegetable patch to plant honeysuckle and forget-me-nots. The prince's earthy, cynical English agent (David Farrar) introduces a disruptive element into the convent in the form of Kanchi (Jean Simmons), an exquisite little kitten, who has been pestering him with her precocious attentions. She evokes the dormant spirit of the Women's House with a sexually charged dance in its lapis lazuli-tiled reception hall. Finally, Sister Ruth (Kathleen Byron) is driven literally mad with desire for Farrar. In an explosion of bottled-up sexuality she discards her white habit and dons a scarlet dress. A vivid slash of lipstick across her lips, her red hair wild against her deathly white face, she descends on Kerr like an avenging fury from a bloodshot nightmare. In the struggle, at the edge of the precipice, she falls

Deborah Kerr's Sister Clodagh confronts Kathleen Byron's renegade nun, Sister Ruth, in Powell and Pressburger's *Black Narcissus* (1947), adapted from a Rumer Godden novel. Ravishingly photographed by Jack Cardiff, *Black Narcissus* is one of the most erotic films in post-war British cinema. Composer Brian Easdale was in charge of the film's sound effects, and the Himalayan setting was created in the studio by designer Alfred Junge, who had first worked with the Archers on *The Life and Death of Colonel Blimp* (1943).

Michael Powell's frequently criticized tendency to lapse into vulgarity was illustrated when David Farrar's crippled, alcoholic scientist grappled with his daemon, in the form of a monster whisky bottle, in *The Small Back Room* (1949).

Moira Shearer in the 20-minute ballet, choreographed by Robert Helpmann, which lies at the centre of Michael Powell's perverse, extravagant masterpiece *The Red Shoes* (1948). The ballet's expressionist sets, haunted by drifting strips of coloured cellophane, were designed by Hein Heckroth.

to her death. Defeated, the nuns leave the palace in a ravishingly filmed sequence as the monsoon breaks.

Jack Cardiff's photography contrasted the white of the nuns' habits with the dominant, lush blues of the interiors, swooning away in the sexual static generated by the sisters. The sound effects were handled by composer Brian Easdale; the climactic struggle at the cliff edge was pre-planned musically and the soundtrack recorded before the images were shot.

Powell's steady progress towards the musical choreographing of a film, and his conviction that composers and film makers had more in common with each other than the latter had with screenwriters, led to *The Red Shoes* (1948). A fantasy set in the world of ballet, it explored in bravura style Powell and Pressburger's romantic belief in the contradictions imposed by Life and Art, using the Lermontov ballet company as a parallel structure to their own film making company, the Archers.

The red shoes of the title are those of Hans Christian Andersen's fairy tale – the diabolic ballet shoes which dance their wearer to death. The potent image provides the inspiration for a ballet commissioned by the Diaghilev-like impresario of the Ballet Lermontov (Anton Walbrook), a man for whom life and dance are one and who has no time for prima ballerinas who are 'imbecile enough to get married'. When choreographer Leonide Massine reminds him that 'you can't alter human nature', he replies – 'You can do better than that, you can ignore it.' But even this fashion-plate Svengali falls victim to a passion for his brilliant protégé Victoria Page (Moira Shearer), the sole interpreter of the Red Shoes ballet. When she marries the ballet's composer (Marius Goring), Walbrook casts them into the outer darkness, while never ceasing to will her return. Ultimately, he achieves both her return and her destruction. The red shoes possess her, and her final leap is from the theatre balcony on to a railway line. Dying, she asks her husband to slip the shoes from her mangled limbs. The ballet goes on without her, a spotlight conveying the dead ballerina's presence on the stage.

Drenched in colour, saturated with overmastering emotions moving in time with the rhythms of the soundtrack, *The Red Shoes* is Powell's attempt to scale the Eiger of total cinema. It is a fairy tale, not far removed from the work of Walt Disney, whom Powell greatly admired; at one point Shearer ascends a seemingly endless, overgrown flight of steps to Lermontov's villa, her tiara and evening gown making her look for all the world like a princess from a Disney film.

The Red Shoes went £200,000 over budget. When it was seen by Rank executives, they were horrified – John Davis stalked out of a screening given by Emeric Pressburger without saying a word. At Universal there was a similar reaction. But far from being a disaster, *The Red Shoes* became Britain's biggest dollar earner, a position it held for many years. It was also the Archers' last film for Rank – in 1949 they moved over to Alexander Korda's British Lion to make *The Small Back Room*.

Rank in Crisis

By the end of the 1940s J. Arthur Rank was in serious trouble. The ambitious post-war expansion programme had bitten deep into his resources and had not been offset by success at the box office – in 1946 Rank's losses on film production alone were £1,667,000. His task – and those of all British film producers – was not made easier by the Entertainments Tax, set at a crippling 38 per cent of box-office receipts. The *coup de grâce*, however, was delivered by the Labour government. Shortly after the war, Michael Balcon wrote about J. Arthur Rank's 'expensive education' in the workings of the film industry and likened his burgeoning empire to 'a sort of giant crammer who demands tremendous fees for getting his pupils through their exams'. But if Rank imagined that he had swotted up the correct answers, he was cruelly mistaken. No sooner had he sat down to tackle the exams when the papers were twitched from under his nose by the men from Whitehall and new unseen ones put in their place.

In 1947 the Treasury, faced with a balance of payments crisis, turned their attentions to the substantial dollar drain represented by the earnings in Britain of American films – in that year alone about £18 million crossed the Atlantic. J. Arthur Rank was in America, negotiating distribution for his films, when rumours began to circulate that the Labour government was contemplating a 25 per cent *ad valorem* duty on American films released in Britain. He returned to persuade the government to change its mind, but without any consultation Hugh Dalton, Chancellor of the Exchequer, announced a swingeing duty of 75 per cent on all films from the dollar area, *paid in advance*, on estimated earnings. In

retaliation the Motion Picture Association of America placed an immediate embargo on the export of new films to Britain. The resulting eight-month deadlock was a disaster for Rank. The imposition of the *ad valorem* duty blasted his distribution arrangements in America and at the same time deprived his cinemas at home of their supply of popular Hollywood films. The Americans, on the other hand, did not suffer unduly. At the time of the introduction of the duty, there were at least 125 Hollywood films stockpiled in Britain, which were not subject to the tax. Along with reissues, which were also exempt, they ensured that the outflow of dollars from Britain was uninterrupted.

The government then compounded their original miscalculation by encouraging Rank (and Korda) to fill the gap suddenly created by their own lack of foresight. This spurred Rank into raising nearly £9½ million for a wildly optimistic investment plan of 47 films. The shareholders of Rank's Odeon theatre chain, accustomed to the steady dividends from the exhibition side of the industry, suddenly found that they were to be involved in production, despite the fact that they had been given a pledge in 1937 that this would never happen.

Sanity seemed to be returning in the spring of 1948 when the new President of the Board of Trade, Harold Wilson, negotiated a two-year agreement with the Motion Picture Association which allowed the Americans to retain $17 million a year of their earnings, a figure which could be increased by the equivalent of British earnings in the United States. A joint control committee was to be set up to supervise the use of the balance of the American money both inside and outside the industry. The *ad valorem* duty disappeared from the statute book in May 1948.

Almost immediately this new initiative was undermined by the Cinematograph Act of 1948, raising the British first feature quota to 45 per cent, which produced another shock wave in the United States and which in any case could not possibly be met by British producers. The sorry chapter of accidents was completed when the embargo occasioned by the original 75 per cent duty was lifted. Harold Wilson had failed to negotiate a phased release of unscreened American films and as a result a flood of eagerly awaited box-office hits like *Gentleman's Agreement*, *The Naked City* and *Body and Soul* attracted far bigger audiences than the product from Rank's stepped-up programme, which was now coming on stream.

Two Korda films of the late 40s. (*Right*) Schizophrenic Kieron Moore threatens suicide in Anthony Kimmins' *Mine Own Executioner* (1947). Burgess Meredith's lay analyst attempts to reason with him from a fire-engine's ladder. Kimmins himself nearly committed professional suicide with (*Centre*) *Bonnie Prince Charlie* (1948), a disastrous million-pound attempt to make a Hollywood-style costumer.

Alexander Korda distributed Herbert Wilcox's *Spring in Park Lane* (1947), box-office proof of the independent producer-director's belief that in the late 1940s audiences 'wanted films about nice people'. The nice people here are Tom Walls, Anna Neagle and Michael Wilding. Nicholas Phipps' sprightly screenplay invigorated a featherweight confection in which Wilding played a peer who masquerades as art collector Walls' footman while attempting to restore his family's fortunes. The public welcomed the lavish sets and popping champagne corks as a relief from the rigours of austerity, but a sequel, *Maytime in Mayfair* (1949), proved less successful.

By 1949 Rank owed the National Provincial Bank some £16 million. Independent Frame had been abandoned, as had the animation and children's film divisions. Gone, too, were the Charm School and Highbury Studios. Independent Producers had broken up: Launder and Gilliat, Powell and Pressburger and David Lean had been lured away by Alexander Korda. These defections were only partly remedied by the arrival of Anthony Asquith with his own production company, Javelin Films.

The crippled juggernaut was hauled back from the brink of disaster by John Davis, a cool-headed accountant who introduced a savage policy of retrenchment. The extravagant Filippo del Giudice had already parted company with Rank and now it was the turn of Sydney Box to go on a year's 'sabbatical'. The Gainsborough Studios at Islington and Shepherd's Bush were closed, the latter being sold to the BBC, and production at Denham was wound down. An edict went out that no film was to cost more than £150,000. Executives who survived the chop had to take a 10 per cent cut in salary.

Korda and London Films

Since the mid-30s Rank and Korda had been seated at opposite ends of a see-saw – when one was up, the other was down. By the end of the 1940s Korda was profiting from Rank's discomfiture. He had returned from Hollywood in 1944, under the banner of MGM–London Films, and reopened the studios at Elstree. He made only one film at Elstree, *Perfect Strangers* (1945) starring Robert Donat and Deborah Kerr, before falling out with MGM. He bought out London Films and struck out on his own, acquiring British Lion, the third largest distribution company in Britain, an interest in Shepperton Studios and a 50 per cent stake in the Warton Hall studio at Isleworth. In America, he negotiated a distribution deal with Twentieth Century-Fox. In the summer of 1948 Korda garnered a loan of £3 million from the newly established National Film Finance Corporation (one of the few Palache recommendations to be followed up). It was stipulated that the money go through the distribution rather than the production side of the industry, and Korda's only rival for the lion's share of the Corporation's operating fund of £5 million was Rank's General Film Distributors. As Rank was cutting back in the face of accumulating debt, Korda got the money.

Korda had retained his old ability to charm

and to wheel and deal but his film making touch was less sure. He chose to direct his first post-war film, a lavishly mounted and stiff adaptation of Oscar Wilde's *An Ideal Husband* (1947), starring Paulette Goddard and Michael Wilding. This was followed by an equally unsuccessful version of *Anna Karenina* (1948), directed by Julien Duvivier. Vivien Leigh was no match for Greta Garbo, Ralph Richardson miscast as Karenin and the inexperienced Kieron Moore hopelessly out of his depth as Vronsky. More successful at the box office was Anthony Kimmins' suspenseful *Mine Own Executioner* (1947), adapted by Nigel Balchin from his own novel and starring Burgess Meredith as a mixed-up alienist treating a violent schizophrenic (Kieron Moore). Kimmins was an interesting film maker, who wrote and directed some of George Formby's best films of the 40s, but his next project for Korda, *Bonnie Prince Charlie* (1948) nearly wrecked his career and Korda's reconstructed empire. David Niven played the Young Pretender in an unflattering blond wig, and that is the only memorable thing to relate about a £1m disaster which was savaged by the critics and ignored by the public.

By 1949 Korda had become more of a film financier than the film maker he had been in the 1930s. The most prestigious recruit to British Lion during this period was Carol Reed, then at the high point of his career. Reed's first post-war film was *Odd Man Out* (1947), adapted from F.L. Green's novel by R.C. Sherriff. Extravagantly praised at the time of its release, it now seems too overwrought to be entirely successful. It is built around the last hours of a reluctant Northern Irish gunman, Johnny McQueen (James

During the late 40s, Carol Reed's career reached a peak, from which there was a slow falling away. 'I believe in everything we're trying to do, but this violence isn't getting us anywhere.' James Mason's dying gunman receives the dubious ministrations of Elwyn Brook Jones and F.J. McCormick in *Odd Man Out* (1947). The film displayed a very British reaction against political violence which was echoed in Ealing's *The Gentle Gunman* (1952), which also dealt with the IRA, and Thorold Dickinson's *Secret People* (1952) – his second film at Ealing – which was set in pre-war London and was centred on the assassination of a Fascist dictator by a group of left-wing emigrés.

Bobby Henrey, Ralph Richardson and Michele Morgan in *The Fallen Idol* (1948), Reed's first collaboration with Graham Greene.

The Third Man (1949). Orson Welles gives Joseph Cotten a little lecture on Switzerland, democracy and cuckoo clocks as they ride the giant ferris wheel, high above the scuttling, ant-like figures hurrying through the streets of post-war Vienna.

Mason), on the run after being fatally wounded in a raid on a linen mill to secure funds 'for the party'. Mason takes an unconscionable time to die and some of his encounters, notably with a crazed artist played at full eye roll by Robert Newton, go way over the top. The dying gunman is propped up amid the decaying Georgian splendour of Newton's lodgings, surrounded by ranks of his appropriately popeyed portraits, while the artist strives to catch the intimations of death in his face. After this experience, Johnny's end at the hands of the police is a merciful release.

The theme of a man 'doing the wrong thing for the right reason' appealed to Reed, and the moral dilemmas implicit in the film make a logical connection with the director's successful association with the novelist

Graham Greene. Their first film together – and Reed's first of a five-feature contract with Korda – was *The Fallen Idol* (1948), adapted by Greene from his story 'The Basement Room'. In an empty, echoing embassy, an eight-year-old boy (Bobby Henrey) has been left in the care of his hero, Baines the butler (Ralph Richardson). Baines' unpleasant wife (Sonia Dresdel) is found dead and the young boy, who knows Baines is having an affair with a younger woman (Michele Morgan), assumes Baines must have murdered her. His loyal attempts at a cover up only serve to implicate his hero. Subtly plotted and beautifully played, *Fallen Idol* was a more highly controlled film than *Odd Man Out*, though it does contain two bravura passages: a game of hide-and-seek in the darkened embassy; and the little boy's panic-stricken flight through the London streets after witnessing Mrs Baines' death.

The conflict between innocence and experience was again explored by Reed and Greene in *The Third Man* (1949), a story developed from a single sentence which several years before Greene had scrawled on the back of an envelope: 'I had paid my last farewell to Harry a week ago, when his coffin was lowered into the frozen February ground, so that it was with incredulity that I saw him pass by, without a sign of recognition, among the host of strangers in the Strand.' From this flimsy beginning, Greene cast *The Third Man* as a novel (he found writing for the screen immensely difficult) and then worked with Reed to turn it back into a screenplay. This was not the only hiccup in the film's gestation. David O. Selznick, who had some money in the film, was unhappy with Reed's choice of Orson Welles as Harry Lime and tried to persuade Reed to replace him with, of all people, Noel Coward.

The Third Man is set in occupied post-war Vienna, whose faded Baroque elegance provides a peeling shell for a seamy world of black marketeers, fixers and displaced persons. Everything and everyone is for sale in a city where the brutalities of occupation are papered over with the politest cynicism. Into this shadow land blunders the naïve Holly Martins (Joseph Cotten), a writer of pulp Westerns down on his luck and looking for his old friend Harry Lime. He is told that Lime has been killed in a street accident but after the funeral is informed by the British Major Calloway (Trevor Howard) that Lime was a racketeer, peddling adulterated penicillin which had caused the death of many children. Martins sets out to find the truth and in the process finds Lime, who turns out to be the mysterious 'third man' glimpsed at the scene of the accident. He betrays Lime to the authorities to save the enigmatic Anna (Alida Valli) whom both men love, from being deported behind the Iron Curtain. A chase through the sewers of Vienna ends when Lime is cornered like a rat and shot by his friend. After Harry has been finally laid to rest, Martins waits for Anna at the end of the long, leaf-strewn avenue leading to the cemetery. But there is no climactic clinch – she walks past him without a word.

The Third Man is one of Graham Greene's 'entertainments', brilliantly realized by a director at the top of his form, and not to be taken too seriously. Greene himself has written: 'We had no desire to move people's emotions; we wanted to entertain them, to frighten them a little, to make them laugh. Reality, in fact, was only a background to a fairy tale.' In addition, the themes of *The Third Man* were overlaid with another fairy tale. In the final count, the film is gobbled up by Welles' Harry Lime, a bankrupt Citizen Kane on the run from his creditors and hovering portentously over a pygmy Europe.

In telling this 'fairy tale', Reed assembled all the psychological and concrete elements of *noir* cinema – uncertainty, betrayal, rain-slicked streets, enveloping shadows and tilted camera shots – with enormous skill. Much of *The Third Man* was shot with a wide-angle lens which gave the buildings on location a distorted, nightmarish quality and emphasised the glistening wet streets (kept continually hosed down at considerable expense by Reed's crew). Many of the film's most telling moments were conceived by Reed: the mortally wounded Lime's hands groping agonisingly up through the sewer gratings (they were in fact Reed's hands); Valli's walk, silent, past Cotten at the film's bleak conclusion; and the discovery of the zither player Anton Karas, whose music gives *The Third Man* its exotic flavour and punctuates its moods. There are also some extremely good black jokes. At one point Martins is suddenly bundled into a car and driven at breakneck speed through the night, not to his assassination but to an arts club whose members mistakenly imagine him to be a famous author. As Martins waits for his final rendezvous with Lime, a huge Quasimodo-like shadow creeps across the face of a building, followed by its owner, an old man selling balloons.

The Studio with the Team Spirit

One satellite of the Rank empire which sailed relatively unruffled through the storms of the late 40s was Ealing studios. Indeed, 1949 was an *annus mirabilis* for Ealing, during which it released three classic comedies – *Passport to Pimlico*, *Whisky Galore!* and *Kind Hearts and Coronets*. The first of these, Henry Cornelius' *Passport to Pimlico*, established the received view of the Ealing output which persists today – the celebration of the 'little man's' mildly anarchic rebellion against the big battalions of free enterprise and bureaucracy.

Ealing, 'the studio with the Team Spirit', was very much the child of Michael Balcon's brand of benevolent paternalism. Balcon owed much to his predecessor, Basil Dean – not least the 'Team Spirit' slogan, which hung on the walls of the studio's sound stages. In 1955, when Ealing moved to MGM's Boreham Wood studios, Balcon was careful to leave behind a plaque which stated, 'Here during a quarter of a century were made many films projecting Britain and the British character.'

When Monja Danischewsky arrived at Ealing in 1938 as Balcon's new head of publicity, the very buildings of the studio seemed quintessentially British: 'It somehow had the air of a family business, set on a village green, in the queen of London suburbs. The administrative block looked like a country cottage and was separated from the studios proper by a little rose garden, tended between crises by Balcon's secretary, Miss Slater.'

Danischewsky's description provides an apt and early example of the interplay between the studio's structure and the films it produced. In Walter Forde's *Cheer Boys Cheer* (1939), the last Ealing feature to be released before the outbreak of war, a small family-owned brewery, evocatively named Greenleaf, fights off a takeover bid by the massive Ironsides brewing combine. A broad comedy, harking back to the Dean era, it nevertheless provided a rough and ready model for the Ealing mainstream of ten years later. It also provides a metaphor for Ealing's subsequent absorption by Rank. In *Cheer Boys Cheer* the two breweries end the film reconciled and united. Balcon's 1944 deal with Rank ensured Ealing's survival, enabling the studio to produce a controlled output of modestly budgeted features while remaining safe within the belly of the monster.

The Ealing ethos placed great store on continuity and loyalty. In the war it carried the studio through the absurdities of *Ships With Wings* to the maturity of *San Demetrio, London*, released in December 1943 and the last Ealing film of the wartime years to deal directly with the conflict. Ealing's films of the mid-war years tapped the sense of purpose and comradeship, and the scaling down of class differences, which characterized the national consensus of the period. Ealing itself – with its small, long-serving work force – came to resemble one of the tightly knit groups whose community of interest was celebrated in its films. Its own posture was that of the quiet understatement found in the words of the judge at the end of *San Demetrio, London* – 'the very modest recital of some gallant gentlemen concerning a memorable achievement'.

In January 1945, as the war drew to a close, Michael Balcon wrote an article for Kinematograph Weekly outlining a bold programme for post-war British cinema: 'British films must present to the world a picture of Britain as a leader in social reform, in the defeat of social injustices and a champion of civil liberties...Britain as a patron of and parent of great writing, painting and music...Britain as a questing explorer, adventurer and trader... Britain as a mighty military power standing alone and undaunted against terrifying aggression.' Later in the article, Balcon described in less bombastic and more practical terms the avenues that the studio should explore: 'contemporary life in Britain in different sectors of our society, films with an outdoor background of the British scene, screen adaptations of our literary classics, films reflecting the postwar aspirations not of governments or parties but of individuals'.

Between the end of the war and the release of *Passport to Pimlico*, a number of films were made at Ealing which pursued these themes: *It Always Rains on Sunday*, *The Loves of Joanna Godden*, *Nicholas Nickleby*. An attempt was also made to make films with a more 'international' flavour: Harry Watt's Australian 'Westerns', *The Overlanders* and *Eureka Stockade*; *Johnny Frenchman*, which dealt with the friendship that war brings between a Cornish fishing village and a rival Breton community; and *Frieda*, a melodrama about a young German girl brought back to England by her English husband during the closing months of the war.

These films represent staging posts on Ealing's uncertain post-war journey. It seems ironic that following Balcon's ringing declaration of intent, Ealing's first film was the

The legacy of war. David Farrar and his German wife Mai Zetterling at the cinema just before the pictures of Auschwitz begin to roll on the Movietone News in Basil Dearden's *Frieda* (1947).

collection of ghost stories, *Dead of Night*. As we have seen in the 'haunted mirror' episode in *Dead of Night* and the resolution of *It Always Rains on Sunday*, when it came to the crunch there was a compulsive pulling back from the brink, an unwillingness to confront the tensions lying beneath the placid surface of British life. (Harry Watt's robust Australian films obviously fall outside this criticism.)

In Basil Dearden's *Frieda* (1947) the arrival in a quiet country town of a young German woman (Mai Zetterling) with the escaped POW (David Farrar) who has married her throws the town and his family into confusion. She has saved Bob Dawson's life in Europe, she is intelligent, beautiful and an anti-Nazi, but with the war not yet over, her acceptance is a long drawn out process. Bob's brother was killed in a bombing raid over Cologne, where Frieda's parents also lived and died. His elder sister Nell (Flora Robson), is a Labour parliamentary candidate who is concerned that the marriage will undermine her hardline attitude towards Germany and lose her votes. The townspeople's reactions vary from the directly hostile to a peculiarly British form of muddled xenophobia: the local builder says his man won't come up to the house to do the repairs as his son was killed in the Ardennes; at the local Labour club, a pompous councillor decides that 'it would be a whole lot easier if the Germans looked like the Japs'.

Frieda's position is made worse by the strangely insensitive behaviour of her husband. He insists they sleep separately until they go through a second marriage ceremony. Significantly, he reoccupies his old bedroom, the one he had when he was a child. He returns to his pre-war occupation of schoolmastering but resigns as soon as some of his pupils boycott lessons because of his 'undesirable associations'. On a trip to the cinema he makes Frieda sit through the Movietone news pictures of the liberation of Belsen. As the election campaign gets under way, he 'accidentally' arrives with Frieda in the market square just as Nell is delivering a speech denouncing all Germans as being guilty of a 'monstrous crime'.

Finally, the living embodiment of Farrar's rigidly repressed doubts and neuroses arrives in the form of Frieda's brother Richard (Albert Lieven), who despite his recently acquired Polish uniform remains a diehard Nazi. Dawson beats him up but not before Richard tells him that 'loyalty, faith and blood' bind him and his sister together and

that 'what you see in me you will see in her and her children, *your* children'. Dawson returns home, wordlessly tosses Richard's swastika into Frieda's lap and tells sister Nell, 'I wish she was dead'.

Frieda wanders off into the winter snow without a coat, obviously set on suicide. She is coolly watched by Nell, who decides that this is clearly the best solution to everyone's problems. At the last moment she relents and tells Bob, who drags Frieda from the river. The film ends with Nell being told by her brother's widow (Glynis Johns) that 'You can't treat human beings as though they were less than human without becoming less than human yourself.'

Despite the comfortable moral of *Frieda*'s conclusion, one is left with the impression that very little has been resolved. At no point in the film has Bob attempted seriously to come to terms with Frieda as a woman, let alone as a German, and there is little indication that he ever will. This stifling of emotion, the unconscious choice not to think things through, also stalks through Charles Frend's reverent handling of *Scott of the Antarctic* (1949), a measured and uncritical account of the classic stiff upper lip cock-up. Reviewing the film in *Sequence*, Lindsay Anderson isolated with merciless precision the standard British technique for dealing with moments of emotional tension: 'When emotion threatens, make your characters talk about something else in a little, uncertain, high-pitched voice.' It is worth isolating the relevant passage from the screenplay and quoting it at some length. Dr Wilson has decided to accept Scott's offer of a place on his expedition. With his wife Oriana, he watches Scott drive away from their country home.

ORIANA: That's the fly you caught the two-pounder on. In the burn at Clachen. Remember?
WILSON: Yes, it's a long time ago now. The gut's all perished. (He shows her that it's so.)
ORIANA: (Her voice a little uncertainly high.) So it has. (From the distance comes the hideous noise of Scott's motor starting. She buries her face in his coat.) Oh darling, darling (Wilson looks up and there is much sadness in his eyes, but Oriana keeps her face buried in his coat. Over the scene, the spluttering of the engine. Fade out.)

Scott of the Antarctic relies heavily on Scott's diaries and they provide the voice-over commentary as the expedition approaches its terrible end. One passage is crucial to the film

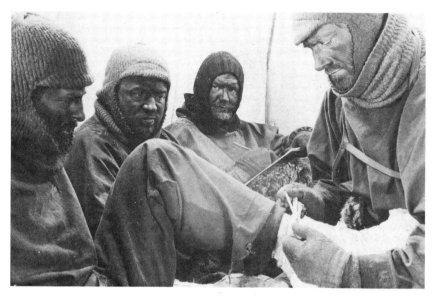

'March 10: Things steadily downhill. Oates' foot worse. He has rare pluck and must know that he can never get through.' Dr 'Bill' Wilson (Harold Warrender) tends Captain Oates (Derek Bond) as 'Birdie' Bowers (Reginald Beckwith) and Captain Scott (John Mills) steel themselves for the end in Charles Frend's *Scott of the Antarctic* (1949).

and by extension to much of post-war British cinema: 'Amongst ourselves we were unendingly cheerful but what each man feels in his heart I can only guess.' One automatically thinks back to Laura Jessop's voice-over in *Brief Encounter* as Dolly Messiter destroys her tender farewell to Alec Harvey: 'Nobody would have known what he was thinking.' And one can also think forward to the moment in *Reach for the Sky* when the camera discreetly pulls away from Douglas Bader's pain-wracked face as he lies in hospital after the amputation of his legs. Later the pain of rehabilitation is 'cheerfully' sublimated in the form of social embarrassment – learning to dance, falling over when playing golf.

Ernest Bevin once criticized the British for their 'poverty of desire', and this tendency to inhibition blocked Balcon's plans for a new cinema of ambitious, outward-looking films tackling big subjects. Instead, Ealing turned inwards, rummaging in its own past to find a more modest approach to the problems of post-war Britain. Charles Barr accurately described Ealing's post-war history in terms of 'an animal emerging from its burrow, blinking in the sunlight, making a few excursions without ever cutting itself off from its base, then scuttling back again into the familiar warm atmosphere of home'. The questing British explorer had become the questing British vole.

Passport to Pimlico

Passport to Pimlico was written by T.E.B. Clarke who two years earlier had been responsible for *Hue and Cry*, an engaging steal from 'Emil and the Detectives' in which a

gang of crooks use *The Trump*, a boys' magazine, to send messages to each other. In a memorable climax, they are brought to book on a bomb site by hundreds of boys who converge on them from all over London.

Passport to Pimlico followed *Hue and Cry*'s framework – a fantasy set against a realistic background. The film opens with an elaborate joke, making heatwave-struck Pimlico seem like a clip from *Torrid Zone*, before picking up the ball from *Hue and Cry* and moving on to children playing on a bomb site. An unexploded bomb is disturbed and detonates to reveal a cache of medieval documents. Eccentric historian Margaret Rutherford confirms that they establish beyond doubt that the inhabitants of Miramont Place are citizens of the kingdom of Burgundy, the result of a grant of land made by Edward IV to the exiled Charles the Rash. 'Blimey, I'm a foreigner,' gulps the local copper. Most accounts of the film then concentrate on the little community's ecstatic realization that they are now free from the constraints of British law and the welter of post-war austerity regulations. The 'Burgundians' toss away their ration books with gay abandon; bookmaker Sydney Tafler openly plies his trade in defiance of the police; the pub stays open all night. In fact, these activities occupy only the first half of the film and are a prelude to its real concern – the return to the solidarity of the wartime communal spirit.

In the wake of the Burgundians' declaration of independence comes an army of spivs; milling crowds pour into this apparent haven of free enterprise, causing chaos in the streets. The inhabitants of Miramont Place are split among themselves. The publican Garland (Frederick Piper) and the local bank manager Wix (Raymond Huntley) are determined to reap the chaotic benefits of their new freedom: 'It's every man for himself!' Garland asserts with evident satisfaction. But Arthur Pemberton (Stanley Holloway), the homely proprietor of the local ironmongers and archetypal Ealing man, is thoroughly alarmed by the undisciplined invasion of the little enclave by forces they cannot control. He suggests that they open talks with the government but is pre-empted by the men in Whitehall, who place their own official cordon round Miramont Place. The spivs are kept out and the Burgundians kept in.

Almost immediately the mood of wartime Britain is evoked as the Burgundians buckle down to deal with this new threat. In a spirit of intense nostalgia, all the apparatus of the Blitz is wheeled out: stringent rationing is

Stanley Holloway as Arthur Pemberton, archetypal Ealing man, in Henry Cornelius' *Passport to Pimilico* (1949). Betty Warren was Mrs Pemberton and Barbara Murray, sporting a delightful utility two-piece, was his daughter Shirley, all set for a characteristically sexless Ealing romance with Paul Dupuis' Duke of Burgundy.

introduced; the children are 'evacuated'; Pemberton and Wix find a common cause and the disagreeable Garland's pub is 'nationalized' (he also suffers the humiliation of being evacuated with the children). Enormous ingenuity and enterprise are displayed in combating the siege. Showers of food are thrown across the barriers by friendly crowds of Londoners. Eventually a compromise is reached. The Burgundians cede their independence and prepare to celebrate at an open-air dinner to which they invite their principal Whitehall adversaries. Each place setting comes complete with a new ration book. As the meal begins, the heatwave comes to an end in a sudden downpour of rain.

The final message of *Passport to Pimlico* is very revealing about Ealing's collective view of post-war Britain. Burgundy/Miramont Place is a model for the nation – at one point Pemberton's wife (Betty Warren) declares, 'It's because we're English that we are sticking up for our rights to be Burgundians.' Pemberton's attitude of nervous horror when confronted with the implications of full-blooded free enterprise and the consequences of 'every man for himself', is shared by Ealing. The fragile unity of Miramont Place is nearly pulled apart by these forces and it is only when the community is sealed off in a time capsule, *circa* 1943, that it 'finds itself'.

Ealing's Renegade Strain

Alexander Mackendrick's *Whisky Galore* and Robert Hamer's *Kind Hearts and Coronets* are often lumped together with *Passport to Pimlico*, but they come from a renegade

Basil Radford's Captain Waggett collapses like a pricked balloon in the cruel ending to Alexander Mackendrick's *Whisky Galore* (1949). Henry Mollinson's customs officer Farquharson is the wry observer. Nine years later the Waggett character was played by Roland Culver in *Rockets Galore* (1958), Michael Relph's limp attempt to revive the Ealing spirit, in which Todday is threatened with a missile base.

Ealing strain. Both of them pull aside the curtain to reveal a world with a harder, more subversive edge than the one inhabited by the cheerful innocents of Miramont Place, and both of them have disturbingly ambiguous endings.

Superficially, *Whisky Galore* bears some resemblance to *Passport to Pimlico*. The islanders of the Hebridean outcrop of Todday are a small, embattled community, plunged deep into Celtic gloom by the wartime shortage of whisky, the 'water of life' without which, for a true islander, life is not worth living. 'I don't think the world has been in such a terrible mess since the Flood,' sighs the island's oldest inhabitant.

As if in answer to their prayers, the SS *Cabinet Minister* – captained by Compton

Exquisite *mise en scène* as over the tinkling teacups Dennis Price anticipates the demise of Valerie Hobson's photographer husband in Robert Hamer's masterpiece, *Kind Hearts and Coronets* (1949). Art direction was by William Kellner.

Mackenzie in a cameo role and loaded to the gunwhales with 50,000 cases of export whisky – runs aground in the fog off Todday. The film recounts the islanders' salvaging of the precious cargo and their fight to keep it as they conduct a running battle with the officer in charge of the local Home Guard, a punctilious Englishman, Captain Waggett, beautifully played by Basil Radford.

As in *Passport to Pimlico*, the community is led by a shopkeeper, Macroon (Wylie Watson), but where Arthur Pemberton was bluff and straightforward, Macroon displays a devious Celtic cunning which progressively humiliates and finally destroys the upright Waggett. The Waggett character is paralleled in *Passport to Pimlico* by the civil servant Gregg (also played by Radford), a man who provides the Whitehall mirror image of Pemberton, a soulmate who can sit down to dinner with him at the end of the film. Waggett and Macroon, however, inhabit completely different worlds and the uncomprehending Englishman is soon reduced to blustering about the islanders' lack of 'sportsmanship'. 'They don't play the game for the sake of the game,' he complains feebly to his English sergeant (Bruce Seton). When the islanders make off with the whisky he exclaims, jowls wobbling in horror, 'Once you let people take the law into their own hands, it would mean anarchy,' a sentiment with which Pemberton would have heartily agreed. But the islanders are allowed to get away with it and to inflict a final humiliation on Waggett by framing him for whisky smuggling. Waggett subsides like a pricked balloon, the unmistakably savage laughter of his wife (Catherine Lacey) ringing in his ears.

Mackendrick later described how during the filming he came increasingly to sympathize with Waggett and to disapprove of the islanders' ways, although this does not seem to have softened the film's harsh ending.

Robert Hamer's *Kind Hearts and Coronets*, the third of the three great comedies of 1949, is a small masterpiece, under whose cool and ironic surface lurk all the sexual and emotional drives customarily muffled by Ealing's self-imposed limitations. Its elegant script was adapted by Hamer and John Dighton from Roy Horniman's Wildean novel of decadence *Israel Rank* and its smooth visual surface is provided by the photography of Douglas Slocombe.

Dennis Price, in the best performance of a sadly blighted career, was Louis Mazzini, the son of the younger daughter of the Duke of Chalfont disowned by her family – the d'Ascoynes – after running off to marry a penniless Italian singer (also played by Price in the opening sequence). Young Louis suffers the humiliation of knowing about his noble blood while having to work in a draper's shop. Snubs from the family come thick and fast. When Louis' mother dies, he is refused permission to place her in the family vault. An obnoxious junior d'Ascoyne (the first of the eight celebrated cameos played by Alec Guinness) secures his dismissal from the draper's on the grounds of insolence. He is also dismissed as a social inferior by his landlord's daughter Sibella (Joan Greenwood) and his heartfelt proposal of marriage treated as an amusing aberration. Louis decides to take his revenge by murdering all eight of the d'Ascoynes who stand between him and the dukedom.

First to go is the tormentor of the draper's shop, Ascoyne d'Ascoyne, whose punt Louis propels over a weir at Maidenhead. Pondering on the unfortunate death of Henry's female companion, Louis reflects, 'I was sorry about the girl but found some relief in the reflection that she had presumably, during the weekend, already undergone a fate worse than death.' Henry d'Ascoyne, a keen amateur photographer, is blown up in his darkroom; the doddering Canon d'Ascoyne succumbs to arsenic in his Cockburn's '69, administered by Louis posing as the Bishop of Matabeleland; suffragette Aunt Edith's ballooning activities are brought to a sudden end by a well-placed arrow; General d'Ascoyne is disposed of with a booby-trapped pot of caviar as he repeats for the thousandth time the details of his most celebrated campaign; and Admiral d'Ascoyne disposes of himself, contriving through sheer pigheadedness a spectacular collision during manoeuvres and going down with his ship. Louis is now heir apparent to the Chalfont title, a rising power in the d'Ascoyne family bank and the fiancé of the statuesque Edith (Valerie Hobson), widow of the photographer cousin. He secures the title by luring the Duke into one of his own mantraps and then finishing the job with a double-barrelled shotgun – whereupon the decrepit banking uncle, Lord d'Ascoyne, expires with shock on hearing that he has succeeded to the dukedom. But Louis' enjoyment of the title, and the glacial charms of Edith, is shortlived. Sibella's bankrupt husband Lionel (John Penrose) has died in mysterious circumstances after a quarrel with Louis and the new Duke of Chalfont is charged with and convicted of the one murder he did not commit. Sibella agrees to produce Lionel's suicide note and secure Louis' release but only if he in turn will agree to get rid of Edith and make her his duchess. Self-possessed and cool, Louis steps out of the prison gate to be greeted by Sibella and Edith who are waiting in separate carriages. As he deliberates on his choice, a reporter from *Tit Bits* (Arthur Lowe) enquires about his memoirs. His memoirs... Louis comes to with a start and the camera moves back to his cell, where on the table lies the pile of papers recording his rise to the dukedom. Written while he awaits hanging, they have been left behind in the excitement of his release.

It is the memoirs which provide the film's framing device – we are introduced to them at the beginning of the film as Louis pens them in the death cell, surrounded by a deferential collection of prison officials. They provide the film's commentary and many of its most felicitous snatches of dialogue, delivered with deadpan relish by Dennis Price. Much more than this, they are used to create a brilliant interplay between word and image. As Louis recounts the problems of disposing of the Admiral, the voice-over is accompanied by an almost subliminal shot of him poring over the elaborate plans of a torpedo. Everyone who has seen the film remembers the moment when a small column of smoke appears over Valerie Hobson's shoulder as she swaps genteel small talk with Price over tea in the garden. The smoke announces the death of her husband in his darkroom, but Price allows the conversation to continue until the carefully chosen moment when he draws it to Hobson's attention. The delight lies in the contrast between the unruffled surface and the tensions underneath.

At the time of its release, *Kind Hearts and Coronets* was stigmatized by Lindsay Anderson as being 'emotionally quite frozen'. But the coolly considered confidences which pass between Louis and Sibella positively crackle with barely concealed sexuality. They are in keeping with the mood of the film and with the historical period within which it was set. Passion is never far away. During his affair with the married Sibella, Louis warns her that she is 'playing with fire'. Sibella replies, 'At least it warms me.'

Robert Hamer left Ealing shortly after completing *Kind Hearts and Coronets*. He made several interesting films between 1949 and 1960, including *The Spider and the Fly* (1949) and *Father Brown* (1954), with Alec Guinness as the priestly detective, but he never recaptured the brilliance of his early masterpiece. His career ended with a pot-boiling comedy, *School for Scoundrels* (1960) based on the writings of Stephen Potter.

Alexander Mackendrick stayed at Ealing until 1955 before returning to his native America (he was born in Boston and brought up in Glasgow) to make his last important film, *Sweet Smell of Success* (1957). At Ealing he made three more comedies – *The Man in the White Suit*, *The Maggie* and *The Ladykillers* – and *Mandy* (1952), an intensely moving account of a deaf child's struggle to communicate.

Mandy Miller, the little girl who played the title role in *Mandy*, also appears in *The Man in the White Suit*, a film which stands at a crucial moment in Ealing's post-war history. A strange young research chemist, Sidney Stratton (Alec Guinness), infiltrates the Birnley textile mill and creates a completely indestructible, dirt-resistant material. The mill owner (Cecil Parker) has the material made up into the luminous white suit of the title, a garment which seems to wear its owner (Guinness) rather than the other way round. Sidney's triumph is short-lived. Far from being hailed as a benefactor of mankind, he is confronted by an unholy alliance of capital and labour determined to protect their markets and their jobs. An immensely aged robber baron, Sir John Kierlaw (Ernest Thesiger) is summoned from London to save the situation. But even this wheezing Victorian grand-paterfamilias, the very embodiment of ruthless market forces, fails to make Sidney grasp the consequences of his disinterested pursuit of scientific research.

Persuasion gives way to violence and then bribery. Birnley's daughter Judith (Joan

93

'By Jove, Holland, it's a good job we're both honest men.' Stanley Holloway, Alec Guinness, Alfie Bass and Sidney James admire their first solid gold Eiffel Tower, cast from their bullion haul, in Charles Crichton's *The Lavender Hill Mob* (1951). A distillation of the Ealing daydream of the ingenious 'little man' pitted against the big battalions of bureaucracy, its screenplay won an Academy Award for T.E.B. Clarke.

Ernest Thesiger's ancient robber baron, Sir John Kierlaw, attempts without success to explain the economic facts of life to Alec Guinness's maverick inventor Sidney Stratton in Alexander Mackendrick's *The Man in the White Suit* (1951). Beefy executive Howard Marion Crawford, Michael Gough and Cecil Parker brace themselves for more old-fashioned methods of persuasion.

Greenwood) is put up to bringing Sidney round. Carrying the suggestion to its logical conclusion she demands a fee for her 'services'. Her father and her fiancé Corland (Michael Gough) are horrified but as they flap around, impaled on the logic of their own cynicism, the splendidly unhypocritical Kierlaw leaps to strike a bargain of £5,000. Having humiliated her menfolk, Judith then reverses the situation by setting Sidney free – she tells him that as the material is indestructible, a single thread from the suit will enable him to climb down from the bedroom in which he is locked.

Pursued through the streets by a posse of executives and trade unionists, Sidney encounters his elderly landlady (Edie Martin, the frail, birdlike old lady who crops up time and again in Ealing films): 'Why can't you scientists leave things alone?' she asks him,

'What's to become of my bit of washing when there's no washing to do?' A chink appears in Sidney's previously impenetrable chain mail of innocence and moments later, as his pursuers close in on him, the white suit begins to fall apart. The film ends on an ambiguous note with a hint that Sidney has discovered a flaw in his original calculations. Perhaps he will become a cuckoo in the nest of another unsuspecting organisation, his joyously bubbling retorts and tubes giving birth to yet more chaos.

The sharper ironies of *The Man in the White Suit* are reserved for the stagnation and fear of innovation which infected post-war British industry and which during the same period slowly overwhelmed Ealing Studios. The film mercilessly shatters the soft option of cheerful consensus which is the message of *Passport to Pimlico*. The alliance between union and management is, in reality, phoney, merely serving their respective entrenched interests. This is brilliantly underlined during a meeting between the shop stewards and Birnley executives which is interrupted by a telephone call for one of the union representatives. The call is taken by Corland, who can barely conceal the amusement in his upper-class drawl as he asks if 'someone called Bertha is in the room'. (There is a remarkably similar moment in Jack Clayton's *Room at the Top*, when snobbish industrialist's wife Ambrosine Philpotts reflects on her future son-in-law Joe Lampton, 'Lampton – what curious names some of these people have.') Management and unions set their faces against change and Britain becomes quite literally a Tight Little Island – the title in the United States of *Whisky Galore*. Significantly, when discussing the role of Birnley with Cecil Parker, Mackendrick advised the actor, 'Model yourself on Mick' – Michael Balcon.

The Blue Lamp

Ealing/Balcon chose the path of consensus. Its history in the 1950s is one of inexorable decline as it clung to a faltering vision of community values and drifted into the celebration of quaintness and whimsicality with which the studio is now automatically associated. The purest distillation of the Ealing philosophy before decadence set in was Basil Dearden's *The Blue Lamp*, scripted by T.E.B. Clarke from a story by Ted Willis. The film opens with middle-aged policeman George Dixon (Jack Warner) showing young recruit Andy Mitchell (Jimmy Hanley) the ropes on his beat. He takes Mitchell under his wing,

offering him a room in his terraced house whose cosy kitchen is presided over by Gladys Henson, brewing endless cups of tea and drying George's socks over the range. It's an almost suffocating picture of Ealing's idealized version of working class life – the little terraced house, the kitchen, the garden at the back where Dixon keeps his pigeons and grows begonias, all the comfortable private rituals of English life. This domesticity is extended to the police station – choir practice under the baton of Welsh constable Meredith Edwards, relaxed banter in the canteen and the avuncular figures of Sergeants Clive Morton and Campbell Singer on the desk.

In and out of the station's swing doors process a reassuring crowd of old ladies looking for their lost dogs, grubby little urchins and picturesque drunks. On the mean streets down which George Dixon plods, police work seems to consists principally of tiptoeing thoughtfully past slumbering night watchmen and moving on chirpy Cockney barrow boys. A well-regulated balance is struck between the police and the local criminal fraternity, represented by wide boy Mike Randall (Michael Golden), basking like a somnolent pike in the smoke-filled recesses of the billiard hall. But, as the introductory commentary tells us, a new virus is abroad, a breed of post-war criminals 'who lack the code, experience and self-discipline of the professional thief...a class apart, all the more dangerous because of their immaturity'. Oh for the days of the 'decent' thief, as played by Mervyn Johns in *The Bells Go Down*.

The new breed of criminal is represented by the youthful Tom Riley (Dirk Bogarde), a cigarette dangling insolently from his lips and

'This thing works!' Jack Warner's PC George Dixon advances towards the hysterical Tom Riley (Dirk Bogarde) and into television history in Basil Dearden's *The Blue Lamp* (1950), scripted by T.E.B. Clarke from a story by Ted Willis. Although Dixon died halfway through the film, his stolid, avuncular presence dominated *The Blue Lamp*, prompting Ted Willis to resurrect this monument to old-fashioned community policing in a television series which ran on and on until Sergeant George Dixon became the oldest policeman in the world.

In the 1950s, the Ealing style spawned a number of imitators. The one that got away: Kay Kendall and Kenneth More in Henry Cornelius's *Genevieve* (1954), which the Ealing expatriate offered to his old studio but which was eventually made, on Michael Balcon's suggestion, at Pinewood. Although centred on the rivalry of two vintage car owners (More and John Gregson) in the London to Brighton rally, *Genevieve*'s machinery took second place to a sophisticated British version of an American-style marital comedy. The script was by William Rose and the charming harmonica score by Larry Adler.

The Battle of the Sexes (1960), directed by Charles Crichton. American efficiency expert Constance Cummings introduces time clocks to the ancient Scottish firm of MacPherson, producers of handwoven tweeds, to the alarm of Robert Morley and Peter Sellers. Masquerading as a comedy, the film was an unconsciously depressing account of the deep-rooted British unwillingness to contemplate change.

a pistol in his pocket. Dearden even takes a timid shot at suggesting that Riley gets a sexual kick out of crime as he waves his revolver under the nose of his cowering girlfriend (Peggy Evans), but this is no *Gun Crazy*, and the mood quickly passes.

Riley and another young punk (Patric Doonan) pull a robbery at the local fleapit but the heist goes horribly wrong when George Dixon arrives on the scene. 'This thing works!' squawks Riley as he brandishes his revolver at the stolid figure advancing steadily towards him. Panicking, he shoots and fatally wounds Dixon, who dies in hospital several days later.

Riley has broken the 'code' so carefully spelt out at the beginning of the film and the police and the underworld unite to track him down. He is finally cornered at a greyhound track, the signals of the tic tac men reporting on his progress through the crowd. In a memorable image he is carried into the arms of the waiting police by the cheerful crowd spilling out of the stadium at the end of the meeting. The film ends where we came in, with Andy Mitchell, well on the way to filling George Dixon's shoes, giving directions to passers-by in the street, the time-honoured ritual of the British bobby. If *The Blue Lamp* can be viewed today with intense nostalgia, then the film itself looks nostalgically back to the deferred pleasures of the wartime years. The scenes in the police station remind one irresistibly of the camaraderie of *The Bells Go Down* and the relaxed intimacy of substation 14-Y in *Fires Were Started*.

The year following the release of *The Blue Lamp*, 1951, saw the Festival of Britain, that self-consciously insular celebration of the nation's long, slow convalescence from the war. Memories of the struggle were beginning to fade and with them the consensus politics of the 1940s. A Conservative government came to power in 1951 and intimations of affluence were in the wind. A mood was passing away which had dominated the five years following the war and through which the Ealing films had been filtered. It reflected the editorial line of the *News Chronicle* or the *Guardian* and found its home among the radical middle class, many of whom (and Michael Balcon among them) voted Labour for the first time in 1945 as part of a 'mild revolution'. It was embodied in Alastair Sim's 'penny doctor' in *Waterloo Road*, the gentle standard-bearer of the philosophy which Michael Frayn brilliantly characterized as belonging to the post-war 'herbivores'. However, the bomb sites on which the children of London played in *Hue and Cry* were soon to provide the lucrative sites for office blocks run up by acquisitive 'carnivores' like *Waterloo Road*'s Ted Purvis. By 1960, ten years after Ted Riley's capture at the greyhound track, Basil Dearden can only recall the old certainties of *The Blue Lamp* as a nervous tic on cashiered officer Terence Alexander's face in *The League of Gentlemen*, as his bitchy wife Nanette Newman lolls in a bubble bath and tells him, 'The war's been over a long time – nothing's rationed any more. There's plenty to go round.'

The safely enclosed pastures of Ealing provided ample grazing for herbivores and, as the studio was such an organic structure, this was reflected at all levels, even in the posters it used to advertise its films. The improving impulse at Ealing led to the commissioning by advertising chief St John Woods of a wide range of leading artists, including Edward Ardizzone (*Nicholas Nickleby*, *The Magnet*), John Piper (*Painted Boats*, *Pink String and Sealing Wax*) and Mervyn Peake (*Black Magic*, an entry in the Monogram Charlie Chan series distributed by Ealing). The results make up a unique record in cinema history.

Ealing in Decline

One of the most popular exhibits at the Festival of Britain was Roland Emmett's fanciful railway, a charming conceit which turned public transport into Gothic folly. The notion of picturesque uselessness haunted Ealing's declining years. In the opening shot of Charles Crichton's *The Titfield Thunderbolt* (1953) a powerful express train thunders over

Basil Dearden's *The League of Gentlemen* (1960). Jack Hawkins briefs the seedy gang of ex-officers he has assembled for a bank robbery which will be conducted like a military operation. Clockwise round the table: Bryan Forbes (who also wrote the screenplay), Roger Livesey, Richard Attenborough, Nigel Patrick, Kieron Moore, Norman Bird and Terence Alexander. A parody of films like *Cockleshell Heroes* (also written by Forbes), it combined the old Ealing whimsy of *The Lavender Hill Mob* with the cynicism of the materialistic late-50s.

a viaduct while beneath its arches chugs an aged tank engine, veteran of the world's oldest branch line, now threatened with closure. A loophole in the 1947 Transport Act enables the locals to establish an independent railway company – happy days when you needed 'at least £10,000' to start a railway line. On the eve of the Board of Transport test, their coach company rivals sabotage the ancient puffer. As a last resort, the antediluvian Titfield Thunderbolt herself is dragged from the Science Museum and put on the rails. After completing the trials, this second cousin to Stevenson's Rocket wheezes triumphantly into the mainline station to a cheerful cacophony of welcoming whistles.

The Titfield Thunderbolt is Ealing gone flabby. There is no longer the dynamism of the real community of Miramont Place or

A sentimental treatment of ancient, obsolete machinery went hand in hand with Ealing's decline. Railway-mad clerics George Relph and Godfrey Tearle wrestle with the museum-piece steam engine in Charles Crichton's *The Titfield Thunderbolt* (1953).

American tycoon Paul Douglas about to throw his cargo overboard as Alex Mackenzie runs his ramshackle steamer aground in Alexander Mackendrick's *The Maggie* (1954). The small boy, Dougie, was played by Tommy Kearins.

Todday – Titfield is merely a fantasy land. The money to open the line is supplied by an alcoholic millionaire (Stanley Holloway) so that he can avoid tiresome licensing laws and start drinking in the bar car at 8.30 in the morning. The line is run principally to fulfil the fantasies of the railway-mad vicar (George Relph) and preserve the status of the young squire (John Gregson). The affectionate plundering of past Ealing films, which enlivened *The Lavender Hill Mob* (1951) with a parody of the car chase in *The Blue Lamp*, becomes merely mechanistic. A laboured attempt is made to replay one of the most famous scenes in *Whisky Galore!* – the furious montage sequence which coincides with the arrival of the excise men as bottles of whisky are hidden at lightning speed in every conceivable place, from the guttering on houses to a baby's cradle. In *The Titfield Thunderbolt* the trackside water tank is sabotaged on the train's trial run. The passengers run all over the country, commandeering every bucket and bowl – including a baby's bath – from a neighbouring farm, to fill up in a nearby stream. All this is mildly amusing but it lacks the internal logic of the sequence in *Whisky Galore*. The passengers on the train obstinately remain unknown figures in a landscape. Like Titfield itself, they exist in a vacuum.

Ancient machinery, already long past obsolescence. In Alexander Mackendrick's *The Maggie* (1954), a rusting old coastal puffer, plying the Clyde and captained by a seedy and incompetent old rogue (Alex Mackenzie), obtains by trickery a cargo of furniture bound for the holiday home of an American millionaire Calvin B. Marshall (Paul Douglas). The

devious Captain Mactaggart insists on carrying out his commission and the American's attempts to recover the cargo are thwarted at every turn. In company with his Waggett-like English subordinate Pusey (Hubert Gregg) he is strung along, deceived and humiliated and, with the destination in sight, forced to throw all the furniture overboard to save the Maggie after she has run aground. The crates are broken open and Calvin B. Marshall's white baths and wash basins float down to their watery grave like monster fragments from Sidney Stratton's indestructible suit. By changing from his business clothes to an oily old sweater and by throwing his furniture overboard, the hapless Calvin B. Marshall has 'joined the team' in Ealing fashion but in an ambivalent way characteristic of Mackendrick. His parting shot to Mactaggart is, 'If you laugh at me for this, I'll kill you with my bare hands.'

The Maggie is Mackendrick's least satisfying Ealing film, but it still has a cutting edge which had vanished from the work of T.E.B. Clarke. Clarke's last screenplay for Ealing, written during the brief twilight at Borehamwood, was *Barnacle Bill* (1957). It starred Alec Guinness as a bogus seadog commanding the end of a run-down Victorian pier which he has registered as a ship for the chronically sea sick. The film's attempts at humour are made all the more poignant by an opening sequence in which Guinness impersonates his long line of naval ancestors, a sad reminder of *Kind Hearts and Coronets*. The giveaway lies in the pier's whimsical designation as RMS *Arabella*, the initials could stand for the state of Ealing – Really Motionless Ship.

Alexander Mackendrick's ability to work within the Ealing tradition while at the same time subverting it was fully realized in his last film for the studio. *The Ladykillers* (1955) is a surreal masterpiece in which all the sentimental Ealing notions of age and tradition are compressed with wicked irony into a lopsided house in St Pancras and the frail old lady who lives there – Katie Johnson. Mrs Wilberforce lives in a Victorian penumbra, surrounded by her genteelly twittering old friends (among them Edie Martin), her parrot named General Gordon and memories of her husband Captain Wilberforce who, like Admiral d'Ascoyne, went down with his ship. Her whole life is deftly put into context in one brief line – her 21st birthday party in Pangbourne was ruined by the announcement of the death of Queen Victoria. The gang of crooks who infiltrate this crumbling monument to Victorian values, in the guise of

End of the pier and end of the line as Alec Guinness' phoney seadog is carried in triumph from the wreck of the Really Motionless Ship *Arabella* in Charles Frend's *Barnacle Bill* (1957).

a string quartet, are paralysed by her moral innocence. When she discovers the massive haul of bank notes from the robbery masterminded by Professor Marcus (Alec Guinness with a set of false teeth that would have done justice to a sabre-toothed tiger) they decide to kill her. They end up killing each other. The house itself, with its clanking water system and banks of Victorian bric-a-brac, mesmerizes them. Like the dinner guests in Bunuel's *Exterminating Angel*, they struggle to escape but are held in its dreamlike grip, going down under the accumulated weight of triumphant British inertia.

The last two members of the gang – the mad professor and the gangster-like Louis (Herbert Lom) – dispose of each other. Louis topples backwards into the belching smoke of the railway sidings, closely followed by the professor whose skull has been split with a sickening crunch by a descending railway signal. Mrs Wilberforce wakes up to find herself alone with all the money. She goes down to the police station – straight out of *The Blue Lamp* with kindly Jack Warner at the desk – to tell her story. But of course they don't believe her – it's just one of her fantasies which always turn out in the end to be 'dreams'. On her way home, she absentmindedly gives a pound note to a pavement artist who specializes in portraits of Winston Churchill.

The Ladykillers was released at the same time as the studios on Ealing Green were sold to the BBC in order to repay a loan from the National Film Finance Corporation. The partnership with Rank came to an end when John Davis indicated there was no room for an independent Ealing setup at Pinewood.

Ealing was relocated in the bleak acres of the MGM studios at Borehamwood. Only seven more Ealing films were made there before the end. As Michael Balcon recorded: 'To comfort myself, I used to say that it was people who counted, not buildings. This was not strictly honest, as over the years there had developed at Ealing a spirit which had seeped into the very fabric of the place.'

'All families should stick together,' says the eponymous hero of Michael Relph's *Davy* (1957) as he turns down a chance of a career in opera to stay with his uncle's tatty music hall act, the Mad Morgans. *Davy* was among the sad cluster of Ealing's last films and, like its hero, the studio had made its choice in the 1950s, stifling ambition and insisting on family loyalties at the expense of experiment

The last great film made at Ealing, Alexander Mackendrick's *The Ladykillers* (1955). Peter Sellers, Danny Green, Cecil Parker, Alec Guinness and Herbert Lom fail hopelessly to put the frighteners on frail but indomitable Katie Johnson. This tribute to the suffocating and triumphant inertia of British tradition was scripted by an American, William Rose.

Wobbling of jowl, fluting of voice, fluttering of harassed hand, Cecil Parker was the master of disconcerted flappability. In *Dear Mr Prohack* (1949), he played a stingy civil servant who inherited a fortune and fell prey to Heather Thatcher's scheming Lady Maslam. In John Paddy Carstairs' *The Chiltern Hundreds* (1949), he was for once the soul of unflappability as Beecham, the perfect butler, who stands as a Conservative against the Labour candidacy of his young viscount master. Here he solicitously anticipates the reaction of peer of the realm A.E. Matthews to the news that he is a 'bloated capitalist' as he helps out his wife, Marjorie Field, in the kitchen.

and change. The Ealing philosophy, like the music hall, was dead on its feet but could not bring itself to admit it. *Davy* was directed by Michael Relph, who had come to Ealing as an art director in 1942, and produced by Basil Dearden, who had stayed exclusively with the studio after joining it as a writer in 1937. They are archetypal members of the Ealing 'family', with its slow progression through the ranks and its emphasis on group loyalty, which in the end produced enervation and stagnation. Yet Ealing exercised a strong hold, like the old house in *The Ladykillers*. With the exception of Robert Stevenson (who left Ealing in 1939 to pursue a successful Hollywood career) the careers of all the long-serving Ealing directors fizzled out or became fossilized after they left the studio. One of the most tragic examples was Seth Holt, who joined Ealing in 1944 as an assistant editor and died in 1971 while shooting *Blood from the Mummy's Tomb*. He waited until 1958 before getting the chance to direct his first, and Ealing's penultimate, film. The result was a stylish thriller, starring George Nader and Maggie Smith, which anticipated the films of the 60s. Its title was *Nowhere to Go*.

Alarms of the 50s

The optimism of the post-war years ebbed away as British cinema moved into the cultural dead zone of the 1950s. On both sides of the Atlantic the film industry was in decline. In Britain between March 1948 and March 1950 employment in major British studios fell from 7,253 to 4,104. In the summer of 1950 the government introduced the Eady

Plan to offset the imbalance caused by the Entertainment Tax which in 1950 absorbed £37 million out of gross receipts in British cinemas of £105 million. Under the Plan the British Film Production Fund was established to distribute money raised from a levy on cinema takings, after a proportion of Entertainment Tax had been removed, with the abolition of the tax on seats costing up to seven pence (old money!). As the Eady levy was channelled on 'a purely automatic and objective basis', calculated on the money a film earned before any fees were deducted, it naturally tended to reward box-office successes, the films which were least in need of a subsidy. The quota was also lowered to a more realistic 30 per cent.

Eady money was used to finance the Children's Film Foundation, run by Mary Field, and Group 3, an interesting but shortlived experiment headed by John Grierson and John Baxter. Group 3's aim was to produce well-made second features – at about a quarter of the normal cost – encouraging new talent in the industry. The experiment lasted from 1951 to 1954 and produced at least one good film, Philip Leacock's *The Brave Don't Cry* (1952), a reconstruction of the Knockshinnock mining disaster in the best dramatized documentary tradition. But the bulk of its output slid into sub-Ealing fantasy and whimsical comedies like *Poet's Pub* (1949), *Brandy for the Parson* (1952) and *You're Only Young Twice* (1952).

Government intervention, however constructive, could do nothing to halt the steady decline in cinema audiences and the closure of many theatres. Between 1954 and 1960 the number of people who went to the cinema each week slumped by over half from 24.5 million to about 10 million. Television played an important, but by no means the only role in accelerating cinema's wasting disease. In December 1949 the first regional television station was opened at Sutton Coldfield, serving Birmingham and the Midlands. At that time there were about 340,000 television licence holders in Britain but soon the number spiralled upwards, reaching 10.5 million in 1960. The televising of the Coronation in 1953 and the opening of the first commercial stations in September 1955 were two important events which had an adverse effect on the cinema-going habit. Ealing attempted to exorcise the threat in a feeble satire, Anthony Pelissier's *Meet Mr. Lucifer* (1953), in which a pantomime demon king (Stanley Holloway) gets a knock on the head and finds himself in conference with Old Nick himself (the voice of Geoffrey Keen) who has decided that people are getting far too much enjoyment from television and should be made to suffer for their newly acquired habit. The film remains of historical interest as it provides glimpses of a number of television stars of the time, including announcer Macdonald Hobley, TV chef Philip Harben and the dyspeptic Gilbert Harding (who had already undertaken an irascible dramatic role in Ealing's 1952 *The Gentle Gunman*). By the end of the decade television loomed so large that hardly a film went by without some media star of the time muscling in on the action. Alan Whicker thrust his microphone under the strikers' noses in *The Angry Silence* (1960); Malcolm Muggeridge chaired the riotous chat show at the end of *I'm All Right Jack* (1959); and Macdonald Hobley hung on grimly to compère the beauty contest in *The Entertainer* (1960).

As cinema audiences declined, theatres began to close. In the heady days of 1946 there had been 4,709 theatres in Britain: 14 years later the number had fallen to 3,034 and by the early 70s it had plummeted to 1,552. Many of the great behemoths of the 20s and 30s, which in their heyday held audiences of up to 4,000, were split up, converted to other uses or demolished. As they frequently occupied prime urban development sites, they were in many cases replaced by the new barbarisms of affluence, office blocks and supermarkets. Rank and ABC, which had been busily diversifying in the 50s, also introduced tenpin bowling and bingo into the dream palaces where in the past packed houses had

thrilled to Douglas Fairbanks in *The Thief of Bagdad* or shed a tear over Margaret Lockwood and Stewart Granger in *Love Story*. As the film business contracted, it was inevitable that hard-headed executives like John Davis would see the loss-making white elephants as business assets rather than as a social service.

The Rank Formula

This approach enabled Davis to turn Rank's 1949 debt of £16 million into a 1959 profit of £7 million. Films took a back seat to investment in photocopying machines, leisure activities and commercial television, and the Rank product became associated with safe, pedestrian family entertainment. (Indeed, the Rank cinemas banned all X-certificate films, a policy which had a considerably inhibiting effect on the range of subjects film makers could tackle.) In the new regime a comfortable niche was established by competent journeymen like director Ralph Thomas, whose partnership with producer Betty Box led to a string of films which reflected the middle-of-the-road values of the period. They opened the decade with *The Clouded Yellow* (1950), an efficient and at times atmospheric Hitchcockian 'double chase' thriller starring Trevor Howard and Jean Simmons. A long, well-handled passage in which Howard and Simmons flee across country while a manhunt closes in on them is reminiscent of *The Thirty-Nine Steps*, a classic which Thomas and Box remade with qualified success in 1959. Kenneth More – who had a small role in *The Clouded Yellow* – was an amiable Richard Hannay, but no substitute for Robert Donat.

Thomas could be relied on to turn in a well-crafted film and operated across the range of genres. *Above Us the Waves* (1955) celebrated the wartime feats of midget submarines; *Campbell's Kingdom* (1957) was a robust actioner, set in Canada (but filmed in Italy) starring Dirk Bogarde and Stanley Baker, who spent the 50s playing an assorted bunch of high-voltage heavies. Bogarde's early screen career had been to confined to melodramas in which he spent most of the time being chased all over the countryside. In Charles Crichton's quirky thriller *Hunted* (1952) he was a murderer on the run with an orphan runaway (Jon Whitely) in tow. In *Desperate Moment* (1953) he played a European refugee framed for murder by black marketeer Albert Lieven. When not being pursued Bogarde was sinking up to his knees in dreadful rubbish like Val Guest's *Penny*

Jean Simmons at the exciting climax of Ralph Thomas' Hitchcockian thriller, *The Clouded Yellow* (1950).

Princess (1952). In this weird piece of hokum, American shopgirl Yolande Donlan finds she has inherited the small European state of Lampidorra, falls in love with cheese salesman Bogarde and gets involved in a scheme to market Lampidorra's alcoholic cheese.

Bogarde was confirmed as a star – Rank's biggest – by Ralph Thomas's hugely successful 1954 comedy *Doctor in the House*. He played Simon Sparrow, a serious-minded young medical student at St Swithins teaching hospital, an institution which is virtually the private fief of James Robertson Justice's peppery surgeon Sir Lancelot Spratt, a bearded Ena Sharples of the operating theatre. The film affectionately recounts the mild student antics of those distant duffel-coat days and concludes with Sparrow entering the ranks of the medical profession. His

friends Grimsdyke (Kenneth More) and Benskin (Donald Sinden) – surely the oldest medical students in history – fail their exams yet again. In the sequel, *Doctor at Sea* (1955), Sparrow becomes a ship's doctor aboard the SS *Lotus*, bound for South America under ferocious Captain Hogg, inevitably played by James Robertson Justice. The film was given a breath of fresh air by the casting of French starlet Brigitte Bardot as a nightclub singer who finds her way aboard. The role had originally been offered to Kay Kendall but Bardot brought a brand of pert sexuality to the part which was virtually unknown in British films of the time. There were further 'Doctor' films but they were increasingly tepid affairs, which only served to underline the cul-de-sac into which the talented Bogarde was shunted in the 50s. His final

A British 'Western'. Charles Tingwell, Chips Rafferty and Gordon Jackson in *Bitter Springs* (1950), the third of three robust films made by Harry Watt in Australia for Ealing. The first, *The Overlanders* (1946), reconstructed an epic cattle drive from Northern Territory to Brisbane. *Eureka Stockade* (1949) was set in the gold rush of 1853 and dealt with the conflict between the prospectors and the colonial government – individualism against benign authority, a characteristic Ealing theme. *Bitter Springs* followed the fortunes of a pioneer family of the early 1900s, their acquisition of land and the resulting clash with the local aborigines, who depend on the water the settlers need.

Barbara Murray, James Robertson Justice, Dirk Bogarde, Michael Craig and Sidney James plot the downfall of the villainous Stanley Baker in Ralph Thomas's efficient actioner *Campbell's Kingdom* (1957).

Rank contract film was Roy Baker's *The Singer Not the Song* (1960), a bizarre 'Western' in which Bogarde played a Mexican bandit, dressed from head to foot in black leather, terrorizing John Mills' Irish priest. Bogarde later remarked, 'It was pure camp: I played the bandit like Gloria Swanson's Queen Kelly.' The following year he made the controversial *Victim* and shattered forever his matinée idol image. He reflected, with relief, as he entered a new stage in his career, 'I wasn't the bouncy, happy doctor with a little perm in the front lock of my hair and my caps in and my left profile – every set was built for my left profile, nobody ever saw the right side of my face in something like 30 pictures. I was the Loretta Young of England. And so that all broke. The caps came out, the hair was never permed again and a different audience came.'

The same audiences went year after year to the hugely successful series of 'Carry On' films, the first of which was *Carry On Sergeant* (1958), produced by Peter Rogers, directed by Gerald Thomas and scripted by Talbot Rothwell. William Hartnell played Training Sergeant Gumshawe, on the verge of retirement and unwisely accepting a bet that his last platoon will pass out as the star squad. His heart sinks when he sees his charges, who range from Gerald Campion's tubby beatnik to Kenneth Williams' toffee-nosed intellectual. The recruits shamble chaotically through their training but at the last moment pull themselves together and, somewhat unconvincingly, pass out at the head of the intake. 'Half-baked', was one critic's view but the public reaction was one of wholehearted approval and the 'Carry On' saga rolled on uninterrupted, at the rate of one or two films a year, until 1974. Among the regulars, and now sadly missed, were the crumple-faced Sidney James and the majestic Hattie Jacques, the latter usually in hot pursuit of the spindly Kenneth Williams. Amongst the cross-fire of *double entendres* a lively performance was always guaranteed from the most prominent parts of Barbara Windsor's spectacular anatomy.

Running alongside the 'Carry On' films was the popular series of Norman Wisdom comedies, big money earners in their day but now very tired stuff through which to sit. The first was the 1953 *Trouble in Store*, directed by the veteran John Paddy Carstairs, in which Wisdom's put-upon 'little man' progressively reduces a department store to chaos. He helps a lady burdened with suitcases to leave the store – she turns out to be a

Dirk Bogarde and a delightful young Brigitte Bardot in *Doctor at Sea* (1955), the second in the successful series created by Ralph Thomas and Betty Box. The other 'Doctor' films were *Doctor in the House* (1954), *Doctor at Large* (1957), *Doctor in Love* (1960), *Doctor in Distress* (1963), *Doctor in Clover* (1966) and *Doctor in Trouble* (1970). Bogarde dropped out for the last two, which starred Leslie Phillips.

Ramrod-straight Sergeant William Hartnell casts a beady eye over unprepossessing National Serviceman Kenneth Connor in *Carry on Sergeant* (1958).

shoplifter. He sets himself on fire at the staff dance and ruins the manager's speech but redeems himself by foiling a plot to rob the store and wins the hand of Lana Morris. The notion of an attractive young starlet falling for this maudlin sub-Chaplinesque figure was as weird as George Formby's conquest of such 40s lovelies as Googie Withers and Phyllis Calvert. One of the redeeming features of *Trouble in Store* was the performance as the store manager of Jerry Desmonde, Sid Field's straight man and a master of his craft. Wisdom was one of the first comics to transfer from television to the cinema and it is pleasing to note that in recent years he has returned to television in a new guise as a considerable character actor.

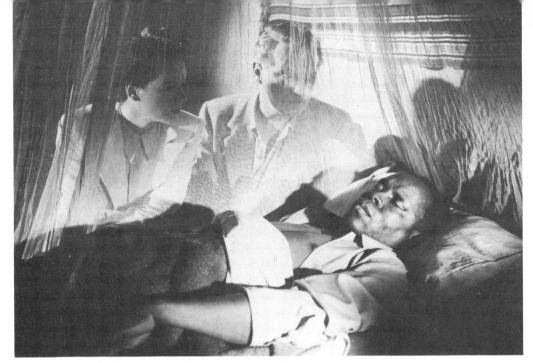

Winds of change.
The transition from Empire to Commonwealth was an important political theme of the post-war world. *Men of Two Worlds* (1946), a Two Cities production directed by Thorold Dickinson, was based on a story by Joyce Carey. Kisenga (Robert Adams), an African concert pianist, returns to his native village in Tanganyika and challenges the power of its witch doctor, Magole (Orlando Martins), who opposes the plans of the District Commissioner (Eric Portman) to move the tribe to an area free of the tsetse fly. Magole places a curse on Kisenga, who falls ill, the result of 'thousands of years of Africa in his blood'. Portman and nurse Phyllis Calvert (*right*) watch at his bedside while outside the villagers sing the choral sequences of one of his African symphonies. Magole's powers are broken and Kisenga decides to stay with his people.

Centre
In Harry Watt's *Where No Vultures Fly* (1951), Anthony Steel and Dinah Sheridan played a young couple fighting to establish a game reserve in Kenya and defeating the machinations of Harold Warrender's ivory smuggler. The film's tone of liberal paternalism was repeated in Watt's *West of Zanzibar* (1954), in which Sheila Sim took over Sheridan's role as Steele's wife. Dressed in crisp linens, with neatly knotted paisley cravat, Big Bwana still knew best. This point of view was carried to absurdity in Wolf Rilla's *Pacific Destiny* (1956) in which Denholm Elliott battles with man-eating sharks, quells a Samoan witch doctor and teaches the natives cricket as a substitute for war.

More sympathetic was Zoltan Korda's faithful adaptation of Alan Paton's South African novel *Cry the Beloved Country* (1951), in which Canada Lee (*right*) gave an outstanding performance.

The Old Faithfuls

The 1950s saw a shift towards comedy on the part of two of the most important film-making partnerships of the previous decade, the Boultings and Launder and Gilliat. Both teams signed off their work of the 40s with some efficient thrillers before moving into a string of highly successful comedies.

John Boulting's *Seven Days to Noon* (1950) looked back to the wartime documentary tradition and forward to the present-day unease over the nuclear arms race. Barry Jones played a physicist driven to moral crisis and mental collapse by his work on nuclear weapons at a top-secret research establishment. In the grip of an apocalyptic religious fundamentalism, he steals a prototype nuclear device which is small enough to fit into his Gladstone Bag. He then delivers an ultimatum to the government – if they do not destroy their stockpile of nuclear weapons within a week, he will detonate the stolen device and take central London with him. A tract for our own troubled times. The film gains in resonance from its presentation of the nuclear blackmailer not as a crazed Fu Manchu type but as a desperately ill old man padding through a succession of seedy lodging houses. The unseen device is made all the more nightmarish by being carried around in a reassuringly shabby doctor's bag. The evacuation of London as the deadline approaches is handled with an ironic restraint which recalls the war years. The corralling of stray pets in makeshift pens at the end of deserted streets is a grisly touch reminiscent of the pathetic sacrificial victims which were

tethered around the fringes of nuclear test sites to measure the ravages of blast and radiation. The film is nearly thrown off balance by the standard wet young couple of the time – the scientist's assistant and daughter (Hugh Cross and Sheila Manahan) – but there is a pleasant echo of Hermione Baddeley's fuddled old barfly of *Brighton Rock* in Olive Sloane's faded actress teetering on the brink of prostitution.

After *The Magic Box* (1951), *High Treason* (1951), and *Seagulls over Sorrento* (1954), the Boultings embarked on a series which lobbed a few mildly satirical grenades over the battlements of various British institutions. Ian Carmichael played the earnest innocent,

'Dark, dark, dark amid the blaze of noon.' Barry Jones' deranged scientist, haunted by visions of the Apocalypse and stalking the streets of a deserted London with a nuclear device in his bag, in the Boultings' *Seven Days to Noon* (1950). Paul Dehn's screenplay won an Academy Award.

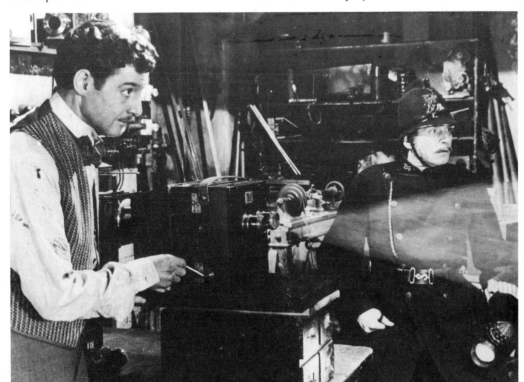

Robert Donat as the film pioneer William Friese-Greene and his astounded constabular guinea pig (Laurence Olivier) in John Boulting's *The Magic Box* (1951), the British film industry's contribution to the Festival of Britain. In spite of the efforts of screenwriter Eric Ambler, cameraman Jack Cardiff and producer Ronald Neame, *The Magic Box* failed to animate the story of a man whose contribution to film was marginal and who ended his career in poverty-stricken obscurity.

Innocent's progress. Eager-beaver Egan (Peter Jones) explains to the confused Stanley Windrush (Ian Carmichael) exactly why they are dressed up in Wehrmacht uniform in *Private's Progress* (1956), the first of the Boultings' mildly satirical digs at the Establishment.

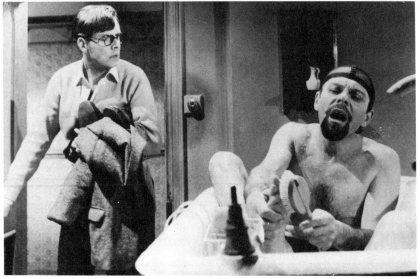

Ian Carmichael bursts in on Terry-Thomas in *Lucky Jim* (1957), a muted adaptation of Kingsley Amis' sourly humorous novel of life at a redbrick university.

Stanley Windrush, placed at the centre of *Private's Progress* (1956), his brand of well-meaning naïveté ultimately torpedoing the efforts of the Machiavellian schemes all around him. We encounter Windrush fumbling his way through the lower depths of the war effort. His less than soldierly bearing condemns him to a far-flung holding unit whose members (including Richard Attenborough, Kenneth Griffith and Ian Bannen) display immense energy and ingenuity in avoiding any work. 'Bein' educated sort of limits you,' reflects Attenborough as he racks his brains for a new line in column-dodging for the hopeless Stanley. The CO, Terry-Thomas, surveys the awkward squad with characteristically petulant resignation: 'You're an absolute shower – and so am I – you've got to be to command rotters like

you,' he snorts.

The old boy network comes to Stanley's aid in the form of crooked cousin Brigadier Tracepurcel (Dennis Price), who drafts him into a cloak and dagger operation to snatch looted art treasures from behind the German lines. There's only one slight problem – Stanley's training at interpreters' school has been in Japanese. Inevitably, the witless Windrush is used as a dupe to 'divert' a lorry-load of old masters to Tracepurcel's shady art-dealing business. We leave him as he is gently led away by the men from the Fraud Squad.

The legal system was next on the Boultings' list in the 1957 *Brothers-in-Law*. The same year also saw their disappointing adaption of Kingsley Amis' novel of provincial university life, *Lucky Jim*, whose pointed social observation was watered down into farce. Two years later, in 1959, the Boultings launched more effective sallies against British industry and the mandarins of the Foreign Office.

I'm All Right Jack provided a corrective and a contrast to the Boultings' almost hysterically McCarthyite *High Treason* (1951) in which a motley gang of leftwingers plot to seize a number of power stations as an advance guard of a Russian invasion. In *I'm All Right Jack*, we have moved from austerity to affluence, from the world of the cheese ration and petrol coupons to the consumer paradise of bubble cars and television quiz shows. The film's cheerful cynicism is part and parcel of the era in which the British were blandly assured by Prime Mininster Harold Macmillan that they had 'never had it so good', a phrase which was soon to take on a whole new meaning with the revelations of the Profumo affair. Stanley Windrush is once more tossed to the wolves by Dennis Price's Tracepurcel, this time in an engineering factory. In no time at all he has contrived to produce a strike which not only serves the trade union ambitions of shop steward Fred Kite (Peter Sellers) but also forms part of a deep-laid and devious plot to make a financial killing for Tracepurcel and Cox (Richard Attenborough), two camelhair-coated and brandy-swilling swindlers limbering up for the asset-stripping bonanza over the horizon. The film is stolen by Peter Sellers' Fred Kite, a creation of genuine pathos as he ruminates on his idealized vision of the Soviet Union – 'All them cornfields, and ballet in the evenings.'

The chicanery moved to the Foreign Office in *Carlton-Browne of the FO*. Terry-Thomas was the diplomat of the title, a chinless wonder whose head is full of the minutiae of Debrett and Sporting Life but very little else. An international crisis blows up in the long-forgotten former colony of Gaillardia - so forgotten, in fact, that the last governor has stayed at his post since 1916, ignorant of the fact that the island is independent. Carlton-Browne is summoned from his desk at Miscellaneous Territories, appointed Special Ambassador and despatched to Gaillardia to find out why teams from every first and second-rate power are swarming over the island and digging holes all over the countryside. He makes a sacrifice, almost equal to that of Charters and Caldicott in *Crooks' Tour*, by foregoing Ascot Week to undertake the mission. Arriving to a full two-gun salute at the island's ramshackle airport Carlton-Browne and his gung-ho military aide Major Bellingham (Thorley Walters) fall into the clutches of the oily Prime Minister Amphibulos (Peter Sellers) who quickly reveals that all the fuss is over huge deposits of cobalt. A familiar diplomatic solution is proposed; the island will be partitioned between the British protégé, the young king (Ian Bannen), and the rebellious Grand Duke (John Le Mesurier, looking rather uneasy in top-boots and sheepskins). A football pitch marker is solemnly wheeled out and wobbles its way over mountains and through jungle to establish the frontier. The arrangement is short-lived, however, as it rapidly emerges that all the cobalt is in the the Grand Duke's part of the island. 'We've got the wrong half!' snaps Permanent Secretary Raymond Huntley, as Britian promptly withdraws her support from the hapless Bannen, who is in London on a goodwill mission. He is left in no doubt

Envoy extraordinary Carlton-Browne (Terry-Thomas) succumbs to a pincer movement from sultry Julie Hopkins and the oily Amphibulos (Peter Sellers), prime minister of Gaillardia, in *Carlton-Browne of the F.O.* (1959). The Boultings' final satirical efforts, *Heavens Above* (1963) and *Rotten to the Core* (1965), were out of joint with the mood of the Swinging 60s.

as to the change of heart as the sprays of flowers which decorate his hotel suite are smartly removed on the orders of Her Majesty's Government. Located as it is in the middle of a typically British comedy, this devastatingly cynical exercise of *realpolitik* only sinks in if one pauses to think about it, as does our next step, the despatch of a task force to secure 'our. interests'. This tinny echo of the Suez affair proves just as disastrous. Our elite commando unit wander round in circles in the jungle for hours before putting in a copybook pincer movement on their own headquarters. 'Are all campaigns like this – an utter shambles?' inquires the quivering Carlton-Browne as he takes refuge beneath a table.

Sidney Gilliat's 1950 thriller *State Secret* was a reminder of the Launder-Gilliat work of the 1930s. Surgeon Douglas Fairbanks Jr is flown into the Eastern European State of Vosnia to operate on its dictator General Niva (Walter Rilla). When the patient dies, Fairbanks has to flee the country, aided by singer Glynis Johns. The film was remarkable for its gallant attempt to create a complete language for the Vosnians to speak, and to sing. No doubt anticipating the advent of the Eurovision Song Contest, Glynis Johns warbled 'Me rah nah day en pahpeer dahz van me de ra mess oo' (I'm going to buy a paper doll that I can call my own).

The release of *State Secret* overlapped with Frank Launder's minor comedy classic *The Happiest Days of Your Life* adapted from John Dighton's successful West End farce. As the result of a bureaucratic blunder, St. Swithin's girls' school is accidentally billeted on Nutbourne College for young gentlemen. As the

Wetherby Pond, headmaster of Nutbourne College and Miss Whitchurch, headmistress of St Swithin's, cope with a crisis in Frank Launder's *The Happiest Days of Your Life* (1950), adapted from John Dighton's play. Margaret Rutherford and Alastair Sim were at the top of their form in this charming comedy, which also introduced Joyce Grenfell as a gauche games mistress and Richard Wattis as a harassed civil servant, roles which typecast them in films for the rest of their careers.

The immortal Alastair Sim in Mario Zampi's comedy *Laughter in Paradise* (1951), in which a wealthy prankster leaves £50,000 each to four relations on certain conditions. Sim played a scholarly hack who dictates Mickey Spillane-type shockers in a smoking jacket beneath a bust of Shakespeare. He has to commit a crime and serve no less than 28 days in prison to collect the money. His attempted smash and grab raid is dignified by a brick wrapped up in a neat parcel. The film is worth seeing just to enjoy Sim's voice ringing the changes on lines like, 'a convulsive terror shook her frame and Petal moaned'.

respective headmistress and headmaster are Margaret Rutherford and Alastair Sim, the scene is set for a delicious comedy animated by a battery of character comedians at the top of their form. 'There's a slight hiatus in the porridge,' announces Rutherford after disaster strikes yet again in the kitchen. Trotting loyally at her heels is Joyce Grenfell's toothy, jolly-hockey-sticks Miss Gossage, urging her charges to 'call me Sausage!' This lovely actress was later stereotyped in similar gawky roles which prevented her from displaying her considerable range. In one of the most charming moments in the film, Grenfell idly traces her surname (with dots under each letter) in the thick layers of dust in the college hallway. Richard Wattis' portrayal of the harassed civil servant Arnold Billings also led to a string of similar roles, virtually making

him an axiom of British cinema, along with Diana Dors' good time girls and James Robertson Justice's irascible professors. Frank Launder's keen eye for telling social detail is much in evidence. As a mysterious delivery of trunks (belonging to St. Swithins) arrives at Nutbourne, Alastair Sim lugubriously observes, 'That's what comes of nationalizing the railways.'

Frank Launder's *Lady Godiva Rides Again* (1951) followed the fortunes of Pauline Stroud, who wins the Fascinating Soap Beauty Contest and with it a film contract at an establishment not a million miles away from the Rank Charm School. The film opens with a wickedly accurate picture of a boring Sunday in a provincial town as the camera moves across rainy, deserted streets and the windswept railway station, where the tannoy gleefully announces, 'There are no trains standing on platforms one, two, three or four and there will be none for hours and hours because it's Sunday afternoon in our town.'

In 1952, Launder and Gilliat produced *Folly to be Wise,* an adaption of James Bridie's play *It Depends What You Mean,* with Alastair Sim re-creating his stage role as the hapless Captain Paris, chaplain and entertainments officer in an army camp. Determined to spare the men further musical torture at the hands of the May Savitt Qualthropp String Quintet, he organizes a brains trust. But an innocent-sounding question posed by Private Jesse Killigrew (Janet Brown) – 'Is marriage a good idea?' – leads to a vicious sniping match and then a brawl between two panel members, local sculptor Roland Culver and writer Colin Gordon, who is his wife's boyfriend.

Peter Martyn, Janet Brown, Alastair Sim and Martita Hunt in Frank Launder's *Folly to be Wise* (1952).

The accelerating chaos enables Sim to deploy his full range of twitches, double-takes and long, reproachful slow burns, as the brains trust yaws wildly off course to the delight of the assembled soldiery.

After the polished but dull *The Story of Gilbert and Sullivan* (1953), a 21st birthday celebration for London Films, Launder and Gilliat moved into broad farce with *The Belles of St Trinians* (1954). The film was based on Ronald Searle's famous cartoons of truculent, anarchic, pigtailed little schoolgirls, whose own origins lay in the sketches Searle made of his Japanese guards when he was a prisoner of war. Presiding over the film's rampaging gymslip-clad hordes was Alastair Sim as the long-suffering and stately Miss Fritton, facing with admirable calm such minor irregularities as the stabling of a racehorse in the dorm. Sim also played Miss Fritton's scapegrace brother Clarence, an older, more devious version of Ted Purvis, and George Cole provided a memorable distillation of no-holds-barred spivvery as Flash Harry.

The success of *Belles of St Trinians* led to three more comedies in which the young girls wrought their own particular brand of havoc. In *Blue Murder at St Trinians* (1957), the schoolgirls merrily cheat their way through a Unesco schools competition and win a trip to Rome to participate in a water polo match. The plot bore a distinct resemblance to the 1937 Will Hay vehicle *Good Morning, Boys,* made at Gainsborough when Launder was a script editor there. Sadly, Alastair Sim did not appear in the last two St Trinians films, *The Pure Hell of St Trinians* (1960) in which the school's collection of busty sixth-formers find themselves in an Arabian harem, and *The*

Great St Trinians Train Robbery (1966) where the school is relocated and finds itself sitting on the proceeds of the crime of the century.

In between the St Trinians sagas, Launder and Gilliat directed and produced some of the more diverting comedies of the 50s. In *Geordie* (1955), Bill Travers is transformed from an 8-stone weakling into an Olympic hammer-throwing champion by physical culture expert Henry Sampson (Francis de Wolff). In *The Green Man* (1956), vacuum cleaner salesman George Cole stumbles across a murder in deepest suburbia. The film contains a marvellous performance by Colin Gordon as an asinine BBC radio announcer, Reginald Willoughby-Pratt. Rounding on George Cole, he issues the ultimate threat, 'By Heaven, I'd thrash the life out of you – if I didn't have to read the nine o'clock news.'

George Cole's Flash Harry, lurking underneath several gallons of pomade, is treated with icy hauteur by Alastair Sim's Miss Fritton in Launder and Gilliat's comedy classic *The Belles of St Trinians* (1954). A flavour of St Trinians' mood of cheerful anarchy is provided by the prop list for a day's shooting: 'practical gramophones and jive records, lurid novels, male pinups, set of dice, pack of cards, poker chips, money, cigarettes...home perm set, Elizabethan axes, golf clubs, croquet mallets, hockey sticks, bed posts, pieces of wood and other weapons'.

The series was a staple of Hollywood's B-movie factories but, with the exception of the 'Doctor' and 'Carry On' films, the British output was more homely and shortlived. During an overland journey to South Africa, Jack Warner reaches for the beer and wishes he was back in his South London local in *The Huggetts Abroad* (1949), the third film based on the Cockney family who first appeared in *Holiday Camp* (1947). From left to right, Dinah Sheridan, Kathleen Harrison, Jimmy Hanley, Susan Shaw, Petula Clark and fellow traveller Hugh McDermott.

'You filthy swine, you won't get away with this.' Radio detective Dick Barton (Don Stannard) is trussed up in a fetching suit of armour by evil Sigmund Caspar (Geoffrey Wincott) and threatened with a phial of cholera germs in *Dick Barton, Special Agent* (1948), directed by Alfred Goulding. Hammer-Exclusives' other radio spin-offs were *The Man in Black* (1950), *A Case for PC 49* (1951), *Life with the Lyons* (1954) and *The Lyons in Paris* (1955).

Margaret Rutherford's Miss Marple poses as an elderly housemaid to solve a murder mystery in *Murder, She Said* (1962), the first of three films based on Agatha Christie's genteel spinster detective. Conrad Phillips (*left*) and Thorley Walters were among the suspects in this entry. All these films were directed by George Pollock, the others being *Murder at the Gallop* (1963) and *Murder Ahoy* (1964).

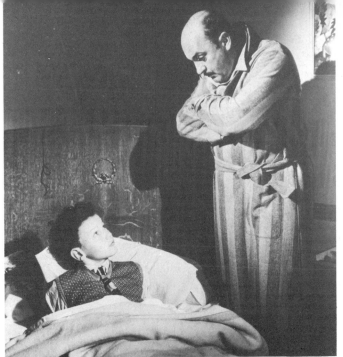

Richmal Crompton's pint-sized anarchist William Brown (William Graham) is taken to task by his long-suffering father (Garry Marsh) in *Just William's Luck* (1947), which was followed in 1948 by *William Comes to Town*. The rest of the family were Jane Welsh (Mrs Brown), Hugh Cross (brother Robert) and Kathleen Stuart (sister Ethel). Both the William films were directed by the tireless Val Guest, who began his career as a scriptwriter for Will Hay in the 30s, graduated to directing with the 1943 *Miss London Ltd*, and was still hard at work in the early 1980s.

John Bentley as Francis Durbridge's smooth sleuth Paul Temple and Dinah Sheridan as 'Steve' in *Calling Paul Temple* (1948), directed by Maclean Rogers. There were two more entries in the series, *Paul Temple's Triumph* (1951) and *Paul Temple Returns* (1952). B-hero Bentley also starred as John Creasey's Toff in *Salute the Toff* and *Hammer the Toff* (both 1952).

Derrick de Marney as Peter Cheyney's hard-boiled private dick Slim Callaghan and Delphi Lawrence as his secretary in Charles Saunders' *Meet Mr Callaghan* (1954). In 1948 Michael Rennie played Callaghan in *Uneasy Terms*, an engagingly hamfisted British attempt to emulate the Hollywood thick-ear style.

The Captive Heart (1946), directed by Basil Dearden. Basil Radford's Major Dalrymple – a racehorse trainer in civilian life – runs the book at an unconventional race meeting behind the barbed wire of Offlag 27. Jimmy Hanley is his clerk and Guy Middleton the hopeful punter.

Jack Warner was cast against type in Ealing's *Against the Wind* (1948), directed by Charles Crichton. He played a treacherous member of an SOE group sent to help the Resistance in occupied Belgium. The film's most effective moment came when Simone Signoret receives a tip-off and instantly shoots him dead as he whistles cheerfully away in front of the shaving mirror.

The Smallest Show on Earth (1957), produced by Launder and Gilliat, directed by Basil Dearden and with a screenplay by William Rose, was an Ealing stray looking for a home. Bill Travers and Virginia McKenna inherit a decrepit provincial cinema, the Bijou, complete with equally ancient ticket lady Margaret Rutherford, janitor Bernard Miles and an alcoholic projectionist, Peter Sellers. They fight to save it from being forced out of business by the town's big chain cinema, an *art deco* battleship whose uniformed commissionaire rules the queues outside with a rod of iron. Ironically, at the time the film was made, the Bijou's rival was as obsolete as the indomitable old fleapit.

Launder and Gilliat's 1959 *Left, Right and Centre*, directed by Sidney Gilliat, struck a more topical note, venturing into the political arena and aiming shafts at all shades of the political spectrum as TV personality Ian Carmichael, the Conservative candidate at the Earndale by-election, drives his workers to despair by falling in love with the Labour candidate, Patricia Bredin.

The War Film

The war film is the nearest thing the British cinema has to the Western. Like the Western, it has its own signs and symbols – the drink left on the mantlepiece of the officers' mess during a scramble in *Angels One Five* (1952), which one knows will never be reclaimed; a farewell letter propped up by a bedside in *The Dambusters* (1955). It also has its own language: ironic understatement by the officers – 'Forgive me for not coming down to the station to meet you, we were unavoidably detained,' drawls POW John Mills to the new arrivals in *The Colditz Story* (1955); and passive stoicism from the men, summed up in the wounded Mervyn Johns' 'Mustn't grumble, sir', as officer Basil Radford cheerily asks 'How's tricks, Evans?' in Ealing's *The Captive Heart* (1946).

The Captive Heart, directed by Basil Dearden, was made before its time – in the immediate post-war years there was an understandable desire to make films about peace rather than war. Nevertheless, it remains one of the most interesting of British war films and the starting point for any discussion of many of the themes explored in the 1950s. *The Captive Heart*'s mood is speedily established as the Oxford Light Infantry, whistling 'There'll Always Be An England', march into captivity in Germany. Later, on parade, the men drown out the Germany victory march 'Wir fahren gegen England', blaring out on the public address system, with a rousing version of 'Roll Out The Barrel'. The first scene anticipates *The Bridge on the River Kwai* (1957) and the second looks back to *In Which We Serve*. The film's measured documentary approach – with much location shooting in Germany – vividly conveys the discomfort and boredom of camp life: the men huddling in blankets in winter, and Corporal Jack Warner sacrificing his carefully carved wooden ship to the stove so that the lads can have a brew up. As Mervyn Johns reads out a letter home, the camp slowly becomes 'a little piece of England', the camera moving over a montage of the men's communal and individual activities – gardening, camp concerts, a picture of the King being stuck up on a wall. In Ealing fashion, the men receive greater attention than the officers; Jack Warner and Jimmy Hanley are significantly paired in a 'father and son' relationship that was to be repeated in *The Boys in Brown*, the Huggett films and *The Blue Lamp*. Warner plays a prototype George Dixon, a slow-moving, middle-aged man whose relaxed manner conceals considerable self-assurance. When asked by one of his mates how to spell 'sufficient', he replies, 'Same as a sergeant major's blessing, two Fs and one C.' Hanley is a brash young spiv, a former burglar, who is soon put in his place by Warner: 'One sniff of a barmaid's apron and you'd be on your hands and knees, sonny.' He nevertheless quickly becomes part of the team. When, in defiance of the Geneva Convention, the POWs are manacled after a British commando raid on Sark, he picks the locks with practised ease. Later he breaks into the commandant's office to substitute the name of a Czech officer (Michael Redgrave) for his own on the repatriation list, thus saving him from the SS. Redgrave has escaped from a concentration camp and assumed the identity of a dead British officer. In order to maintain the deception, he corresponds with the dead man's widow (Rachel Kempson). Ignorant of the fact that the man whose identity he has taken is estranged from his wife, he writes a series of tender letters and eventually falls in love with her. The film's focus is inevitably blurred by the breaking up of the self-contained world of the camp and the portmanteau-style unravelling of the threads of the principal characters' family lives in Britain. Nevertheless, *The Captive*

Deserter Nigel Patrick confronts his portrait as a war hero in *Silent Dust* (1949), directed by Lance Comfort.

Heart remains one of Basil Dearden's best films and one of the best of the POW genre.

The return of the prisoner of war, with all its attendant upheaval and crisis, was a popular theme of the period. In *The Years Between* (1945), Michael Redgrave returns 'from the dead' to the consternation of his wife Valerie Hobson, who has taken his place in the House of Commons. The roles were reversed in Herbert Wilcox's *Piccadilly Incident* (1946). Anna Neagle meets and falls in love with Michael Wilding during an air raid. They marry but are soon parted as Neagle takes ship for the Far East. She is reported missing after the fall of Singapore but in fact is stranded on a Pacific island. When she returns to London, she finds Wilding married again and with a small son. She is conveniently disposed of in another air raid and the film ends with a gloomy epilogue outlining the problems of illegitimacy.

In Lance Comfort's *Silent Dust* (1948), blind self-made millionaire businessman Stephen Murray builds a cricket pavilion in memory of his war hero son (Nigel Patrick), whose arrogant portrait hangs over the fireplace. However, Patrick has not fallen in battle but rather fallen by the wayside, as a deserter. He returns as a stubble-chinned, grubby, trenchcoated fugitive to extort money from his wife (Sally Gray). The film has an agreeably 'noirish' feel with Patrick lurking upstairs until Murray, in a sequence in negative with rasping voice-over, pieces together the small clues which lead to the realization that his 'dead' son is alive and hiding in his house.

The lives of the women who stayed at home during the war were celebrated in Roy Baker's *The Weaker Sex* (1948) in which

Ursula Jeans played Martha Dacre, mother, housewife, firewatcher and assistant at the local British restaurant. A plodding family saga, it contained a memorable performance from Thora Hird as a comical daily. At their Borehamwood studios, MGM made *The Miniver Story* (1950), a post-war sequel to the exploits of Home Counties heroine Greer Garson, with Walter Pidgeon repeating his role as her patient husband. (This was one of a number of Anglo-American productions of the period, which enabled the big American studios to spend earnings which remained 'frozen' in Britain. Other films included Warner's *Captain Horatio Hornblower RN* (1951), directed by Raoul Walsh, and Twentieth Century-Fox's *The Mudlark* (1950), directed by Jean Negulesco.)

Several films faced up to the problems and

legacies of the wartime years. In *No Room at the Inn* (1948), partly written by Dylan Thomas, Freda Jackson played a slatternly and sadistic landlady who terrorizes her pathetic little evacuee charges.

The end of the war left hundreds of thousands of displaced persons stranded in bleak camps all over Europe and in the process provided a ripe field for drama. Mai Zetterling starred in Terence Fisher's *Portrait from Life* (1948) as an amnesiac forcibly adopted by a notorious SS man. She is tracked down in a refugee camp by Major Guy Rolfe. The following year Zetterling turned up again in George Provis' *Lost People*. In this melodramatic piece, a disused German theatre serving as a dispersal centre for displaced persons is thrown into chaos by rumours of bubonic plague. At Ealing Charles Crichton's *The Divided Heart* (1954) followed the search by a Yugoslav mother (Yvonne Mitchell) for her baby, taken from her during the war by the occupying Germans and given to a childless mother in the Fatherland (Cornell Borchers). The climax comes in the court of the American Control Commission when judge Alexander Knox returns the boy (Michael Ray) to his real mother, adding that the son is not being handed into the custody of the mother, but the mother into the custody of the son.

For some the excitement of the war years could never be recaptured. Attempts to do so inevitably led to crime and disillusionment. At the beginning of Basil Dearden's *The Ship that Died of Shame* (1955), George Baker's voice-over tells us, 'The beginning, like almost everything else about me, went back to the war.' A former motor torpedo boat

Patrick Holt, Guy Rolfe and Sybilla Binder bend anxiously over amnesiac refugee Mai Zetterling in *Portrait from Life* (1948), directed by Terence Fisher.

'The beginning, like everything about me, went back to the war.' Richard Attenborough and George Baker pick up 1087's final cargo, the *M*-like child murderer, in Basil Dearden's exploration of post-war disillusion, *The Ship That Died of Shame* (1957), adapted from a novel by Nicholas Monsarrat.

commander, he is picked out of the peacetime gutter by his ex-No 1 Richard Attenborough, now a shady 'businessman', and set up in their old ship, 1087. Times have changed. Instead of sneaking into remote French inlets to shoot up German installations, Baker, Attenborough and Bill Owen (the wartime coxswain) now go in at night to pick up smuggled brandy. The consignments become progressively more dodgy. Currency forged by the Germans during the war is taken on board. 'It could have gummed up the works pretty badly if they'd been circulated during the war,' remarks Attenborough nonchalantly. 'So now we're doing the work for them,' accuses Baker. At this moment, 1087's engines mysteriously pack up. She is beginning to 'lose heart' in her ignominious role and, as the work spirals down through gun-running to picking up a child murderer on the run, she increasingly refuses to answer the wheel. When a French patrol boat catches them in the fog off Honfleur, Attenborough pushes the murderer overboard. Back in port, he suggests that they cut and run to Portugal, but before they can set sail stolid customs man Bernard Lee confronts Attenborough and his partner, Roland Culver, in the latter's seedy garage. Culver's is the best performance in the film, a washed-up major who 'didn't fancy working for the plebs after fighting for them'. He shoots Lee on the spot – 'Never want to do a lot of talking with one of these in your hands,' he says, eyeing his Webley with an infinitely bleak malice, and joins Attenborough on the trip to Portugal. They hit a storm and 1087's engines grind to a permanent halt. Culver is shot in a fight and Attenborough tossed overboard by the lurching boat, her whirling propellors grinding down on his head. The stricken ship smashes up on the rocks and Baker and Owen scramble ashore to face the music.

P.O.W.s

By 1950, the time was ripe for the revival of the war film proper. The passage of time had dulled people's memories and was beginning to force the British to come to terms with their changed position in the world. The Empire was breaking up and Britain was now relegated to the position of a second-division power, still exhausted by her enormous effort in the war and lagging behind the economic recovery that was taking place in Europe. It was hardly surprising that the film which set the mood for the 1950s war cycle was a prisoner-of-war story, Jack Lee's *The Wooden Horse* (1950). It created its own 'little piece of England', peopled with good-natured and ingenious types whose sense of humour could always be relied upon to keep them one step ahead of their German captors. In contrast with the films of the later war years, the emphasis shifted away from the men and back to the officers, stiff-upper-lip types who found little to complain about in their Stalagluft after the rigours of public school. As Jocelyn Brooke wrote in *The Orchid Trilogy*: 'And one realized that war would be like this: like the end of the school holidays, going back to the red, unfriendly house with its laurelled drive and empty, polished rooms … but at this school, of course, the holidays might never come.'

Escape was the answer, the means inevitably enterprising and frequently based on a true story. *The Wooden Horse* was a faithful adaptation by Eric Williams of his account of the escape of three British airmen – Leo Genn, David Tomlinson and Anthony Steel – by means of a tunnel dug under the diversion of a gymnastic vaulting horse. The planning and execution of the breakout were skilfully handled by Jack Lee, a veteran of wartime documentaries.

Albert RN (1953) was based on another true story, in which naval POWs devised a remarkably lifelike dummy – which could even smoke a cigarette – to cover their escape. It was directed by Lewis Gilbert, an efficient narrative craftsman whose name is almost synonymous with war films of the 50s: *The Sea Shall Not Have Them* (1954), *Reach for the Sky* (1956), *Carve Her Name With Pride* (1957)

The dummy smokes. Jack Warner, in a rare role as an officer, contemplates the lifelike *Albert RN* (1955), directed by Lewis Gilbert. From left to right, an impressive array of familiar character actors: Eddie Byrne, Michael Balfour, Guy Middleton, Robert Beatty, Moultrie Kelsall, William Sylvester and Paul Carpenter.

Some optimistic tunnelling is interrupted by Dennis Shaw's Leutnant Priem in Guy Hamilton's *The Colditz Story* (1957). Lionel Jeffries and John Mills muster a measure of British calm as Bryan Forbes emerges from the tunnel. Guy Hamilton brought the war film cycle to an end in 1969 with the ponderous *The Battle of Britain*, whose host of ageing stars outnumbered the aircraft on display.

and *Sink the Bismarck* (1950).

Albert RN was considerably enlivened by the presence of Anton Diffring, one of the minor film icons of the period, as an unpleasant Nazi. He turned up again in Guy Hamilton's *The Colditz Story* (1955), which was based on Major Pat Reid's memoirs of his escape from Colditz Castle, the medieval fortress in which the Germans locked up persistent escapers. The film is full of the clichés of the genre, with much twitting of the humourless Germans by assorted British hearties. 'Don't shout, you self-inflatable little man,' says Ian Carmichael reproachfully to a bellowing guard. Later, when Richard Wattis is interrogated after an unsuccessful escape attempt, he covers up by launching into a story from *Alice in Wonderland*, an echo of the 'Jaberwocky' theme in *Pimpernel Smith*. One quality which *The Colditz Story* has in abundance, and which is shared by many of the war films of the mid and late 50s, is an unrelieved visual greyness, which contrasts sharply with the skilfully pointed detail of *The Captive Heart*.

The last of the classic POW adventures of the 1950s was Don Chaffey's stylish *The Danger Within* (1958), set in an Italian camp during the long, hot summer of 1943, where there is a traitor at work among the tunnellers. The cast lists boasts most of the stalwarts of the genre – Richard Todd, Bernard Lee, Michael Wilding, Richard Attenborough and Donald Houston. In the same year, Hammer released *The Camp on Blood Island*, directed by Val Guest, whose heavy-handed, sensationalist treatment of Japanese atrocities verged on exploitation. Far more effective was Jack Lee's understated adaptation of Neville

Shute's novel *A Town Like Alice* (1956), which followed the harrowing march of a group of British women to an internment camp in Malaya.

These films were inevitably overshadowed by David Lean's *The Bridge on the River Kwai* (1957), a three-million-dollar epic produced by Sam Spiegel. It set the pattern for Lean's later films – *Lawrence of Arabia* (1962), *Doctor Zhivago* (1965) and *Ryan's Daughter* (1970) – meticulously planned, hugely expensive and resoundingly empty international superproductions.

It is 1943 and the new arrivals at Camp 16, in Siam, are welcomed by its commandant Colonel Saito (Sessue Hayakawa). 'Be happy in your work,' he urges them in measured and heavily accented tones reminiscent of Bela Lugosi. The work in question is the building of a bridge over a river to connect the Bangkok-Rangoon railway. But the senior British officer, Colonel Nicholson (Alec Guinness), defies Saito's instruction that the officers should work alongside the men, in breach of the Geneva Convention. 'Without law, there is no civilization,' he primly tells Saito, who despises the British for having surrendered and has his own code to observe. 'What do you know of Bushido, the soldier's code?' he demands, tossing away Nicholson's battered copy of the Geneva Convention and snapping the luckless colonel's baton. Nicholson is led away to solitary confinement in a corrugated iron sweat box, to the strains of 'For He's a Jolly Good Fellow', sung by the other ranks. Having established these apparently irreconcilable points of view, the film gradually brings them together. Nicholson wins his minor victory and the British officers are allowed by Saito to supervise the building of the bridge. Initially, its construction is a task to be undertaken to rebuild the battalion's morale, but soon it is dominated by Nicholson's blimpish preoccupation with showing Saito just what the Tommy is really made of. In a demonstration of Western efficiency, Saito is even smugly told that the bridge is incorrectly sited and will collapse under the weight of the very first train. The obsessions fuelled by Nicholson's and Saito's two different codes are slowly brought together: if the bridge is not built on time, Saito will have to commit *hara-kiri* and Nicholson will have failed to impress on his Japanese captors the endurance and craftsmanship that won the British an empire. All this is ironically observed by William Holden's Shears, a cynical American prisoner who lies about his rank to obtain preferential

Alec Guinness' Colonel Nicholson and his Japanese counterpart Saito (Sessue Hayakawa) make an alarming discovery in David Lean's *The Bridge on the River Kwai* (1957).

'Use your bayonet in his guts!' Richard Harris, Kenji Tagaki and John Rees in Leslie Norman's pallid version of Willis Hall's caustic play *The Long and the Short and the Tall* (1961). It followed Hammer's *Yesterday's Enemy* (1958) in attempting to show that the good old British Tommy was as capable of committing atrocities as the faceless enemy.

treatment reserved for officers and disobeys Nicholson's orders not to try to escape – as the British were ordered to surrender, escaping is also apparently contrary to the Geneva Convention. Having regained the safety of India, it is only with the greatest reluctance that Shears agrees to accompany a commando raid on the bridge led by Major Warden (Jack Hawkins). Their efforts are nearly thwarted by Nicholson, who discovers the commandos' dynamite leads, exposed in the river's shallows. In the desperate fight that follows his discovery, it is the fatally wounded Nicholson who blows up the bridge as he collapses on the commandos' plunger. Saito and Shears are also killed and the bridge collapes spectacularly just as a fully loaded supply train puffs across. Watching from the bank, James Donald's medical officer despairingly cries, 'Madness, madness!'

If *The Bridge on the River Kwai* is a film of ideas, they are pretty basic ones. It is, in fact, a glossy adventure story handled by a master of narrative film. However, on some levels it fails as lamentably as any of the Monogram or

Tempers reach flash point in the desert in J. Lee Thompson's excellent *Ice Cold In Alex* (1958), with John Mills, Anthony Quayle, Sylvia Syms and granite-jawed NCO Harry Andrews. A small group of officers and nurses fleeing across the desert pick up an Afrikaner (Quayle), who turns out not only to be a spy but also by far the most efficient at getting them to the end of their trek and the chilled lagers of the title.

The enemy also got all the best tunes in Roy Baker's *The One That Got Away* (1957), in which Hardy Kruger played the cocksure PoW Franz von Werra, who after several unsuccessful escape attempts in Britain, finally managed to give his captors the slip in Canada and gain the safety of the neutral United States. Michael Goodliffe is his interrogator and Terence Alexander waits at the door.

'You've picked up something here, sir.' Brewster Mason, Nigel Stock and Richard Todd examine the effects of low flying on their Lancaster in Michael Anderson's *The Dambusters* (1955).

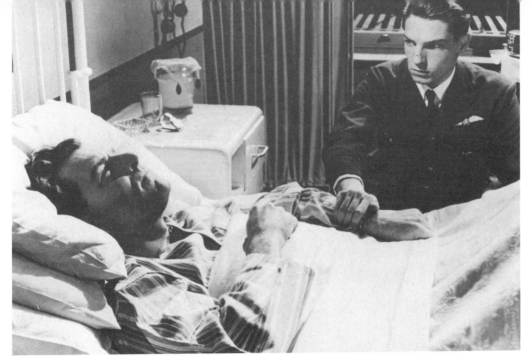

'No one could tell what he was really thinking.' The words come from *Brief Encounter*, but might equally well have been applied to Kenneth More's portrayal of Douglas Bader in Lewis Gilbert's *Reach for the Sky* (1956). The gritty concern is provided by Lyndon Brook.

PRC action Bs of the 40s. Warden's commando expedition is a joke from beginning to end. Warden himself is an academic who is temperamentally and physically unfit for the job, and the expedition winds its way at a leisurely pace through the jungle, complete with beautiful female bearers. Hardly a day's march away from their destination, Warden and Shears are still shouting their heads off in tones loud enough to be heard back in Delhi, let alone in Camp 16.

Despite these failings, *The Bridge on the River Kwai* moved away from the 1950s stereotypes of wartime heroism. No film did more to establish the clichés which were later mercilessly guyed by Peter Cook and Alan Bennett in *Beyond the Fringe* than George More O'Ferrall's *Angels One Five* (1952). It starred John Gregson as a cackhanded and obstinate Hurricane pilot, T.B. 'Septic' Baird, whose painful Battle of Britain apprenticeship and budding romance are cut short in a dogfight over southern England. The tousle-haired young pilots at Marston station rush whooping to their kites, lovingly maintained by comic working-class types. 'You're an idiot, Wailes,' Flight Lieutenant 'Batchy' Salter (Humphrey Lestocq) beams at his aircraftsman (Harry Goodwin). 'Yes, sir,' is the reply, accompanied by an equally fatuous grin. The ending is calculated to leave not a dry eye in the house, from helpless laughter. As Baird's plane splutters to its doom over Marston, its fuselage and pilot full of lead, the dying pilot comes over the line to the operations room. 'Tell the CO (Jack Hawkins as Group Captain 'Tiger' Small) that the race around the airfield will have to be (very quietly) postponed (long pause, cut to

agonized faces of WRACS) indefinitely.' Hawkins grabs the phone and, jaw rigid with suppressed emotion, growls out, 'Tiger to Septic. Message received, over and out.'

Michael Anderson's *The Dambusters* (1955) was in the same mood, but thanks to a thoughtful screenplay by R.C. Sherriff it remains a superior film. Neatly divided into two parts, the first follows the invention and testing by Barnes Wallis (Michael Redgrave) of the legendary 'bouncing bomb', developed to deal with the major strategic targets of the Ruhr dams. The second covers the training of the crews who are chosen to deliver it, and builds up to the night of the raid, led by Wing Commander Guy Gibson (Richard Todd). Michael Redgrave gave a persuasive performance as the ultimate 'back room boy',

By 1960 Kenneth More was sailing a desk, rather than striding the bridge, in Lewis Gilbert's *Sink the Bismarck!* Dana Wynter worships from afar while Robert Desmond gets on with the *Times* crossword. The film's portrayal of the *Bismarck*'s captain (Karel Stepanek) as an unstable Nazi fanatic was a throwback to the days of *Ships With Wings*.

119

Trevor Howard and Anthony Newley in *Cockleshell Heroes* (1955), directed by Jose Ferrer, one of many celebrations of the British flair for small-scale operations which tipped the strategic balance.

combining eccentric scientific genius with a cosy rural eccentricity in his half-timbered refuge from the blasts of war. Anderson and Sherriff skilfully chart the narrow dividing line between inspiration and obsession as Wallis doggedly pursues his plan for driving a bullet deep into the heart of the Nazi giant rather than trying to 'kill him with a million peashooters', a graphic description of the strategic bombing offensive. There is a detailed evocation of the research and development war (without the pessimistic undertones of *The Small Back Room*) – chilly test tanks and windy firing ranges populated by sceptical Ministry men in bowler hats and flapping raincoats. One of the key images of 50s British cinema is that of Redgrave's lonely figure heading out over Reculver sands, trousers rolled up, to feel with his toes for the shattered fragments of a failed prototype. There is a mild understatement, too, in the classic manner. 'How could I possibly get the RAF to release a bomber for you,' a pompous civil servant tells Wallis. 'Well, if you tell them I designed it, do you think it might help?' is the *sotto voce* reply.

As the raid approaches, the camera lingers on the small, quiet rituals of the men as they kit up. Their contained nervousness is captured in a long, slow, tracking shot of the crews waiting by the tarmac, sprawled on the grass, playing cricket. When the survivors return, the cost of the operation is all too evident: exhausted, silent crews, empty tables in the mess, the camera roaming through the bedrooms of the dead, halting on

a travelling clock ticking away in the surrounding silence. Gibson walks off alone to write to the parents of those who did not come back.

The Dambusters was one of several films of the period which recreated, with varying degrees of accuracy, a small-scale operation with big repercussions. Jose Ferrer's *Cockleshell Heroes* (1956), made for Irving Allen and Cubby Broccoli's Warwick production company, provides an interesting contrast. The operation here is the disabling of the harbour at Bordeaux, which is providing a refuge for fast German merchant ships. The men to do it are a bunch of raw Marines who have to be trained from scratch. In contrast with the sober grey tones of *The Dambusters*, *Cockleshell Heroes* uses Technicolor and Cinemascope. It also plays up the humour in a long initiative test in which the motley band of volunteers are dropped 400 miles from base dressed as German soldiers and with no money. The principal subplot involves the prickly relationship between the unit's easygoing CO (Ferrer) who is not a regular soldier, and his hidebound second-in-command (Trevor Howard), a seasoned professional who joined up in 1918. 'One does not address the rank and file as "gentlemen", even if they are gentlemen,' he reflects wearily after a chaotic briefing.

Psychological warfare was a field in which the eccentric British genius could be guaranteed to run rings round the Germans. In Ronald Neame's *The Man Who Never Was* (1956) a corpse carrying false plans for the

Officer for a day in Michael Anderson's *Yangtse Incident* (1956). Leading Seaman William Hartnell goes to face the ribbing of his shipmates in a lieutenant's uniform after being asked by Captain Richard Todd to attend a meeting with the Chinese People's Liberation Army. James Kenny and Richard Leech share the joke. The film was based on a real-life incident of 1949 in which a British cruiser, HMS *Amethyst*, was bottled up by the Chinese communists on the Yangtse River and forced to run the gauntlet of their artillery.

invasion of Sicily was successfully foisted on the Germans. Clifton Webb and Gloria Grahame were foisted on the film to give it added international appeal. *I Was Monty's Double* (1958), directed by John Guillermin, recounted one of the more bizarre episodes of the war, in which a humble provincial actor, M.E. Clifton-James, was enlisted by British Intelligence to impersonate General Montgomery and make a highly visible tour of North Africa in order to mislead the Germans into thinking that the invasion of Europe would be launched in the Mediterranean. Clifton-James recreated his wartime exploits with disarming modesty, giving the performance of his life as a man very nearly out of his depth, but just clinging on by sheer will power to deliver the goods, even fooling a lecture theatre full of high-ranking American officers.

A different kind of courage was displayed in Herbert Wilcox's *Odette* (1950), in which Anna Neagle played Odette Churchill GC, a Frenchwoman married to an Englishman and living in England with two children, who is sent to France as an agent. She is soon captured, along with her commanding officer (and future husband) Captain Peter Churchill (Trevor Howard), is tortured, refuses to divulge any information and is sentenced to death. The sentence is not carried out and she finds herself in Ravensbruck concentration camp. Anna Neagle looked laudably haggard and bedraggled throughout the film but her regal, stately presence never quite convinces. Peter Ustinov nearly upsets the whole film

with some ill-timed comic relief as a clumsy radio operator.

The torch of passive suffering was picked up by Virginia McKenna, one of the ice maidens of 50s British cinema, in Lewis Gilbert's *Carve Her Name with Pride* (1958). McKenna played the resistance worker Violet Szabo, who died in Ravensbruck. Paul Scofield gave a pleasantly sceptical performance as her operator.

A more acerbic view of the tangled morality of resistance work was taken in Anthony Asquith's *Orders to Kill* (1958) in which a young agent (Paul Massie) is increasingly afflicted with doubt about his mission to assassinate a French resistance worker suspected of being a traitor. Irene Worth gives a chilling, if slightly theatrical, performance as Massie's underground contact who denounces what she sees as his weakness – 'Were you ordered to find out whether he was innocent or guilty before you killed him?'

'What a shambles we've made of this whole rotten business.' Sunday on the beaches in Leslie Norman's *Dunkirk* (1958). Sean Barrett, Bernard Lee and John Mills kneel to pray.

Top
Paul Massie and Irene Worth in Asquith's bleak examination of the twisted morality of licensed assassination, *Orders to Kill* (1958).

Above
Peacetime soldiers. Noelle Middleton, David Niven and Raymond Francis in Anthony Asquith's court martial drama, *Carrington VC* (1955).

Asquith, Lean and Reed

Orders to Kill marked a temporary halt in the decline of Asquith's career. Along with the other major British film makers of the 1940s – David Lean and Carol Reed – the following decade witnessed the progressive drying up of his talent. After the war Asquith resumed the collaboration with Terence Rattigan which had begun in 1939 with *French Without Tears*. Their partnership produced *While the Sun Shines* (1947), *The Winslow Boy* (1948) and *The Browning Version* (1950). The last is a measured film in which Michael Redgrave gives an acutely observed performance as a failed public school master, Arthur Crocker-Harris, driven by ill health to resign and take up a menial position at a crammer. He is hated

by his colleagues and his pupils and despised by his wife (Jean Kent) who is having an affair with a fellow master (Nigel Patrick). He is brought round to facing up to himself when one of his pupils (Brian Smith) unexpectedly presents him with a copy of Browning's translation of Aeschylus's *Agamemnon*, and on speech day Redgrave gives a moving confession of his life's failure.

Asquith's post-war work was essentially threatrical rather than filmic, which served him well in his faithful translation to the screen of Oscar Wilde's *The Importance of Being Earnest* (1951). Less successful was *The Final Test* (1953), an oddity adapted from a Terence Rattigan television play in which Jack Warner, at 59, played a veteran England batsmen going out to hold the rampant Australian attack at bay in the second innings at Lords. As Raymond Durgnat has remarked, Asquith's films of this period have an 'Edwardian' flavour abvout them, an irony when one considers that the director was a pillar of the technicians' union, ACT. *The Net* (1952) was a muted reply to David Lean's *The Sound Barrier* (1951) in which the development of a new aircraft is threatened by Soviet agents. The Cold War also provided the background to *The Young Lovers* (1954), a thriller-cum-romance in which an American diplomat (David Knight) falls in love with the daughter of an East European ambassador (Odile Versois). *Carrington VC* (1955) and *Libel* (1959) were both stodgy courtroom dramas. In the former David Niven played a war hero whose battles with the red tape of the peacetime army lead to a court martial. *Orders to Kill* was sandwiched between two elegantly realized adaptations of Shaw's plays, *The Doctor's Dilemma* (1958) and *The Millionairess* (1960).

After his triumphs of the 40s, David Lean directed two commercial failures, *The Passionate Friends* (1949) and *Madeleine* (1950), both of which starred his wife, Ann Todd. In 1952 the Cineguild partnership broke up and Lean made *The Sound Barrier* for Alexander Korda. The film was dominated by Ralph Richardson's portrayal of a designer obsessed with producing a supersonic aircraft and nearly destroying his family and his own humanity in the process. It is a war film in disguise, with the elusive sound barrier standing in for the enemy. Test pilot Nigel Patrick's icily controlled reports of 'Buffeting! Buffeting!' as he flies the prototype remain a cherished call sign of the early 50s. Lean followed *The Sound Barrier* with a charming adaptation of *Hobson's Choice*

A feast of knees, unequalled since *The Boys in Brown*, in Ronald Neame's *Tunes of Glory* (1961).

Michael Redgrave (centre), Jean Kent and Nigel Patrick at his most dapper in Anthony Asquith's *The Browning Version* (1951).

Ralph Richardson, Ann Todd and Nigel Patrick watch helplessly as Denholm Elliott plummets to his death on his first solo flight in David Lean's *The Sound Barrier* (1952).

Clad in white from head to foot, Peter O'Toole's T.E. Lawrence rides off to a bloodbath in David Lean's *Lawrence of Arabia* (1962).

(1954), in which Charles Laughton's drunken bootmaker went deliciously over the top. *Summer Madness* (1955) was a technically accomplished 'international' film, a glossy rerun of *Brief Encounter* set in Venice with leathery spinster Katharine Hepburn softening under the svelte charms of heart-throb Rossano Brazzi. This was a stepping stone on the way to *The Bridge on the River Kwai* and the great empty spaces of *Lawrence of Arabia* (1962). Lean's examination of the legend of T.E. Lawrence was a bravura display of technical skill and organisational ability, but the accumulating series of exquisitely photographed desertscapes only emphasise the shrivelled imagination at the heart of the film. During *Lawrence of Arabia*'s longueurs one yearns for Charters and Caldicott to stumble over the next dune, still trying to cope with the vagaries of Spindles Tours. Buried in the middle of the film is its facile massage. Arriving at the Suez canal after a nightmarish crossing of the desert, Lawrence is hailed from across the water by a man on a motorcycle (Lawrence's eventual nemesis). The motorcyclist is muffled against the desert sand, his face invisible; his repeated question, snatched away on the wind, is 'Who are you?'

Carol Reed's career had reached a high point with *The Third Man*. For his next project he turned to Joseph Conrad. *The Outcast of the Islands* (1951) starred Trevor Howard as a disgraced trickster pursuing a downward spiral in a small East Indian river village. By now an element of strain had crept into Reed's work, transmitted in the feverishly paced acting and editing. Reed then returned to familiar territory in *The Man Between* (1953). Set in a snow-shrouded postwar Berlin, it entangled a young Englishwoman (Claire Bloom) in the activities of East German black marketeer James Mason, whose speciality is enticing West Germans wanted by the Communists through the Iron Curtain. A neglected work, it inevitably suffers from comparison with *The Third Man*. Reed brought all his vast technical skill to his first colour film, *A Kid for Two Farthings* (1955) a tepid East End fairy tale written by Wolf Mankowitz, in which a small boy buys a goat thinking it is a unicorn. After the American Technicolor spectacular, *Trapeze* (1956), a routine circus story starring Burt Lancaster and Gina Lollobrigida, Reed made a metaphysical war film, *The Key* (1959), with a typically pretentious script by Carl Foreman. Sophia Loren played a mysterious refugee, the key to whose flat has been held by a succession of tugboat captains who operate in the North Atlantic. They have all died in action and now it is the turn of William Holden to acquire the key from its latest owner, Trevor Howard.

In 1959 Reed was reunited with Graham Greene for *Our Man in Havana*, a Cold War fable which swung uneasily between whimsy and menace. The mild-mannered Wormold (Alec Guinness) is a British expatriate running an electrical goods store in the Cuban capital. In a gentlemen's lavatory he is recruited as a spy by Noel Coward's imperturbably inept agent Hawthorne. To keep his new masters happy, Wormold invents a fantastic tale of secret installations in the rain forest, and to add weight to the deception supplies intelligence with some modified diagrams from the maintenance manual of his latest line, the Atomic Pile Hoover. All this is calmly swallowed back in Whitehall and Wormold's gentle fantasies eventually lead to a series of murders. To avoid further embarrassment he is extracted from Havana and placed in charge of training agents in the minutiae of secret service fieldcraft.

The film is thrown off balance by its sudden transition from comedy to tragic irony, but it is full of marvellous performances: Ralph Richardson's magisterially incompetent intelligence chief, only dimly aware that the East and West Indies are on different sides of the globe; Paul Rogers as a hail-fellow-well-met travelling salesman

with a sinister secret; and the American comedian Ernie Kovacs' alarmingly capricious police chief, musing on the expediencies of torture. The film's weakest link is Alec Guinness, who plays throughout in his most saintly and self-effacing manner, delivering an almost invisible performance. Reed handled the comedy elements in sprightly fashion. Particularly memorable is a long tracking shot, at a sales convention, in which a poisoned lunch plate meant for Wormold but heading straight for a US senator is frantically headed off by a waiter (John Le Mesurier) in the pay of the Russians.

William Holden and Trevor Howard in Carol Reed's moody, metaphysical war drama, *The Key* (1958).

Ralph Richardson's 'C' accepts Wormold's bogus plans with the bland assurance of the cosmically incompetent in Carol Reed's final collaboration with Graham Greene, *Our Man in Havana* (1959). Noel Coward gazes calmly out of the window, Maurice Denham and Raymond Huntley are the doughty Cold War warriors, and Maureen O'Hara is Wormold's glamorous contact in Cuba.

125

A busty combination of old-fashioned music-hall vulgarity and new 1950s affluence, Diana Dors was once referred to by an unkind critic of the 1960s as 'forgotten but not gone'. In fact she was always a far more considerable actress than was suggested by her reputation as a perennial starlet and wearer of the famous mink bikini. After her debut in *The Shop at Sly Corner* (1946), she quickly graduated to playing a string of basically good-natured floozies and good time girls.

In Gainsborough's *A Boy, a Girl and a Bike* (1949), she tangled with Honor Blackman over a supercilious Patrick Holt. Megs Jenkins and Leslie Dwyer are behind the counter.

She was behind bars in J. Lee Thompson's saga of a women's prison, *The Weak and the Wicked* (1953). Three years later she was in the death cell in the same director's *Yield to the Night* (1956), an anti-capital punishment drama, loosely based on the Ruth Ellis case, in which Dors played a woman sentenced to hang for the murder of her boyfriend Michael Craig's mistress.

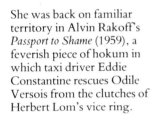

She was back on familiar territory in Alvin Rakoff's *Passport to Shame* (1959), a feverish piece of hokum in which taxi driver Eddie Constantine rescues Odile Versois from the clutches of Herbert Lom's vice ring.

Michael Powell has recalled that when he was setting up *The Battle of the River Plate* (1956) the only question Twentieth Century-Fox asked was, 'Is Jack Hawkins going to play the admiral?' Hawkins' air of grizzled authority was a buttress of 1950s cinema.

Right
In *Man in the Sky* (1957) he was a test pilot struggling to save a blazing prototype.

Top
In *Angels One Five* (1952), he brought John Gregson's wayward young fighter pilot down to earth.

Above
As Captain Ericson in *The Cruel Sea* (1953) he was allowed a brief moment of uncharacteristic emotion after depth-charging a U-boat in waters which contain the helpless survivors of one of its victims. The fellow officer is Donald Sinden. *The Cruel Sea* established Hawkins as Ealing's dominant leading man of the 1950s.

C3 INTO THE 60s

The mid-50s found British cinema at its lowest ebb since the crisis of the mid-30s. The confident vision of a revitalized industry outlined in 1945 by Michael Balcon had shrunk to the formula films of Rank and the faltering whimsy of Ealings's declining years. War films provided a reassuring massage for a fragile national ego battered by the realities of post-war international politics and the humiliation of Suez. Significantly, two big films of 1958, Roy Baker's *A Night to Remember* and Leslie Norman's *Dunkirk*, were meticulously produced and constipated anatomies of disaster, filmed in a documentary style that looked back to World War II. Like the 'unsinkable' Titanic in *A Night to Remember*, the brave

hopes generated by *Henry V* and *Brief Encounter* had slid beneath the waves. *Dunkirk*, in particular, seems drained of all energy by the cultural isolation and inertia of the 1950s, ending with a long, dull and ugly sequence of drilling troops which, rather than suggesting the new unity of the wartime years, seems to anticipate the endless boredom and bull of post-war National Service.

The mood of the period found its perfect expression in the downturned and grumpy little mouth of Elizabeth Sellars as she bickers with her test pilot husband Jack Hawkins in their ghastly suburban home in *Man in the Sky* (1957); or the impossibly wet and conformist young couple, John Fraser and June Thorburn, in another Hawkins film, *Touch and Go* (1955). These feeble incarnations of the mid-50s notion of youth are caught up in furniture designer Hawkins' sudden decision to emigrate with his family to Australia when his 'modern' designs are rejected by his tradition-minded boss. The suffocating ties of home and suburb exert their inexorable gravitational pull and the film ends with the Fletcher family, having decided to stay in England, being observed from the rooftops by their old black cat, Heathcliff.

As Charles Barr has pointed out, the cat is an unconscious reminder of the sensuality which the British cinema chose either to bury or to ignore. The rare moments when it forces its way to the surface are, in the process, made all the more remarkable: a five-minute cameo of a super-bitch by Mary Morris in *Train of Events*: Joan Greenwood's kittenish Sibella in *Kind Hearts and Coronets*; Kathleen Byron running her hands deliriously over the furniture in David Farrar's bungalow in *Black Narcissus*; the confident sexuality of Joan Collins' teenage offender in *I Believe in You* (1952); Trevor Howard's infatuation with Elsa Martinelli in Guy Hamilton's *Manuela* (1957).

Frank Lawton, the chairman of the line, confronts the captain of the *Titanic* (Laurence Naismith) in Roy Baker's painstaking *A Night to Remember* (1958).

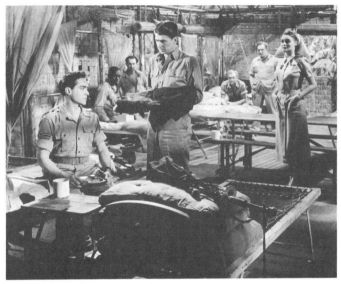

American visitors.
Patricia Neal watches as Ronald Reagan presents Richard Todd with a Cameron Highlander's kilt in Vincent Sherman's *The Hasty Heart* (1949). Todd played a prickly Scottish soldier whose discovery that he has only a short time to live finally brings him the first friendships of his life, with his hospital mates. The film was part of a major Associated British production programme in partnership with Warners.

Hammer Films

When the bottle was finally uncorked, the first genie to emerge took the unlikely form of a small independent production company at Bray, near Maidenhead – Hammer Films. There was little in Hammer's early years to suggest the explosion of success that would overtake the studio in the late 50s. Nevertheless, they provide an interesting insight into the underbelly of the post-war film industry.

Hammer's association with the horror film goes back to *The Mystery of the Marie Celeste* (1936) starring Bela Lugosi and made for the original Hammer Productions Ltd founded by Will Hammer in 1934. By 1939 Hammer had gone out of business, although its films were reissued by the Exclusive Distribution Company during the war. The ABC circuit's post-war need for a regular stream of British B films encouraged the reforming of Hammer as a production subsidiary of Exclusive and it was not until February 1949 that Hammer Film Productions Ltd was registered. The studio then began producing a

The mountainous Mike Mazurki and Richard Widmark found themselves in London in Jules Dassin's *Night and the City* (1950). A strange cross between *Thieves' Highway* and *Oliver Twist*, it set small-time crook Widmark on a doomed bid to sew up the wrestling racket in a London heaving with Dickension grotesques, including an old man who rents out crutches to bogus beggars.

Despite the close attendance of Diana Dors, the endless cups of tea seem to have exerted a morbid influence on Victor Mature in *The Long Haul* (1957), directed by Ken Hughes. Mature played an ex-GI who falls foul of Patrick Allen's heavy, Joe Easy, and is forced into a fur-smuggling racket.

Four British Bs.
A young Christopher Lee, Peggy Evans and Ethel Coleridge in *Penny and the Pownall Case* (1948), made at Rank's Highbury Studios and directed by Slim Hand. Lee played a cartoonist who turns out to be a member of an organisation responsible for the escape of German war criminals.

Below
Hollywood B heavy Jack La Rue (with gun) was imported to play the mixed-up hood Slim Grissom in *No Orchids for Miss Blandish* (1948).

Above right
Dermot Walsh, Jacqueline Hill and Ballard Berkeley in *The Blue Parrot* (1953), directed by John Harlow. Walsh's film career got off to a good start in *Hungry Hill* and *Jassy* (both 1947) but he quickly slid into second features. He was married to Hazel Court, with whom he co-starred in *Ghost Ship* and *Counterspy* (both 1953). Ballard Berkeley is better known as The Archers' Colonel Danby.

series of amiable second features, some of them based on popular radio series of the time. Dick Barton was the BBC's answer to the Hollywood serial hero Dick Tracy and in 1948 Hammer brought him to the screen in *Dick Barton, Special Agent*. Athletic Don Stannard took over from the radio's suave Noel Johnson as the clean-limbed spy smasher. His knockabout companions Snowy and Jock were played by George Ford and Jack Shaw, and Gillian Maude was the simpering Jean. In his first screen adventure, Barton defied snipers, a set of poisoned pub darts and the machinations of fugitive Nazi war criminals to foil the evil Dr Sigmund Caspar's plot to introduce deadly bacteria into Britain's water supply. In those less complicated days, jaws jutted, trench coats remained firmly belted at all times and trilbies

were only removed in the direst of emergencies. Nevertheless, as Barton spends much of the film sporting a decidedly louche black shirt with white tie – which doubtless would have been the envy of *Good Time Girl*'s super-spiv Jimmy Rosso – one is left with the feeling that things are not quite 100 per cent. There were two more Barton films, *Dick Barton Strikes Back* (1950) and *Dick Barton at Bay* (1950), before the series came to an end when Stannard was killed in a car crash.

Another radio hero, Archibald Berkeley Willoughby, alias PC 49, turned up in *A Case for PC 49* (1949). Brian Reece's slow-thinking, upper-class flatfoot stays resolutely two or three steps behind a complicated plot in which model Della Dainton, the 'Glorious Soap Queen' arranges for the murder of her hapless fiance, Jimmy Pewter, to collect on

Adrienne Corri, Hugh McDermott, Joseph Tomelty and Hazel Court are menaced by Nyah, the alien invader in David Macdonald's *Devil Girl from Mars*, a Danzigers' space epic of 1954. Patricia Laffan was magnificent as the strapping Nyah, a totally emancipated spacewoman clad from head to foot in black PVC. She does not hesitate to unleash her paralyser ray gun and giant robot on the hapless inmates of a remote Scottish hotel as she scours the countryside for some husky earthling studs to service her Martian matriarchy. The film contains the immortal line, 'Mrs Jamieson, may I introduce you to your latest guest, Miss Nyah. She comes from Mars.'

his will. Christine Norden was in splendidly florid form as the devious Della and Michael Ripper – later to become a Hammer stalwart – made an early appearance as an ex-con framed for the murder.

From producing low-budget films aimed at the home market, Hammer moved on to making B features for the much bigger American market. *Cloudburst* (1951) with Robert Preston, initiated a long series of films in which fading American stars – usually playing amnesiac Canadian airmen or visiting American cops – thronged the streets of London, discovering corpses in Mayfair with every reel change. Richard Carlson, Louis Hayward, Cesar Romero, Dane Clark and Zachary Scott were among the leading men who slid into the backwaters of the British B feature. Some of the plot lines in these American-bolstered epics have a weird charm all their own. In Bernard Knowles' *Park Plaza 605* (1955) – not a Hammer film – Tom Conway (of Falcon fame) played debonair private dick Norman Conquest, whose full-blooded drive off the golf tee brings down a carrier pigeon bearing the mysterious message, 'Contact eight o'clock this evening, Room 605, Park Plaza Hotel', and plunges him into a diamond smuggling racket. In *Three Steps to the Gallows* (1954), poor old Scott Brady finds himself in a thriller which built up to a slightly less than gripping climax among the exhibits at the British Industries Fair at Olympia.

Many of the Hammer Bs were made as part of a co-production deal with the American producer–distributor Robert L. Lippert. The first of these was *The Last Page* (1952), in which a haggard George Brent was a bookseller blackmailed by a busty young Diana Dors and her confederate Peter Reynolds. This was the first film directed for Hammer by Terence Fisher and in the same year he directed Paul Henreid and Lizabeth Scott in *Stolen Face*, in which demented plastic surgeon Henreid remodels the face of a psychopath (Mary Mackenzie) to resemble ex-girlfriend Scott. From here it was a short step into science fiction fantasy, and in Fisher's *Four-Sided Triangle* (1953) mad doctor Stephen Murray sets about duplicating Barbara Peyton after she leaves him for colleague John Van Eyssen.

One film which stands out from the Hammer output of those years is Ken Hughes' *The House Across the Lake* (1954), an assured little melodrama out of the school of *Double Indemnity*, in which an American hack writer (Alex Nicol) becomes a pawn in the game of a *femme fatale* (Hillary Brooke) to dispose of her millionaire husband (Sidney James).

The flat-rental B market began to dry up with the accelerating closure of cinemas and Hammer moved a rung or two up-market and into the field of science fiction which it had tentatively explored in *Four-Sided Triangle* and *Spaceways* (1953). Val Guest's *The Quatermass Xperiment* (1955) was adapted from Nigel Kneale's powerful television serial. An early example of the TV spin-off, it also indicates Hammer's flexible handling of genre films. Brian Donlevy was imported to play Professor Bernard Quatermass, whose rocket into space returns with only one member of the crew left on board. The film's opening sequence is strongly suggestive of Hammer delights to come. As a typically wet young 50s couple embrace tepidly in a haystack, their laughter is suddenly drowned by

131

The National Health gets an alarming new customer in Val Guest's *The Quatermass Xperiment* (1955). Richard Wordsworth was Victor Carroon, the astronaut possessed by an alien slime who is tracked down by Jack Warner's dogged Inspector Lomax. The other Quatermass films were *Quatermass II* (1957) and *Quatermass and the Pit* (1967).

Top
Howard Duff and Eva Bartok find love across a crowded space rocket in *Spaceways* (1953), directed by Terence Fisher, a British reply to the American space operas *Rocketship X-M* (1950) and *Destination Moon* (1950).

Above
Shirley Ann Field with one of the radioactive children in Joseph Losey's *The Damned* (1961).

a shuddering roar; as they run for cover, Quatermass's rocket plunges to earth, obliterating their little love nest and burying itself in the ground like a gigantic, defiant phallus.

Donlevy's performance is a delight. Surrounded by stalwart British character actors like Jack Warner, Gordon Jackson and Bryan Forbes, he crashes on regardless, as if he has just walked off the set of *The Glass Key*. More subtle was Richard Wordsworth's haunting portrayal of Victor Carroon, the sole survivor of the rocket flight, whose body is being slowly invaded by an alien intelligence and transformed into a monstrous perambulating Venus fly trap. His confrontation with a small child on a lonely bombsite is an obvious nod in the direction of the Frankenstein myth, although his end is pure science fiction. Having located a comfortable billet in

the roof of Westminster Abbey, the pullulating alien mass interrupts a live TV broadcast before being roasted to a crisp on an outside broadcast gantry as the current from all of London's power stations is driven through the scaffolding.

Donlevy was back again as the indomitable scientific delinquent in *Quatermass II* (1957). The power of Nigel Kneale's original material to generate a strong sense of unease – and some moody, low-key photography by Gerald Gibbs – triumphed over Val Guest's plodding direction. Quatermass discovers a factory on the eerie, windswept expanse of Wytherton Flats which exactly duplicates his own project for sustaining life on the moon. It turns be the launching pad for an alien plan to work a change in the earth's environment. The advance guard of the invasion is already in place, in the form of the British establishment, most of whom have been taken over by the alien intelligence. *Quatermass II* is full of pleasingly subversive touches – when Quatermass asks what the mysterious plant is for, he is blandly reassured that it is developing a new food source for Third World countries.

By the time of *Quatermass II*'s release, Hammer had altered course again and moved into the neglected field of the horror film. By the late 40s the steam had long since gone out of the classic Universal horror cycle and the studio's gallery of monsters were subjected to the grisly fate of starring alongside the studio's popular comedy duo, Abbott and Costello. Sensing that the public preferred more sympathetically 'human' monsters to an endless diet of extra-terrestrials, Hammer turned to the Frankenstein theme. Terence Fisher – who under the terms of his contract was owed a film by Hammer – got the luckiest break of his long career when he was offered *The Curse of Frankenstein* (1957). Jimmy Sangster wrote the screenplay, plundering Mary Shelley's original which lay safely in the public domain. As Universal had copyrighted Jack Pierce's celebrated make-up, Hammer's Phil Leakey created an entirely new face for Christopher Lee's monster. The solution was delayed until the eve of the first day's shooting – too late for Leakey to make detailed casts of Lee's skull – and as a result he had to work directly on Lee's face on each day of shooting. The results were disappointing, although they bore a passing resemblance to Mary Shelley's original description of Baron Frankenstein's creation. It was the Baron himself who was the film's finest creation, becoming, in Peter Cushing's hands, an arrogant aristocratic polymath whose blend of relentless dandyism and sadism was in the true Byronic tradition.

Despite a hostile critical reaction, *The Curse of Frankenstein* was 1957's biggest dollar-earner from a British studio. Hammer were quick to produce a sequel, *Dracula* (1958), in which the part of the aristocratic vampire was played by Christoper Lee, an actor who had knocked about playing small roles since his days at the Rank Charm School. He can be glimpsed briefly as a naval officer in *Scott of the Antarctic*, a customs officer in *Innocents in Paris* and an SS officer in *Private's Progress*. Lee's immense height and powerful physical presence – which had previously limited him in British films – enabled him to create a strikingly elegant, forceful and very British vampire, far removed from Bela

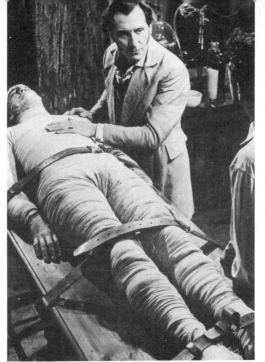

Lugosi's hissing mid-European exotic. His entrance is particularly effective, the camera moving towards him as he walks slowly down a darkened staircase to reveal not a fang-toothed fiend but a disconcertingly urbane aristocrat.

Following the success of *The Curse of Frankenstein* and *Dracula*, Hammer turned Bray into a highly efficient film factory whose production-line methods more closely resembled those of a 40s American studio like Republic or Monogram than any equivalent in post-war British cinema. This enabled Hammer to drive deep shafts into the seams of all the classic horror cycles – the Mummy, the Werewolf, Dr Jekyll and Mr Hyde – but at the same time led to an increasingly banal approach to their own successful formulae. In the hands of a prolific but limited director like

Above left
The dandy as super-hero. Peter Cushing as Baron Frankenstein, Robert Urquhart as his assistant Paul Krempe and Christopher Lee as the monster in Hammer's *The Curse of Frankenstein* (1957).

Above right
Christopher Lee's Count Dracula gets tough with junior vampire Valerie Gaunt when he discovers her gorging on John Van Eyssen's vital bodily fluids in Terence Fisher's *Dracula* (1958).

Left
The Mummy strikes. George Pastell gets summary treatment from Christopher Lee's bandaged monster in *The Mummy* (1959), directed by Terence Fisher.

133

Norman Ward makes a surprise return visit to his native Cornish village in John Gilling's atmospheric *Plague of the Zombies* (1966). As well as running briskly through all the horror themes, Hammer were adept at plundering other genres: Grand Guignol (*The Nanny, Fanatic, The Anniversary*); swashbucklers (*The Pirates of Blood River, Devil Ship Pirates, The Scarlet Blade*); fantasy (*She, One Million Years BC, Slave Girls*); and psychological thrillers (*Paranoia, Taste of Fear*).

Terence Fisher, a hardening of the arteries quickly set in. Fisher's *Brides of Dracula* (1960) is often cited as one of the best of the Hammer horror cycle but its dismal failure at almost every level seems only to underline the limitations of both director and studio. After his initial triumph as Count Dracula, Christopher Lee shrewdly declined to undertake the role again for ten years (in the event, it turned out to be seven). Thus in *Brides of Dracula* we are lumbered with David Peel's Baron Meinster, a sub-vampire who looks like an overfed Surrey estate agent. In the original *Dracula*, Fisher had played up the underlying sexuality of the vampire myth with a degree of skill, but the potential of the sequel's promising scenario – a vampire loose in an academy for young gentlewomen – was completely muffed. Peter Cushing's Dr Van Helsing talks about ridding the mountains of the undead just as a Rentokil man might discuss ways of dealing with an infestation of cockroaches. Veteran character actresses Martita Hunt and Freda Jackson battle away gamely but the rest of the cast supply the standard range of Hammer stereotypes – pompous members of the bourgeoisie, cowering peasantry muttering into their beer, all of them more in keeping with *Maria Marten*

and the Red Barn than the Gothic tradition and a mid-European setting. Only in the closing moments, when Meinster meets his end trapped in the cruciform shadow of a windmill's sails, does the film spring startlingly to life. An efficient and painstaking journeyman like Fisher, a former editor who handled everything from Gainsborough first features to quickies at Highbury Studios, was an ideal interpreter of Hammer's conveyor belt product. By the same token, it was this plodding professionalism which smothered the possibilities for exploring the surreal and bizarre which had been tantalizingly opened up by the studio's success. It is all the more ironic, therefore, that the same director should have handled *Dracula*, with its hints of sexuality, and Gainsborough's *The Astonished Heart* (1949), in which Celia Johnson played a woman even more passive and abjectly repressed than Laura Jessop. Perhaps Fisher's most interesting film – co-directed with Anthony Darnborough – was Gainsborough's *So Long at the Fair* (1950), an atmospheric Gothic thriller set in Paris during the 1889 Exposition, which hindsight can identify as a horror film in disguise. Two Hammer films of the period, both directed by John Gilling, struggle free from the straitjacket imposed by

CHAPLIN.

NORMAN WARD.
12TH FEB. 1860. · AGED 28 YEARS.

Vincent Price as Matthew Hopkins in Michael Reeves' *Witchfinder General* (1968), a film which demonstrated the director's feel for the English countryside and his ability to extract a straightforward performance from one of cinema's greatest hams. Reeves' promising career was ended shortly afterwards by suicide, earning him the tag of the Penrose Tennyson of the 60s. His other films were *Sisters of Satan* (1965) and *The Sorcerers* (1967).

tight shooting schedules, over-familiar sets and inept supporting players. *The Reptile* and *Plague of the Zombies* (both 1966) are efficient entertainments, sharing a Cornish background, and intermittently generate an effective, dreamlike atmosphere. The celebrated sequence in *Plague of the Zombies*, in which the dead, bathed in a baleful green light, scrabble their way from the grave, planted the germ of an idea in the mind of a young American *cinéaste*, George A. Romero, which led to *Night of the Living Dead* (1968).

Peeping Tom

The most remarkable handling of the horror theme during this period was Michael Powell's *Peeping Tom* (1959), a film universally execrated at the time of its release but now recognized as one of the landmarks of post-war British cinema. At the time it must have seemed an unlikely assignment for Powell. His films of the 50s had included two unsatisfactory ventures for Alexander Korda, *Gone to Earth* (1950) and *The Elusive Pimpernel* (1951); a return to *The Red Shoes* territory with a flamboyant, expressionist filming of Offenbach's *The Tales of Hoffman* (1951); a whimsical version of *Die Fledermaus, Oh Rosalinda!* (1955) set in post-war Berlin; and two quirky war films, *The Battle of the River Plate* (1956) and *Ill Met by Moonlight* (1957), the first marking the end of his association with Emeric Pressburger.

Peeping Tom was the third in a series of Eastman Colour exploitation films produced by Anglo-Amalgamated and aimed at titillating audiences with a mixture of voyeurism and sadism. In Authur Crabtree's *Horrors of*

the Black Museum (1958) Michael Gough was a crime reporter who commits a series of murders to satisfy his readers' insatiable demands for the gory details of death. The films opens with an attractive woman taking delivery of a pair of binoculars; when she uses them hidden springs activate a pair of spikes which gouge out her eyes. In another episode, the camera records with awful glee the death of a prostitute, guillotined in her own bed. In Sidney Hayers' *Circus of Horrors* (1959) Anton Diffring played a rogue plastic surgeon who flees Britain after a botched operation. He uses his skill to remould the disfigured features of various outcasts and drop-outs, who are then put to work as star performers in his circus. When they become troublesome, they are disposed of in a series of gruesome accidents, a disturbing reflection

Roman Polanski's *Dance of the Vampires* (1967). Jack MacGowran's antiquary and vampire hunter Professor Arbronsius and his assistant (Roman Polanski) encounter cinema's only Jewish vampire in the form of Alfie Bass's benighted innkeeper. Polanski's elegant pastiche of all the horror clichés boasted a magnificently languid and world-weary vampire in Ferdy Mayne's Count Krolock.

on the morbid tension created in the real
world of circus by its staple acts of lion
tamers, knife throwers and tightrope
walkers.

After these lurid, tuppence-coloured ex-
ploiters came *Peeping Tom*, a film into which
Michael Powell poured the accumulated experience of a lifetime's film making and
which reflects the major preoccupations of
the director's career. *Peeping Tom's* script was
written by Leo Marks, with whom Powell
had been working on a life of Freud before the
announcement of John Huston's *Freud – The
Secret Passion* forced them to abort the project. Marks, who collaborated on Hammer's
excellent *Cloudburst*, had spent the war
working on codes and cyphers and was the
original of the Paul Scofield character in
Carve Her Name with Pride. His immensely
complex script, with its intricate pattern of
correspondences, pointed ironies and sly in-
jokes about Powell's cinema, dovetailed
perfectly with the director's lifelong preoccupation with the apparatus and ways of
seeing.

A withdrawn and solitary young man,
Mark Lewis (Carl Boehm), works as a focus
puller in a film studio. He also has a part-time
job as a photographer for a newsagent who
specializes in under-the-counter porno-
graphy. Beneath his melancholy politeness
Mark Lewis is an emotional cripple, the result
of his psychologist father's experiments on
him as a child to test the reactions of the
nervous system to fear. Every moment of his
childhood was filmed, including an experiment in which the little boy has a lizard tossed
in his bed. Every room of the big house,
which Mark has inherited and split up into

flats, was wired for sound. Grown-up Mark
is driven to murder women – a prostitute, an
aspiring film actress and a photographic
model, all of whom make their living by
being gazed at. The instrument of death is his
16 mm camera, whose tripod contains a
hidden spike and also accommodates a mirror
in which the terrified victims are forced to
watch their own death throes as they are
impaled – and filmed – by Mark. Terror
squared. Mark strikes up a hesitant relationship with Helen Stephens (Anna Massey)
who lives with her blind mother (Maxine
Audley) in a flat in Mark's house. The mother
penetrates Mark's inner sanctum on the top
floor and while he runs a film of one of his
murders – the victim's tortured face seen over
her shoulder – she intuitively grasps that 'this
filming isn't healthy – get help and stay away
from Helen'. The next day, at the film studio,
he waits on the sound stage for the discovery,
in a trunk on the set, of the body of the
murdered starlet, Viv (Moira Shearer). As he
waits, he talks about the 'peeping tom' syn-
drome to a psychiatrist who has been hired to
cosset a dumbell actress (Shirley Ann Field)
who cannot register any emotion. Moments
later she does, as she discovers the body in the
trunk, and Mark snatches the moment sur-
reptitiously on his camera. By now the police
are following Mark, and he films his tail from
the window of the newsagent's studio before
turning his camera – and the spike and mirror
– on the model stretched out provocatively
on the bed. Back at his flat he finds Helen in
his darkroom watching his 'documentary' in
horror. 'It's just a film, isn't it?' she pleads.
'No, I killed them – you're safe as long as I
can't see you're frightened.' As Mark ex-

plains his compulsion, the police arrive and break in. Amid the popping of pre-set flash bulbs, the whirring of the 16 mm camera and the sinister recordings of his dead father's voice, he impales himself on his own spike. The last words of the film are on the tape recorder: 'Don't be a silly boy, there's nothing to be afraid of.' 'All right, Daddy, hold my hand.'

Peeping Tom's intricate structure contains a series of films within films. The first thing we see is an opening eye, following which we are placed behind Mark's 16 mm camera as he films his encounter with a prostitute (Brenda Bruce), follows her up to her room, watches her undress and then advances towards her with the tripod blade extended. Helen is shown the black and white films Mark's father made while experimenting on his son: dropping the lizard in the bed; shining a bright light in his face; spying on the child, who is himself observing a pair of lovers embracing in the shelter of the house's garden wall; recording his mother's death and funeral, and his father's marriage six weeks later to a busty young floozie. Finally, there is the film in the studio itself, with its evocative title, *The Walls Are Closing In*.

Within this framework there is a web of complex connections. Mark's job as a focus puller is linked with the sexual imagery of his erect, bayonet-like tripod attachment. The camera's spike is echoed in the metal tip in the blind woman's stick and the sharp fastening on the brooch which Mark gives Helen, pinning it on to her blouse himself. The nubile young wife we glimpse briefly in his father's home movie resembles the model Millie, Mark's final victim. When, towards the end of the film, Mark and Helen leave the house at night for a restaurant, they observe a pair of lovers nestling against the garden wall.

Jokes are buried in the rich texture of the film like a plethora of sixpences in a Christmas pudding. The director of *The Walls are Closing In* is played by Esmond Knight, who was blinded during the war. His character's name is Arthur Baden, from which it is a short step to Arthur Baden-Powell, the guardian of the nation's imperial notions of boyhood. Mark Lewis's name is a close anagram of Leo Marks, but in the film Carl Boehm was dressed in Michael Powell's old clothes. The father who appears in the home movies is Powell himself, and the child is played by his son Columba. The opening eye and the camera's mirror recall the closing eye in *A Matter of Life and Death* and the *camera obscura* with which Roger Livesey's doctor spies on

the villagers. One can plunge further back, like Colonel Blimp in the Royal Bathers club swimming pool, to the monster eye on the prow of a ship which glides into view in the opening moments of *The Thief of Bagdad;* and the Archers' logo itself – an arrow thwacking into a target's bullseye. As we watch the removal of Brenda Bruce's body through Mark's 16 mm viewfinder, a detective moves towards us and Mark and inquires what newspapers we work for. The deadpan reply is 'the *Observer*'.

The film is suffused with Powell's red-headed women. Moira Shearer, leading lady of *The Red Shoes*, is killed off in an empty studio after running through a hackneyed, finger-snapping dance routine in front of the waiting, impassive Mark. A model with a stunning profile and a disfigured lip has a tawny mane of hair. Maxine Audley dyed her hair red for the part of the blind woman who intuitively 'sees through' Mark, and her ominous presence recalls the pagan elements in *Black Narcissus* and *I Know Where I'm Going*.

In an interview, Powell remarked that *Peeping Tom* was 'a tender film. Almost a romantic film'. When Helen kisses Mark, he waits till she has gone and then gently brushes the lens of his camera with his lips. It is impossible to hate the film's introverted, fastidious 'monster', who in fact is its Romantic hero. In Powell's words, Mark Lewis is 'an absolute director who is conscious of and suffers from it. A technician of emotion'. Mark's assiduously compiled 'documentary' is the ultimate film and *Peeping Tom* is not so much a reflection on voyeurism as a final exploration of the conflict between Art and Life which is central to Powell's work. As David Thomson has written, 'the Peeping Tom is watching himself'.

The Angry Young Men

While the British cinema languished in the mid-50s, the seeds of regeneration were being sown in the theatre and the novel. In 1956, John Osborne's *Look Back in Anger* burst on to the stage at the Royal Court, spraying shots in all directions at the hallowed institutions of the British establishment, as its anti-hero Jimmy Porter rages through his verbal assault course on life. Of his wife Allison's brother, he has this to say: 'Have you ever seen her brother? Brother Nigel? The straight-backed chinless wonder from Sandhurst?...Well you've never heard so many well-bred commonplaces from beneath the same bowler hat. The Platitude From Outer Space – that's Brother Nigel. He'll end up in the Cabinet one day, no mistake.' This may seem pretty small beer nowadays, but in one speech Osborne had lobbed a whole skip-load of bricks through the French windows which customarily graced the sets of the dull, deferential 'well-made' plays which had dominated post-war British theatre. In Osborne's wake came the heterogenous talents of Harold Pinter, Arnold Wesker and Joan Littlewood, whose first big success at her East End Theatre Workshop was the 1957 *The Quare Fellow*, written by Brendan Behan. John Braine's novel *Room at the Top* set working-class lad Joe Lampton on his journey to the boardroom, while Allan Sillitoe's *Saturday Night and Sunday Morning*, and David Storey's *This Sporting Life* located their heroes in the proletarian environment in which the authors grew up. Ever eager to lay a marker buoy on a new cultural groundswell, the press dubbed the emerging writers and playwrights 'The Angry Young Men', an ironic tag when one considers the dyspeptic mood of the subsequent careers of John Braine and Kingsley Amis, both of whom were dragooned into the club. Osborne himself was involved in a splendid broadside of 1957 against just about everything in the British way of life. His essay in *Declaration*, entitled 'They Call It Cricket', blasted away against 'royalty', religion...the moral funk of the Church, full of bishops sounding like bewigged old perverts at the Assizes...'. Among his fellow contributors to this 'Angry Young Man's Manifesto' were Kenneth Tynan, John Wain and Colin Wilson. The last – catapulted to fame by a pseudo-philosophical book, *The Outsider* – seemed the living embodiment of the notion of an 'Angry Young Man'. Scruffy, working-class, huddled in his duffel coat, Wilson was the identikit rebel of the moment. Musing on his sudden celebrity in the *Daily Mail* in 1957, he wrote: 'How extraordinary that my fame should have corresponded with that of James Dean, Elvis Presley, Bill Haley, Lonnie Donegan.'

Britain Discovers Teenagers

Apart from the charm of linking homespun Lonnie Donegan with a gallery of American giants, Wilson's remark highlights an important economic development of the time – the growth of teenage affluence and with it a 'youth market' waiting to be tapped by enterprising entrepreneurs. Although native idols like Tommy Steele, Terry Dene and Cliff Richard were barely free of pubescent pimples, the mediators of this small revolution were strictly mainstream, old-style showbiz. In Gerald Thomas's *The Duke Wore Jeans* (1958), Tommy Steele played both the Honourable Tony Whitcliffe and his Cockney double in an odd mixture of rock 'n' roll and Ruritanian romance. The same year saw Herbert Wilcox's *The Lady is a Square* in which pop singer Frankie Vaughan helps Anna Neagle to save her symphony orchestra. At the end of the film Vaughan sings Handel's 'Largo' at a National Youth Orchestra concert to a screeching teenage audience. *Idle on Parade* (1959), from Irving Allen and Cubby Broccoli's Warwick stable, was directed by the dependable John Gilling. It starred Anthony Newley as rock 'n' roll star Jeep Jackson, pursuing an erratic National Service career under the despairing eye of Sergeant-Major William Bendix. The pop process was portrayed in traditional Tin Pan Alley terms in Val Guest's *Expresso Bongo* (1959), in which teenage sensation Bongo Herbert (Cliff Richard) is exploited by Laurence Harvey's unscrupulous agent Johnny Jackson. In *Six Five Special* (1958), a portmanteau edition of Jack Good's classic TV show, star-struck Diane Todd hops on board the famous train and, while it clicks 'over the points, over the points', listens to Dickie Valentine, Jim Dale, Russ Hamilton, Joan Regan and Don Lang and the Frantic Five as they rehearse their acts.

Free Cinema

All this manufactured, mild anarchy was a long way from the austere enthusiams of the Free Cinema group which in the 1950s had vigorously campaigned against the debilitated state of an industry summed up in Frederic Raphael's 1967 recollection: 'Who will ever forget those days at Iver where cloistered in the fumed oak dining room (reminiscent of the golf club where no one ever paid his subscription) frightened producers blenched at the smallest tincture of reality.' Among the young film makers attempting to focus on reality was another contributor to *Declaration*, Lindsay Anderson, who since the late 40s had been an influential critic in *Sequence* – which he co-edited from 1947 to 1957 – and then in the British Film Institute magazine *Sight and Sound*. The BFI played an important part in the activities of the Free Cinema group. Its experimental film fund financed several of their

The kids are all right, or Britain discovers the youth market. The CO is not amused by National Serviceman Anthony Newley's unsoldierly conduct, but daughter Anne Aubrey seems to get the joke in Warwick's *Idle on Parade* (1959), directed by John Gilling.

Val Guest's *Expresso Bongo* (1959). A bitter argument explodes between teenage singing sensation Bongo Herbert (Cliff Richard) and his unscrupulous manager Johnny Jackson (Laurence Harvey) when he finds his protégé in the company of scheming American *chanteuse* Dixie Collins (Yolande Donlan).

Gillian Hills, Shirley Ann Field, Peter McEnery and Adam Faith in *Beat Girl* (1960), directed by Edmond T. Greville.

documentaries and organized the six Free Cinema programmes between 1956 and 1959. Other members of the group included Karel Reisz, who in the mid 50s was the BFI's programme planner, Tony Richardson and the cameraman Walter Lassally. It is difficult to tease out a coherent programme from the Free Cinema's polemics and films but their principal tenets can be narrowed down to a belief in art as a personal expression, with the film director as artist, 'poetry' as the supreme quality of a film, and a well-developed hostility to the commercial system, whether it was the 'school' at Ealing or the 'factory' at Pinewood. The group were also keenly aware of developments in European cinema. Like Grierson's bright young men, Anderson started by making industrial documentaries and films for such public bodies as the Central Office of Information and the Fuel Efficiency Service. A more personal note was struck in films like *Thursday's Children* (1953), an account of a school for deaf children in Margate and *O Dreamland* (1953), in which Anderson's middle-class sensibilities seem to have been unsettled by the same seaside town's raw, gaudy funfair. The Ford Motor Company financed *Every Day Except Christmas* (1957), which was co-produced by Karel Reisz, then head of the company's film programme. An exploration of the everyday life of Covent Garden fruit and vegetable market, it recalls the uncritical idealism of the 30s documentary school with its own aim of allowing 'people – ordinary people, not just Top People – feel their dignity and their importance, so that they can act from these principles'. The distance this approach placed between well-intentioned Oxbridge-educated film makers and their working-class subjects also worked against Tony Richardson's *Momma Don't Allow* (1955), an expedition to a jazz club, and Karel Reisz's *We Are The Lambeth Boys* (1958). The latter was a sympathetic account of the lives of the members of a Lambeth youth club. Both films are consistently wide of the mark: *Momma Don't Allow* does not reflect the fact that an interest in jazz was principally a middle-class concern; in *We Are The Lambeth Boys*, the visit by the youth club's cricket team to a minor public school fails to provide a clear picture of class differences. By the late 50s, Free Cinema's earnest backward-looking notions of cinematic 'realism' had been supplanted by television documentary.

The importance of the Free Cinema group lies not so much in the films its members made but in the training and encouragement

it gave them in the dead years of the 50s. Their efforts were paid little attention by the commercial cinema, which by the end of the decade was steeling itself to translate to the screen the successful plays and novels of the mid-50s. Jack Clayton's *Room At The Top* was released in January 1959, after a time lag of nearly three years, when the 'Angry Young Man' image was already tinged with the flush of middle age.

The Tincture of Realism

'I'm working-class and proud of it!' bellows Laurence Harvey's Joe Lampton during the amateur dramatics rehearsal in *Room at the Top*, an appropriately prickly disruption as the thespians stumble through the lines of the kind of 'well-made' thriller which had been knocked sideways by *Look Back in Anger*. Nevertheless Joe is out to escape from his origins in grime-caked Dufton as soon as he can. His hair, cut *en brosse*, gives the impression that his head is a battering ram which he will use to bullock his way to the clerk's dream – 'the girl with the Riviera tan and the Lagonda'. He sets his cap at Heather Sears, the daughter of a local bigwig, but still has to negotiate the minefield of snobbery laid down by her posh boyfriend (John Westbrook). 'Sergeant Observer, I can tell,' he languidly remarks of Joe, when the subject of the war comes up. Both men were POWs but Westbrook escaped, an 'officer's privilege' denied to Lampton.

Joe's eventual assimilation into the boss class is made at the price of a bleak marriage and the death of his mistress (Simone Signoret). As the limousine carries the bridal couple away to the big house at the top of the hill, Joe sheds a bitter tear, not so much for the loss of his social virginity as for the sacrifice of a mature social partner who would have provided one of the normal appurtenances of his new life with the nobs.

Room at the Top was hardly a revolutionary film. Joe's Machiavellian sexuality was a familiar fixture in French cinema, and the theme of an ambitious young man from 'the wrong side of the tracks' had been the staple of many a Hollywood melodrama and the principal theme of John Garfield's career. Moreover, Joe is hardly a horny-handed son of toil. His job in the accounts department at Warley town hall puts him on the rungs of the lower middle class, and his sentimental return to Dufton comes towards the end of the film. His clash with father-in-law Donald Wolfit – a self-made man – is more of a sniping match

across the generation gap than an extension of the class struggle. The snobbery is left to Heather Sears' upper-class mother (Ambrosine Philpotts), whose venomous sallies are calculated to keep Joe firmly in his place.

Jack Clayton's direction was cautious and heir to the studio traditions of British cinema. When Harvey seduces Simone Signoret on the moors above the town, the grass is ruffled by the wind machine and studio lights twinkle in the valley below. When it did venture out into the streets and on to the football terraces, *Room at the Top* revealed the kind of drab, provincial town which provided the background to the lives of most cinemagoers but not to those of the men who made the films. Perhaps the most important element in the film was the statement of the unexceptionable fact that a young Englishwoman could find sex enjoyable. After her coupling with Joe in the boat-house, Heather Sears' breathy 'Isn't is super, Joe – wasn't it wonderful?' exorcised the years in which the sex act had been used as a device to ring the changes on the infinite British capacity for guilt.

The very success of *Room at the Top* – it won two of the 1959 Academy Awards – cast

a spell that would inhibit British cinema at the moment it appeared to be rediscovering itself. In essence *Room at the Top* is no more than a faithful adaptation of John Braine's novel. The commercial cinema was still stranded on the starting blocks by the time the successful novelists and playwrights of the post-Suez period had completed their first lap. Now it was about to hitch a ride on their backs. The brief burst of activity in which film makers 'discovered' northern townscapes and working class life owed its existence to the writers who several years before had sniffed the air and caught a mood which by 1960 was already beginning to evaporate.

John Braine's landmark novel was followed on to the screen by the watershed theatrical experience of the decade, *Look Back in Anger*. The film was handled by a graduate of Free Cinema, Tony Richardson, who had also directed the stage production in London and New York. The producer was Harry Saltzman, a North American entrepreneur with a colourful past in vaudeville, television and UNESCO. He succeeded in coaxing a £225,000 budget from Warners and Associated British-Pathe, a British distribution company part-owned by the American

Upwardly mobile Joe Lampton (Laurence Harvey) beds down with his mistress (Simone Signoret) in Jack Clayton's *Room at the Top* (1957), a 'breakthrough' film with its feet nevertheless planted firmly in the mainstream tradition of British cinema.

Mary Ure suffers in well-bred silence, Richard Burton threatens to inflict his trumpet on everyone, and Claire Bloom plots a takeover at the ironing board in *Look Back in Anger* (1959), directed by Tony Richardson.

studio. With the deal came Richard Burton, already an international star, who owed Warners a film on a 'play him or pay him' basis. Burton was too old, too sure of himself, to convey the vulnerability of Osborne's Jimmy Porter, but he did suffuse the film with a brooding misogyny and a fine rage. Perhaps the best moment in the film is a brief shot of Burton, seen through the rear window of a departing car, thrashing his raincoat on the kerb in a paroxysm of impotent fury. Mary Ure, recreating her stage role of Allison, stayed draped over the ironing board, her pinched face bearing testimony to her self-protective passivity. Claire Bloom gave an icy edge to Helena, 'the unmarried Mother Superior' who temporarily takes over from Allison at the ironing board and in Jimmy's bed.

Nigel Kneale's screenplay took the action out of doors and into the pubs and among the market stalls of the Midlands town where Jimmy lives. Burton defiantly (if rather too professionally) tootles his trumpet in an impromptu jam session with the Chris Barber band at the local jazz club. We see Jimmy at his market stall, defending an Indian stallholder from the prejudice displayed by fellow traders and Donald Pleasance's creepy council inspector. This softening of Jimmy's anger was extended into his relationship with Ma Tanner (Edith Evans) – the old woman mentioned but not seen in the play – who becomes his patron and, as she lies dying, tells him, 'Don't let yourself down.' Jimmy's ambiguous reunion with Allison, when she returns after losing her baby, is set in the town's railway station. The whistling steam engines, now on the edge of obsolescence,

provide an ironic reminder of *Brief Encounter*.

Osborne and Richardson had formed Woodfall Films to launch *Look Back in Anger*. For their next project, a film version of Osborne's *The Entertainer*, they turned to Bryanston Films for finance. Bryanston was a loose confederation of independent film makers formed in 1959 to secure distribution guarantees for their product. Its founder-members included producers Maxwell Setton, Julian Wintle and Leslie Parkyn; Ronald Neame and John Bryan; and old Ealing hands Monja Danischewsky, Michael Relph, Basil Dearden and Charles Frend. Michael Balcon, an independent himself after *The Siege of Pinchgut* (1959) which had concluded the agreement with MGM, was part-time chairman.

With so many of Balcon's old team reunited on the Bryanston board, its programme inevitably acquired a backward-looking Ealing flavour. *The Battle of the Sexes* (1960) dumped a brisk American time and motion expert on the dust-laden ledgers of an ancient Scottish family business. *Light up the Sky* (1960) followed the escapades of a wartime searchlight battery. *Spare the Rod* (1961) was a long-deferred Ealing project which had been held up in the 50s by censorship problems. It was a tame attempt to make a British version of *The Blackboard Jungle* (1955) with Max Bygraves in the Glenn Ford role as a schoolmaster coping with violence in the classroom.

Against this background of cautious film making, stuck in a mainstream that had nearly dried up, the advancing by Bryanston of 75 per cent of *The Entertainer*'s budget of around £200,000 represented a considerable risk. It did not pay off. Despite a remarkable re-creation of his stage triumph as Archie Rice by Laurence Olivier, *The Entertainer* was a critical and commercial flop. Once again the action was opened out by Nigel Kneale, thrusting Olivier's broken-down comedian on to the marine parade at Morecambe where the holiday-makers throng past newspaper placards bearing the latest headlines of the Suez crisis. While his father (Roger Livesey), a former music hall star, entertains his pub cronies with songs redolent of Edwardian jingoism, Archie makes his own contribution to the 'war effort' in his tatty seafront revue. He sings 'This was their finest shower' against a faded backcloth of a battleship, attended by a blowsy and mutinous Britannia who has not been paid for weeks. Britain, like Archie, has been reduced to moral and financial bankruptcy, signing cheques that cannot be honoured, nursing the cheap fantasies peddled by television (Archie's posters claim he is a 'star of TV', although, of course, he has never appeared on the box). Incapable of genuine feeling, Archie is washed-up, 'dead behind these eyes'. As he lies in his stuffy little caravan with the teenage beauty queen he has seduced in a vain effort to raise money for a show, Oswald Morris's camera lingers in huge close-up on his blank face, a mask concealing the husk of a man. As reality crowds in on Archie, even the self-protective jokes turn sour. The policeman who turns up with a telegram is not the tax man Archie has been dodging for 20 years but the bearer of the news that his soldier son Mick has been killed in the Suez operation. But even the galvanized corpse can still twitch feebly. As Archie says bitterly before his last act is brutally cut

'I'm dead behind these eyes.' Laurence Olivier as the broken-down music-hall comic Archie Rice, in Tony Richardson's *The Entertainer* (1960), stumbling through his tatty act in a tatty post-Suez Britain. Tony Richardson directed John Osborne's savage dissection of the national malaise in 1960.

short by the descending safety curtain, 'I have a go, don't I ladies, I have a go.'

Archie Rice's son, Mick, was played by a young and virtually unknown actor, Albert Finney, who was determined, as he told an interviewer at the time, 'To do prestige work in the cinema.' He got his chance in the next Woodfall/Bryanston project, Karel Reisz's *Saturday Night and Sunday Morning* (1960). From the opening moment when we encounter Finney's Arthur Seaton on the production line at the Raleigh bike factory, it is clear that a new, identifiably working-class hero has stepped on to the screen. Arthur is a young bull, thirsting for life. As he tells us in the opening work-bench soliloquy, 'What I'm out for is a good time – all the rest is propaganda.' The world has changed since *Love on*

Albert Finney's flash Arthur Seaton consults Hylda Baker – representative of an older working-class tradition – about a gin-bath abortion for his married girlfriend Rachel Roberts in Karel Reisz's *Saturday Night and Sunday Morning* (1960).

the Dole's portrait of penny-pinching and self-denial. Late 50s affluence has ensured that Arthur's wardrobe is bulging with sharp, Italian-style suits and a matching range of square-bottomed ties. Drinking all comers under the table, sleeping with a workmate's wife (Rachel Roberts) and peppering the fat backside of the local gossip with air gun pellets, Arthur has carved a comfortable niche for himself in the system which has enabled 'the ruddy gaffers' to push his parents around like sheep. But Arthur's randy freedom is as circumscribed as that of the fish he catches at weekends with his mate, Norman Rossington. Like them, he 'can't keep his chops off the bait'. Arthur may have his bit of fun but he is also reconciled to paying the price. Rachel Roberts' pregnancy is terminated in a £40 back-street abortion and Arthur is savagely beaten up by her husband's soldier brothers. A pert little tease, Doreen (Shirley Ann Field), skilfully ensnares him in a marriage which will lead to a new home on a housing estate 'with a bath and everything'. Towards the end of the film Arthur gazes from his bedroom window along the cluttered little back gardens of the terrace which he will soon leave. A rosy, sentimental glow clothes the busy life of the back lane, the noisily playing children, gossiping neighbours, even his old antagonist, Ma Bull, poised at her watching post like one of those fearsome concierges encountered on every floor of Russian hotels. The film closes with Arthur throwing stones at the housing estate shoebox whose neat, blank lines indicate his imminent surrender. Like Rose Sandigate in *It Always Rains on Sunday*, Arthur is about to settle for the 60s equivalent of 'haddock for breakfast' – fish fingers and 'Take Your Pick' on the television.

Karel Reisz's assured handling of *Saturday Night and Sunday Morning* marked a breakout from the cautious bridgehead established by *Room at the Top*. Clayton's film, and *Look Back in Anger*, had not been able to struggle free from the conventions of the studio. Although Tony Richardson wanted Ma Tanner's death in hospital to be an impressionistic touch, he was presented with an elaborate set for the purpose. Laurence Harvey and Richard Burton were established film stars and were not entirely successful in submerging their screen personalities in 'daringly' chosen roles. Albert Finney owed no debts to the commercial cinema or the West End stage and the sheer energy of his performance quite literally turned him into Arthur Seaton – it's impossible to say where the actor ends and the character begins.

Saturday Night and Sunday Morning differed from its forbears in one other important respect. Alan Sillitoe's novel had been adapted for the screen by its author rather than being filtered through the hands of a practised screenwriter. This approach was subsequently adopted in most of the films made during the experiment in social realism but sadly it did not lead to the development by the same writers of *original* screenplays for the cinema of the 60s.

Room at the Top's success galvanized some of the professionals who had laboured in the stony fields of the 50s. In 1958 actors Richard Attenborough and Michael Craig, director Guy Green and actor/writer Bryan Forbes, all of whom were seeking projects more challenging than the routine films on which they

Kenneth More as the bright, well-meaning young works manager who joins a workers' co-operative in Bernard Miles' *Chance of a Lifetime* (1950), which featured a splendid performance from Hattie Jacques as a shopfloor termagent.

were then working, formed Beaver Films to produce a hard-hitting drama built around an unofficial strike. *The Angry Silence* (1961) was not the first British film to deal directly with industrial relations. *The Proud Valley* (1940) and *Hard Steel* (1942) had placed management-union relations in the context of the wartime need for national unity. Bernard Miles' *Chance of a Lifetime* (1950) was a muddled English version of Renoir's *Le Crime de Monsieur Lange* (1935). A breakdown of communications in a light engineering factory leads to a strike. When the factory owner challenges the workers to 'have a go at my job' they take him at his word and set about running the factory themselves. Eventually they run into trouble, the owner returns and, with a few well-placed telephone calls, saves the day. A compromise for the future is reached; the factory owner will share power with the young works manager. In contrast to this blandly optimistic tone, the Boultings' *I'm All Right Jack* (1959) portrayed management and unions as mirror images of each other, equally corrupt and pigheaded.

The Angry Silence made a determined attempt to go beyond these formulas and in doing so it took a provocatively unpopular stand. The film opens with the arrival in an industrial town of Alfred Burke's unnamed (but by implication Communist) agitator. His mission is to cause maximum disruption at the local engineering plant. An unofficial strike is called – virtually on the nod – over the issue of a closed shop. A few dissidents decide to work on, among them Tom Curtis (Richard Attenborough). Soon he is the only 'scab' left. When the strike is called off, he is sent to Coventry by his mates and then

Shop steward Fred Kite (Peter Sellers) is pleased to find that his new lodger (Ian Carmichael) is an 'educated man, like myself' in the Boultings' 1959 *I'm All Right, Jack*.

mown down in a hit and run accident by a thuggish band of fellow workers led by Teddy Boy Brian Bedford. He loses an eye, and his easy-going friend (Michael Craig) is driven to breaking the silence and meting out some rough justice. He corners Bedford in a garage, gives him a savage beating, and then hauls him back to a mass meeting – where the workers are howling down one of their officials – to confront them with their own guilt.

The makers of *The Angry Silence* pulled out all the stops to produce a gritty drama of a man struggling to preserve his individuality and the right to dissent. Ultimately, however, the film suffers from failure of nerve. The workers are presented as hopelessly docile and led by the nose by the malevolently

Michael Craig looks uneasy as Richard Attenborough raises the awkward voice of individual conscience in Allied Film Makers' *The Angry Silence* (1959), scripted by Bryan Forbes and directed by Guy Green.

Faithful clerk Noel Howlett looks on as barrister Dirk Bogarde receives a disturbing message in Basil Dearden's *Victim* (1961), the first British film to tackle the theme of homosexuality. Screenwriter Janet Green carefully wrapped it up in a detective story format, but it remains a worthy effort and marks the point at which Bogarde's over-extended career as a matinée idol came to an end.

scheming Burke, who is forever on the telephone to his unseen bosses in London. Apart from Laurence Naismith's pugnacious director – 'I'm a member of the hard work union' – the management is shown as a bunch of cigar-puffing absentees with apparently little idea of what the factory produces. There is no attempt to present any of the process of negotiation between management and men. Brian Bedford's gang of roughnecks (among them a slouching Oliver Reed) are a convenient mechanism for 'mindless violence', but on the evidence of their behaviour they are more likely to be strike breakers than stalwarts of the picket line. The factory in which they work looks real enough, but sports a curious range of accents, from Michael Craig's faltering South London to the stage northern of Beckett Bould's grizzled old-timer Billy Arkwright (sic) who looks like a dress extra from *How Green Was My Valley*. Guy Green's direction rushes headlong into ripe cliché: 'It's a storm in a teacup,' says Attenborough to his fretting Italian wife (Pier Angeli), whereupon we cut to works manager Geoffrey Keen thumping his enamel mug on the table as he faces up to shop steward Bernard Lee. Throughout *The Angry Silence* there are tinny echoes of other films.

Michael Craig lines up posh Pat from the factory accounts department for a seduction on the grass in a rural setting reminiscent of *Room at the Top*. His role of lodger and mutual comforter in Attenborough's cramped flat resembles that of Cliff in *Look Back in Anger*. The final beating-up and confrontation with the workforce is a reminder of *On the Waterfront*. Thawing attitudes towards sex are reflcted in arbitrary fashion and great play is made at the beginning of the film with the game of 'sex maniacs' which Attenborough finds his children playing.

By 1961 the gradual relaxation of sexual prohibitions enabled solid commercial directors like Ralph Thomas and Basil Dearden to flex their muscles in an arthritic and stylized realism which dealt, in sentimentalized fashion, with social issues of the day. Thomas's *No Love for Johnnie* (1961) was a reworking of *Room at the Top*'s themes in a Westminster setting with Peter Finch as an ambitious and adulterous Labour MP. *Victim* (1962), the fourth film from the Allied Film Makers group, was produced and directed by Michael Relph and Basil Dearden. It tackled homosexuality, wrapping it up in the 'social thriller' format which Dearden and script-writer Janet Green had already used in

146

Dudley Sutton and Colin Campbell in Sidney J. Furie's *The Leather Boys* (1963), which placed a tentative homosexual relationship in the world of bike gangs. An interesting low-budget production, it suffered from being held up by distribution problems.

Sapphire (1959). *Sapphire* had examined racial prejudice against the background of the murder of a coloured music student who 'passed for white'. In *Victim*, a successful barrister about to take silk (Dirk Bogarde), is implicated in a homosexual scandal when a young man (Peter McEnery) hangs himself in a police cell. The two men had been lovers and Bogarde realizes that his former boyfriend had been stealing money to pay off a blackmail ring who had photographed them together. Having refused to return McEnery's desperate phone calls before his arrest, on the assumption that they were blackmail attempts, Bogarde is driven to find and expose the real blackmailers, at the risk of his career and his marriage. From the viewpoint of the 1980s *Victim* contrives to be both timid and melodramatic by turns, but it was made before the recommendations of the 1957 Wolfenden Report had passed on to the statute book and at a time when homosexuality remained an offence punishable with a severe prison sentence and an irresistible hunting ground for blackmailers. As a result the film constructs an elaborately balanced structure of special pleading in which its liberal arguments are posed with ponderous care against reactions of disgust or intolerance. A police sergeant who prides himself on his 'puritanism' is wearily told by his superior that there was a time when that belief was against the law. As he tracks down the blackmailers, Bogarde discovers that the victims range from an elderly hairdresser who tells him 'Nature played a cruel trick on me', to an upper-class member of his own club. The latter, along with his actor boyfriend (Dennis Price), have no intention of

rocking the boat and tell him to shut up or pay up. With heavy irony, the most sinister customer at a gay pub turns out to be an undercover policeman. Presumably in order to show that gays can be naughty, too, an elderly couple who write begging letters crop up at regular intervals. The blackmailers turn out to be a hysterical woman, whose mission is to punish gays for their 'filthy blasphemy', and leather-jacketed bike boy Derren Nesbitt. '*Mens sana in corpore sano*' is his watchword, but as the camera lingers pruriently over the punch ball and print of Michelangelo's *David* in his bedsit, we are left to draw our own conclusions.

Bogarde and Losey

The real importance of *Victim* lay in the change it marked in Dirk Bogarde's career. It launched him on the impressive series of character roles which confirmed the versatility and range wasted for so long in Rank potboilers. In *Victim* Bogarde gave a sensitive performance in a pedestrian film. Two years later, in Joseph Losey's *The Servant*, he was reunited with a director who could fully realize his talent. The American Losey had come to England in 1952 after being blacklisted in Hollywood at the height of the McCarthy frenzy. His first British film, made on a closed set under the name of Victor Hanbury, was *The Sleeping Tiger* (1954), a baroque triangular love story in which Dirk Bogarde's young criminal becomes a guinea pig for psychologist Alexander Knox's theories and the object of his wife Alexis Smith's lust. In the late 50s Losey directed three films which went beyond the limits

McCarthy refugee Joseph Losey's career in Britain began in 1954 with *The Sleeping Tiger*, a low-budget domestic psychodrama which hinted at the work that was to come later in the 1960s. (*Top*), John van Eyssen, Stanley Baker and Hardy Kruger in *Blind Date* (1959), a Kafkaesque thriller in which artist Kruger is framed for his girlfriend's murder and whose underlying theme of Establishment cover-up allowed Losey to explore the ramifications of the British class system. In the 1950s Baker had become a star by way of picturesque villainy, but in Losey's hands he was able to extend his range while retaining his strong physical presence. (*Centre*), *The Criminal* (1960) was a classically constructed gangster-on-the-loose drama which marked the beginning of Joseph Losey's long association with designer Richard Macdonald. (*Bottom*), as enclosed and claustrophobic as the world of prison, *The Servant* (1963): the gentleman's gentleman (Dirk Bogarde) meets his young master (James Fox) for the first time. *The Servant*'s picture of the weakness and corruption which lay behind the well-groomed mannerisms of the upper class were a remarkably precise anticipation of the revelations of the Profumo affair. (*Opposite*), in *Accident* (1967) it was the *bourgeoisie* who fell apart as Dirk Bogarde and Stanley Baker's Oxford academics became infatuated with an icy Austrian undergraduate (Jacqueline Sassard). The film was stolen by Baker's performance as a resoundingly hollow media don.

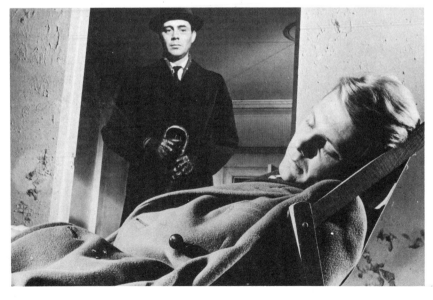

imposed by their thriller format to display a confident, developed style and an increasing grasp of the pervasive influence of class in British society. *Time Without Pity* (1957) was a melodramatic anti-capital punishment tract; in *Blind Date* (1959) the underlying theme is that of an upper-class solidarity which would rather have an innocent man convicted of a crime than allow a scandal to slip out which may touch the establishment. *The Criminal* (1960) with a punchy script by Alun Owen, was a stylish exercise in the gangster-on-the-loose formula, with Losey extracting an explosive performance from Stanley Baker.

The Servant, adapted from Robin Maugham's 1949 novella by Harold Pinter, gave Losey the chance to distill the preoccupations with the subtle gradations of British society which had even infiltrated his run-of-the-mill films like his Rank costumer *The Gypsy and the Gentleman* (1957). In Anthony Asquith's *Tell England* (1931), an 18-year-old officer tells his batman, 'Just fetch my bath water in the morning and brush my clothes and see that my buttons are clean and polish my boots and belt.' Thirty years later the languid habit of command is still there as an effete young Sloane Ranger, Tony (James Fox), hires the obsequious Barrett (Dirk Bogarde) as a manservant to run his newly acquired Chelsea home. Soon the indispensable Barrett installs his 'cousin' Vera (Sarah Miles) as a maid and the process of undermining the young master proceeds to its inevitable conclusion. While Fox toys with a scheme to make a fortune by moving thousands of Middle Eastern peasants to a grandiose new city in the South American rain forest, his own life is pulled from under him – like one of his smart Persian rugs – by the menials who are supposed to cater for his every whim. Discovered in Tony's bed with Vera, Barrett is fired, and then subsequently rehired, by his disintegrating master. The balance of power between the two men is gradually transferred in an elaborate series of games, ranging from the hearty to the sinister, at the height of which Barrett gives Tony his first order, 'Go and pour me a bloody brandy.' Tony's assumptions of superiority have been drained away by Barrett's vampire-like servility and the film ends in an orgy in which the drug-sodden Tony is now only dimly aware that his home, his money and his life have been appropriated by Barrett, who is himself locked in the same vicious downward spiral.

The house in which these games are played out reflects the phases through which the

men's relationship moves. First an empty shell in which the newly hired Barrett discovers the sleeping Tony; later, the smart, trendy home, the arrangement of whose flowers and furniture provides a battleground for the sublimated power struggle between Barrett and Tony's girlfriend Susan (Wendy Craig); next the airless, decaying shambles through which Tony drifts after Barrett has been fired; and finally the ambiguous arena for Barrett's ritualized humiliations of his master.

Pinter's script, in which the space between the words is resonant with tension, evasion and deceit, captures the casual nuances which mark the boundary lines of class and the easy assumptions of those born to privilege. Tony's background is expertly sketched in two short scenes, first in a restaurant and then at his family's country home, in which Pinter's sardonic humour impales the inconsequential hypocrisy of their overlapping conversations. Particularly memorable is Tony's stuffed-shirt father (Richard Vernon), who interrupts a rambling discussion about Argentina to insist that South American cowboys are called 'ponchos'.

The master-servant relationship provided the background for Losey's next film, *King and Country* (1964), adapted from James Wilson's television play *Hamp* and filmed on a low budget, and on one set, for British Home Entertainments. In *King and Country*, Tony's Chelsea home, with its smart facade and squalid interior, is exchanged for the sodden claustrophobia of a dugout on the Western Front in World War I. Private Hamp (Tom Courtenay) is the sole survivor of a unit which joined up in 1914. After three years of hell, he decides quite simply and trustingly to 'walk home'. Now he faces a court martial and death at the hands of a firing squad. 'It won't come to a shooting job,' he tells the officer assigned to defend him (Dirk Bogarde), but as the court casts diffidently around for a solution, the order comes down from HQ that no mercy is to be shown. Hamp is to be shot on the following day, before the battalion moves into the line, to stiffen morale. In a world where death is king even Hamp's ability to survive three years of war is held agains him by the prosecuting officer (James Villiers). While the condemned man awaits his fate, his mates drive a colony of rats from the carcass of a dead horse and subject one of them to a mock trial and execution. A cook staggers down the trenches under the weight of a side of meat

which might just as well be one of his fellow soldiers. Amid the grotesquerie of destruction, a rotting body, slowly sinking into the glutinous mud, dissolves into an eighteenth-century landscape painting hung on the wall of an officer's dugout. The unspoken code operated by the property-owing classes, to which the painting alludes, requires Bogarde to finish Hamp off with a pistol when the firing squad botch the job, putting him out of his misery like an aged Labrador or a hunter with a broken leg. 'I'm sorry, sir,' apologises Hamp before the revolver slides into his mouth.

A New Kind of Star

In *King and Country*, Tom Courtenay's knobbly, anxious face, with its sunken cheeks and sudden slash of a smile, conveyed the inarticulate bewilderment of a simple man whose only crime is to commit an act of sanity in a madhouse. With the emergence of a star like Courtenay in Tony Richardson's *The Loneliness of the Long Distance Runner* (1963), the British cinema had come a long way since the days when the carefully manufactured products of the Rank Charm School were wheeled before the cameras at the Highbury studios. Ironically, it also coincided with the moment when the energy released by *Room at the Top* had almost run its course.

Tony Richardson followed *Saturday Night and Sunday Morning* with an adaptation of Shelagh Delaney's play *A Taste of Honey* (1961), which introduced another newcomer to the screen. Rita Tushingham played Jo, a wide-eyed but resilient waif, pulled from one

Tom Courtenay as the Borstal Boy and James Fox as the captain of the public school's cross-country team in Tony Richardson's *The Loneliness of the Long Distance Runner* (1963).

Two waifs: Murray Melvin and Rita Tushingham in *A Taste of Honey* (1961), directed by Tony Richardson. Uncluttered and moving, the film also has a strong performance from Paul Danquah as the young black sailor whose child Tushingham carried. As Gary Null wrote in *Black Hollywood*, 'Instead of stuffing their black character into a tightly-fitting role as a symbol of heroism, villainy, or anything else, they simply gave him room to breathe.'

seedy lodging house to another by her ageing, good-time-girl mother (Dora Bryan). While Mum sets up home in bungaloid bliss with a flatulent car salesman (Robert Stevens), Jo finds a refuge in a draughty old studio with a lonely homosexual art student (Murray Melvin). They alternately comfort and bicker with each other through the pregnancy resulting from Jo's fling with a young black sailor (Paul Danquah). Tushingham was superb as Jo, vulnerable and yet full of the calculating, aggressive curiosity of a child. 'I'm not very experienced in these little matters,' she tells Danquah before they make love. She insists on accompanying her mother on a trip to Blackpool, dons a weird assortment of the older woman's clothes and pursues the grown-ups like a truculent Cinderella, hurling insults into the steady rain of the British summer. When Melvin suggests moving in with her, she agrees on the condition that he satisfies her curiosity about 'what you do'. Their idyll comes to an end with the return of Jo's mother but, in a final moving image, Jo stands by the local children's bonfire on firework night clutching a fizzing sparkler which symbolizes the life kicking inside her.

In *A Taste of Honey*, Tony Richardson and Shelagh Delaney succeeded in transforming a rather jumbled play into a straightforward and delicately observed film whose industrial landscapes were explored by Walter Lassally's camera with the same guileless curiosity displayed by Jo as she embarks on adult life. For *The Loneliness of the Long Distance Runner*, Richardson went to the opposite extreme, overwhelming Alan Sillitoe's expanded short story with the complete vade-mecum of French New Wave jump cuts, multiple flashbacks and speeded up action. The surface flashiness of Richardson's technique failed to disguise the growing predictability of the short-lived British experiment with social realism. The smoky industrial landscapes had become clichés, and their glum, disadvantaged inhabitants representatives of arguments rather than individuals. There had been a failure to dig beneath the surface, to explore the inner lives of working class people with the insight shown in France by directors like Truffaut. As Penelope Huston wrote, '...the British risk the elimination of surprise; a situation triggers off a reaction and the audience knows in advance what the reaction must be, because it knows – or by now should know – the kind of social thinking at work'. John Schlesingers's first film, *A*

Alan Bates strides through an industrial landscape that was already becoming a cliché in John Schlesinger's *A Kind of Loving* (1963).

Cicely Courtneidge's lesbian veteran of the music hall hovers anxiously over the pregnant Leslie Caron in Bryan Forbes' identikit kitchen sink drama, *The L-Shaped Room* (1962).

Kind of Loving (1963), tinkered with the formula, placing its central characters, Alan Bates and June Ritchie, in a modern factory and a contemporary flat. But the film which made the most whole-hearted attempt to explore its characters' interior landscapes, rather than the industrial topography through which they moved, was Lindsay Anderson's *This Sporting Life*. Richard Harris played Frank Machin, a hulking miner who can only express himself in terms of violence. To get a trial with the local rugby league team, he resorts to smashing one of their star players in the mouth outside a pub. These assault tactics gain him a place in the team and soon earn him a reputation for ruthlessness which leads to the loss of his front teeth in a punch-up on the playing field. The film's complicated structure is built around a series of flashbacks as Machin undergoes surgery for his shattered mouth.

The most serious casualty of Machin's inability to communicate is his relationship with his landlady, Mrs Weaver (Rachel Roberts). Her own emotional inhibitions, underlined in the morbid polishing of her dead husband's boots and the constant tic of smoothing her hair back behind her ear, prevent her from unfreezing and allowing Machin to display the tenderness he clearly feels but cannot express. The relationship collapses and Mrs Weaver dies in hospital of a brain haemorrhage. At the moment of death blood dribbles from her mouth, a reproachful reminder of the violence of the rugby field, with its mud- and blood-spattered titans crashing into each other like primeval monsters, and the violence that the helplessly watching Machin has inflicted on her. In an

explosion of despair he crushes a large spider against the wall as it crawls past the dead woman's head. Already sapped of his own strength on the rugby field – like the Spanish bulls on the poster in his bedroom, their necks bristling with the picadors' lances – Machin is left with a void in his life that cannot be filled.

Mistakenly hailed as a breakthrough when it was made, *This Sporting Life* marked the end of the process which had begun with *Room at the Top*. Films like Bryan Forbes' *The L-Shaped Room* (1962) and Peter Glenville's *Term of Trial* (1962) seemed more like identi-kit assemblages of the genre's clichés than films with a life of their own. When Rank entered the lists with their own laundered brand of realism in Ralph Thomas's *The Wild and the Willing* (1962) the writing was clearly on the wall. *This Sporting Life* was caught by the turn of the tide and left stranded, like a beached whale, on the sandbanks of fantasy which were to mark the changing mood in British society and cinema.

Boom

In 1959 Jocelyn Stevens' *Queen* magazine had breathlessly informed its readers: 'Nearly two thousand million pounds is pouring out of pockets and wallets and handbags (the gold mesh one above costs five guineas from Jarrolds) and changing into air tickets and oysters, television sets and caviar, art treasures and vacuum cleaners, cigars and refrigerators. Britain has launched into an age of unparalleled lavish living. It came unobtrusively. But now you are living in a new world. Turn the page, if you want proof that you are living in a ... BOOM!'

Queen may have catered for a small, London-based readership of about 120,000 but its headlines preached the universal gospel of dreams that money can buy. In the provinces, gold mesh handbags and caviar may not have been at the top of many shopping lists but refrigerators, vacuum cleaners and the Aladdin's cave of consumer durables advertised every night on commercial television beckoned invitingly to those experiencing the new affluence.

With the economic boom came a mood of cheerful cynicism which animated otherwise routine films like Mario Zampi's *The Naked Truth* (1957). Dennis Price was a smooth blackmailer who extorts money by threatening to expose public figures in his scandal magazine. A large cheque, made out to the Distressed Journalists Association, of which he is the founder, chairman and sole member, will forestall the compromising article. His victims range from the old aristocracy, embodied by Terry-Thomas's Lord Manley, to the new media peerage, in the person of Peter Sellers' ghastly television comic Wee Sonny MacGregor. Price's arrest for fraud threatens to expose the peccadilloes of dozens of members of the establishment and Terry-Thomas decides to spring him from jail. The Top People join in with a will and we are treated to the sight of retired colonels and judges puncturing police car tyres and making hoax telephone calls while Terry-Thomas masterminds Price's escape. Brass hats in the RAF and the Royal Navy complete the job as the blackmailer is spirited out of the country. The film's assumption that everyone in the ruling class has something to hide, and can get away with breaking the law to keep it hidden, is a striking anticipation of the revelations of the Profumo affair and the atmosphere of public scandal on to which *Private Eye* gleefully battened in the early 60s.

Consumerism bred its own deep-grained cynicism, peddled by its own most devoted acolytes. In Jay Lewis's *Live Now, Pay Later* (1962), super-salesman Ian Hendry buries June Ritchie under a mounting pile of supermarket goodies before enfolding a plastic window dummy in a loveless embrace. The Hendry character was a fantasist of the never-never, in whose wake came an eager army of profiteers and developers seizing the chance to change the face of Britain, at a profit.

John Schlesinger's second film, *Billy Liar* (1963), turned the camera's unblinking eye on

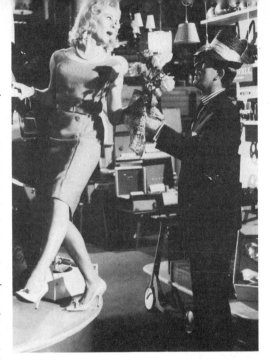

Live Now, Pay Later (1961). June Ritchie and Ian Hendry run amok amid the plastic flowers and two-tone Dansette Deluxes in Jay Lewis' caustic view of the easy-instalment dream world of hire purchase.

the process of transformation. Its northern setting was not that of sooty terraces and smoke-belching factories but the shopping piazzas and supermarkets of the new order. The film opens with a 60s echo of Humphrey Jennings' *Listen to Britain* as the camera tracks briskly over suburban facades and high-rise flats while Godfrey Winn introduces 'Housewives' Choice' and a lucky listener is rewarded with Kenneth McKellar singing 'Song of the Clyde'. Trapped in the oak-panelled splendours of Shadrack and Duxbury's funeral parlour is Billy Fisher (Tom Courtenay), compulsive liar and inveterate dreamer seeking escape in fantasies set in the imaginary state of Ambrosia. He fails to hitch his star to a visiting TV comedian to whom he has sent some scripts but, as one escape route to the bright lights of London closes,

Tom Courtenay returns home at the head of his phantom army in John Schlesinger's *Billy Liar* (1963), adapted from their own play by Keith Waterhouse and Willis Hall.

another opens up. Skipping breezily through the high street traffic, swinging her handbag, making faces at her reflection in the shop windows, comes Liz (Julie Christie), a 'magic girl' who goes where she wants. She persuades Billy to take the train with her to London but at the last moment his nerve fails him. Desperately seeking a way of avoiding doing anything, he rushes off to get some milk from a machine on the platform. As the train moves off, leaving him behind, Billy stands clutching the two icy little reminders of his entrapment. The relaxed and confident Liz has put his suitcase on the platform. Billy trudges back home to his parents' semi-detached. The camera pulls back from the solitary light burning in 'Hillcrest' and, to the swelling strains of the Ambrosian national anthem, reveals Billy marching up the hill at the head of his phantom army.

In Schlesinger's hands *Billy Liar* neatly caught the images of transition and reconstruction that were changing Britain. A palm court orchestra, straight out of *Brief Encounter*, saws away in the tea-rooms while a new supermarket is opened to the skirl of a band of girl pipers. The funeral parlour's senior partner (Finlay Currie) dozes away in Edwardian gloom while his pushy partner (Leonard Rossiter) considers the commercial possibilities of plastic coffins. Billy writes a song called 'Twisterella' which is performed by the band at the local Locarno.

The full-blown fantasy world which finally captures Billy jarred with the naturalism of the rest of the film; more disturbing were the brief explosions of frustration in which he machine-gunned down his parents (Wilfred Pickles and Mona Washbourne) and

employers. Wholly unconvincing, however, was his attraction for Liz, about as likely as George Formby's ability to pull starlets in the 1930s.

The Young Ones

Central to the excitement of the early 60s was the cult of youth. The enthusiasm was as much financial as mystical. By 1960 Britain's population included five million 'teenagers' (young, unmarried people over 15 and under 25) who drew 11 per cent of the nation's personal incomes. Sixty per cent of them went to the cinema at least once a week. ABPC's response to the lucrative youth market was Cliff Richard in *The Young Ones* (1961), a glossy and anodyne chip off the old Mickey Rooney-Judy Garland 'Hey kids, let's put on a show in the barn' school of film making. *The Young Ones*' basic plotline had a touch of topicality, with Cliff playing the son of a property developer (Robert Morley) battling to prevent Dad from building an office block on the site occupied by a youth club. To raise money to buy out the lease the kids put on a show in a derelict theatre which, in time-honoured fashion, is transformed into a passable imitation of the London Palladium in about two hours flat. For those who remember the early 60s, there are some intensely nostalgic moments. The youth club's pirate radio station interrupts the Strand cigarette advertisement on the television to broadcast 'The Girl in my Heart' by the Mystery Singer (Cliff, of course) which sets the nation's toes tapping. In the concert which closes the film, Cliff is backed by the Shadows, with Jet Harris slouching moodily through the Shadow Walk.

There is something engagingly weird about the notion of Robert Morley as Cliff Richard's father and the old monster has a splendid time, convincing himself that the well-scrubbed members of the youth club spend the day 'polishing their coshes' and declaring with heartfelt relish that 'there are never too many offices in London' as he considers placing a Greek temple on top of his latest steel and glass eyesore.

Summer Holiday (1962) was a more ambitious effort to package Cliff Richard as an all-round entertainer. Cliff, Teddy Green, Melvyn Hayes and Jeremy Bulloch take a London Transport bus to Europe, pick up a runaway American singing star, fall in with Una Stubbs' singing group and gingerly pick their way through an endless series of

Forever young. Bachelor Boy Cliff Richard serenades runaway pop star Lauri Peters in Peter Yates' *Summer Holiday* (1962).

ponderously choreographed dance routines. Cliff gets through about 45 changes of polyester shirt, entertains us with 'Bachelor Boy' and reaches journey's end in Athens, where he wanders all over the Acropolis wearing a fish-net tee shirt and singing 'The Next Time'.

There is something depressingly middle-aged about these prim cavortings. *Summer Holiday*'s watered-down pop music, cut loose from its moorings in television, where it was snappily packaged in 'Wham!' and 'Oh Boy!' drifts downstream on the sluggish waters of a played-out Hollywood musical tradition. The energy and pace of the small screen's pop shows and commercials were seized on by Dick Lester, a veteran of Canadian and British television, in his first feature film, *It's Trad, Dad* (1961), a low-budget rock 'n' roll quickie produced for Columbia by Milton Subotsky. *It's Trad, Dad*'s format was a straight steal from the classic string of American rush-release exploitation movies launched in 1956 by B-feature schlockmeister Sam Katzman.

Subotsky himself had produced a memorable entry in the series, the 1956 *Rock, Rock, Rock*. Like its American predecessors, *It's Trad, Dad* was not so much a film as the solution to the logistical problem of cramming as many headliners and young hopefuls' rock acts as possible into a running time of 73 minutes. The stuffy council of a new town decide to halt the wave of 'creeping jazzism' blasting away from the local coffee bar and place a ban on the juke box. The kids respond by doing what the kids in 73-minute rock 'n' roll quickies always do – they plan a show in the town square to show the fuddy duddies that all this jungle music is really good clean fun. Craig Douglas and Helen Shapiro (of the imposing beehive and husky voice) are despatched to London where they gatecrash the BBC Television Centre and a recording studio to recruit stars for the show. Act after act flashes past at lightning speed, some of them real gems: Gene Vincent, all in white, singing 'Spaceship to Mars'; Gary US Bonds, like a sleek young shark in his shiny Italian suit; Gene McDaniels, surrounded by swirling cigarette smoke as he meanders moodily through 'Another Tear Falls'. In contrast, the jazz bands, which were already past their peak of popularity, cut rather sorry figures, although the Temperance Seven strike a mordant note of surreal British humour. Lester filled the film with a non-stop fusillade of sight-gags and jokey references to the fashionable figures of pop art. Acker Bilk's

Paramount Jazz Band are shot through wire mesh, which larkily parodies the big screen-print dots on Roy Lichtenstein's paintings. The coffee bar's 'gardener', tending plastic plants with a pair of garden shears, pauses to snip the offending edges off a customer's overloaded salad sandwich. 'Can't you do something about this character?' Craig Douglas asks the camera, pointing to officious doorman Hugh Lloyd, whereupon a custard pie flies from off-screen straight into the latter's astonished face.

Tom Jones and the American Invasion

While *It's Trad, Dad* fizzed off the screen, Tony Richardson was employing the same bag of tricks in a more ambitious project whose astonishing success was to have momentous consequences for its director and for the style and financing of British cinema.

Tom Jones (1963) wrote an emphatic full stop to Woodfall's association with social realism. The visual tricks which had swamped *The Loneliness of the Long Distance Runner* were now put to use as the punctuation marks in a freewheeling adaptation of Fielding's picaresque novel of eighteenth-century life. The film opens with a jaunty pastiche of silent cinema, complete with titles. Albert Finney's Tom Jones turns to the camera to confide in the audience and at one point is compelled by his natural modesty to hang his hat over the lens. Transitions are made with old-fashioned wipes, frames are frozen with gay abandon. Speeded-up chases run their chaotic course through the inn at Upton. The film was shot entirely on location and cameraman Walter Lassally's use of a blimped Arriflex enabled him to light large areas, so that

A non-stop fusillade of sight gags were paraded by Dick Lester in *It's Trad, Dad* (1962). Disc jockey David Jacobs' microphone lead gets tangled up with Mario Fabrizi's spaghetti as he introduces the acts in television's 'Clique Club' show.

David Warner on his way to a
rendezvous with the
revolutionary firing squad of
his own fevered imagining in
Karel Reisz's *Morgan: A Suitable
Case for Treatment* (1966).

himself takes place against the whimsical
background of the eccentrics around him
rather than that of the real world. Bernard
Bresslaw's constable, playing hopscotch on
the pavement, and Arthur Mullard's wrestler
Wally the Gorilla, Warner's confederate in
kidnapping, seem to have wandered in from
one of Ealing's later efforts. This faltering
touch is emphasized by the application of the
complete apparatus of 60s trendiness – frozen
frames, slow-motion love-making, speeded-
up chases and a hallucinatory sequence at the
end in which Morgan is confronted by a revolutionary firing squad composed of figures
from his past, including Redgrave prettily
decked out in commissar's uniform with
matching submachine gun.

In Jack Gold's *The Bofors Gun* (1967),
David Warner played a different kind of
victim, on the receiving end of a mind at the
end of its tether. Nicol Williamson gave a
blistering performance as a brutal regular
soldier who in one dreadful night destroys
sensitive grammar school boy Warner's
chance of becoming an officer and escaping
from the bleak BAOR camp where they are
stationed. The mayhem caused by Williamson in the base and the guard room reaches a
nightmarish climax when he commits *hara-
kiri* with his bayonet as Corporal Warner gets
his men to fall in for inspection by Sergeant
Peter Vaughan.

Roman Polanski's *Repulsion* (1965) is an
inside-out *Psycho*, charting with great technical virtuosity the surrender to schizo-
phrenia of a young Belgian girl (Catherine
Deneuve) living in South Kensington. Her
Oedipal horror of sexuality drives her to kill
her boyfriend (John Fraser) and slash her

lecherous landlord (Patrick Wymark) to
death with a razor. We follow the descent into
madness through her eyes, from the minutely
observed obsession with cracks in the pavement and distorted view of domestic objects
to the terrifying hallucinations – hands
coming through the walls of the flat – which
crowd in on her. A lingering image of
Repulsion is that of a foetus-like skinned
rabbit rotting away on the flat's kitchen table.

Polanski's next film, *Cul de Sac* (1966), also
had the quality of a bad dream and a triangular plot line reminiscent of his early *Knife
in the Water* (1962). An ill-matched couple
living in a castle on Holy Island (Donald
Pleasance and Francoise Dorleac) are visited
by a pair of gangsters on the run from a
robbery (Lionel Stander and Jack Mac-
Gowran). After the death and burial of the
fatally wounded MacGowran, Pleasance,
Dorleac and Stander play a series of sinister
games with each other which end when
Pleasance shoots Stander and then breaks
down. He ends the film hunched on a rock as
the tide laps over the causeway to the island,
crying feebly for his first wife.

Bryan Forbes explored the dividing line
between sanity and madness in two films of
the 60s, *Seance on a Wet Afternoon* (1964) and
The Whisperers (1967). In the former Kim
Stanley was an unbalanced medium who persuades her submissive husband (Richard
Attenborough) to kidnap a child so that she
may 'divine' its whereabouts. In *The
Whisperers*, Edith Evans played a poverty-
stricken old woman, convinced that she is
being spied on by the 'whisperers' of the title
and nursing delusions of grandeur and a
phantom legacy as she tries to negotiate the

heartless maze of the Welfare State.

Peter Brook's *Lord of the Flies* (1961) dealt with the disintegration and regression of a society in miniature. It was adapted with great skill by Brook from William Golding's allegorical novel in which a band of middle-class English schoolboys are stranded on a desert island after a plane crash during a nuclear alert. Soon the grey flannel suits and choristers' uniforms are reduced to shreds and fall away, taking with them the constraints of the adult world. Ralph – generous, practical, intent on attracting rescuers – is supplanted by Jack, a 'natural leader', whose choristers retain their hats on top of the war-paint as a vestigial symbol of their group's role as hunters. Jack offers the boys 'fun and feasts' and protection from 'the Beast' – the dead pilot whose parachute billows eerily in

Theatre of the absurd in Roman Polanski's *Cul de Sac* (1966). Grotesque gangsters Lionel Stander and the fatally-wounded Jack MacGowran find their Morris Minor cut off by the tide and seek the shelter of Holy Island.

Richard Attenborough and Kim Stanley in Bryan Forbes' *Seance on a Wet Afternoon* (1964), the film which allowed Attenborough, under a thick layer of make-up, to throw off the eternally boyish image which had dogged him since his debut as a cowardly young stoker in Noel Coward's *In Which We Serve* (1942). The commercial failure of *Seance on a Wet Afternoon*, coupled with the poor returns on Basil Dearden's 'problem' picture *Life for Ruth* (1962) led to the break-up of Allied Film Makers and underlined the problems faced throughout the 1960s by the British independent production companies.

the rain forest. The descent into savagery is brought to an end by the arrival of a rescue party of adults. (The boys' reversion to their childish roles as the rescuers march up the beach is curiously reminiscent of Kenneth More's transformation back into the family butler at the end of Lewis Gilbert's 1957 *The Admirable Crichton*). Brook shot the film strictly in sequence and succeeded in extracting at least one memorable performance from the boy who plays Piggy, the kind of pompous, insecure little fat boy who is natural prey for bullies. There is a beautifully orchestrated scene in which he explains with wistful pedantry how the town of Camberley acquired its name. Sadly, the book's central scene in which the wonky little mystic Simon confronts the placatory pig's head, with its buzzing cloud of flies, falls completely flat. From the novel's vision of hell, it dwindles

merely into a small boy staring quizzically at a pig's head.

In Peter Watkins' *Privilege* (1967), Britain itself was falling apart. Now a splendid period piece, *Privilege* was set in the near future. A quasi-Fascist government cynically uses a rock idol (Paul Jones) to control the nation's youth in a series of mass rallies linked with the state-controlled church. He is prompted by his girlfriend (Jean Shrimpton) to rebel against this manipulation but is quickly discredited by the government.

Watkins was one of a number of directors (Ken Russell, Kevin Billington, Ken Loach, Jack Gold) who moved into feature films in the late 60s after gaining their initial experience in television. While working for the BBC, Watkins made two films which remain classics of their kind: *Culloden* (1964) was a reconstruction of the defeat of the Young

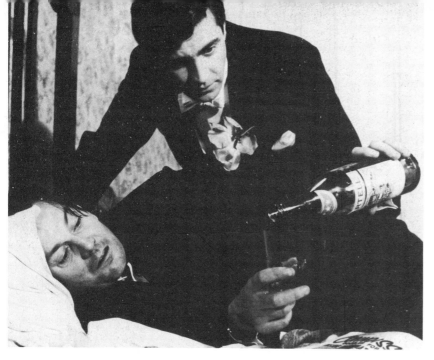

Alan Bates' ruthless Young Pretender to the crown offered by the property boom finds his remittance man mentor (Denholm Elliott) sunk deep in brandy-sodden gloom in Clive Donner's *Nothing But The Best* (1964).

increased by £700 million and Charles Clore, the biggest developer of them all, became a household name. Clive Donner's *Nothing But The Best* (1964), scripted by Frederic Raphael, held up a mirror to the superficial values of a society in which 'old' and very new money mingle in a get-rich-quick marriage of convenience and in which an impostor can gain entry into the ruling class by presenting the correct outward appearance to the world. Unlike Joe Lampton, Alan Bates' young thruster Jimmy Brewster is working-class and determined to conceal it. To make his way in a smart West End estate agents ('property sharks in the nicest possible way') and to marry the boss's daughter (Millicent Martin) he needs a dancing master, someone to teach him the codewords and call signs of the upper classes. He acquires the perfect tutor in Denholm Elliott's Charlie Prince, definitive remittance man and occasional forger of cheques, who is persuaded to turn Brewster into a forgery of himself. Raphael's script brilliantly compresses the transformation as Brewster is provided with the bogus background and vocabulary which will establish him automatically as a Top Person. Cambridge is chosen as his *alma mater:* 'If pressed, better say you read history – you don't know any do you? – excellent – always refer to historians by their Christian names.' Brewster smacks a squash ball around the court with growing assurance while Prince drills into him the kneejerk responses to fit every occasion: 'What's wrong with the British workman? Too bloody middle class by half. Bloody management? It ought to pull its finger out. Negroes are ...? Very fine cricketers. Americans? Let us down over

Suez. French? Let us down in 1940. Germans? Best bloody infantry in the world.'

When Charlie becomes troublesome, he is disposed of by Brewster – strangled with his old Etonian tie – and bricked up in his landlady's basement. There he becomes Brewster's nemesis. When he returns from his honeymoon to take up a fraudulently acquired directorship, he finds the building being demolished as part of a property deal he has set up. As the inevitable discovery is made, Jimmy Brewster is already formulating an alibi.

In a society whose feverish pursuit of the appearance rather than the substance of affluence had become a fetish, one had to keep on one's toes to avoid being caught out by the shifting sands of fashion. When porky deb's delight William Rushton frets over the vexed question of whether 'Rembrandt is hip or square this year', a whole world of brittle values is encapsulated. Nothing is ever what it seems. The camera pulls back from the façade of a stately home to reveal that it is the lid of a biscuit tin proffered by Brewster's mother in her Wapping home. Brewster's property deals pile middle men and money men on top of each other in an increasingly delicately balanced house of cards which, like many a paper empire, threatens to collapse at the slightest puff of wind. Slick, knowing and deceitful, *Nothing But The Best* is deliberately fashioned like one of the television commercials of which Donner was a leading exponent. It is a world in which anything, no matter how bogus, can be successfully packaged if the 'image' is right.

If 'image' was everything, then the opening of John Schlesinger's *Darling* (1965) was the perfect expression of the narcissism of the image makers. As the titles roll, Julie Christie's gigantic face is slapped over the withered bodies of starving children on a London advertisement hoarding. Having caught the train south in *Billy Liar*, Christie turned up in the capital as a model who drifts opportunistically through the shallows of chic London society, mouthing the trendy clichés of the moment and moving from one bed to the next with the blithe self-assurance of the truly superficial and self-absorbed. The loss of a lover registers on the same scale of fleeting remorse that she feels after killing her goldfish by drunkenly bombarding their bowl with stolen delicacies from Fortnum and Mason. They are neatly boxed up, tossed into the Thames and float downstream, instantly forgotten. She finally gets her comeuppance in an empty marriage to an elegant

Italian aristocrat. From now on life will be an endless round of public and private duty – good works delivered from *en haut* by the new *principessa* under the watchful eye of husband and the Press. A British newsreel catches her standing uneasily by the beds of the local senile and demented.

'Darling's' image of herself is defined by the men she is with. The three men through whose hands she passes in London are all professional image makers: Dirk Bogarde's liberal television pundit, sensitive, concerned, straight out of 'Late Night Line Up'; Laurence Harvey's sleek marketing executive, a professional voyeur for whom everything except real feeling comes via his expense account; Roland Curram's gay photographer, with whom Christie competes for the same lover on a holiday in Capri. Frederic Raphael's script fixes London's smart set with the same jaundiced gaze he employed in *Nothing But The Best*. At a grotesque charity function, gay peers salivate over liveried black boys while tottering tipsily past a portrait of the Queen taking the salute at the Trooping of the Colour. Curram and Christie walk into Fortnum and Mason, a cathedral of conspicuous consumption, to the sound of sacred organ music.

Image maker and image: Laurence Harvey's sleek executive and Julie Christie's model contemplate the grotesque sculpture outside the Glass Corporation's headquarters in John Schlesinger's *Darling* (1965).

'What's the going price of integrity this week?' Orson Welles and Oliver Reed in *I'll Never Forget Whatsisname* (1967), Michael Winner's gleefully cynical trip round the advertising world.

163

Lucy Bartlett and Charlotte Rampling's wet suits prove altogether too much for wimpish little Colin (Michael Crawford) as his lecherous lodger Tolen (Ray Brooks) ponders on how to teach him *The Knack* (1965). Charles Wood wrote the energetic screenplay for Richard Lester's reworking of Ann Jellicoe's play.

Michael Caine and Shelley Winters indulge in some frolicsome foreplay in Lewis Gilbert's *Alfie* (1965).

Permissiveness *à la mode*

Richard Lester's *The Knack* (1965), sand-wiched between his two Beatles films, *A Hard Day's Night* and *Help!*, switched the emphasis from the sour, middle-aged deca-dence of the television studios and Mayfair gaming clubs to the youthful anarchy of Carnaby Street. Lester's sensitive antennae had divined the permissiveness in the air but *The Knack* stops short well on this side of innocence. In the title sequence, the camera snakes up the queue of identical, mini-skirted 'dolly birds' waiting on the stairs for the seal of sexual approval from the voracious Tolen (Ray Brooks) and stops at his door. Rita Tushingham's provincial ingenue rushes all

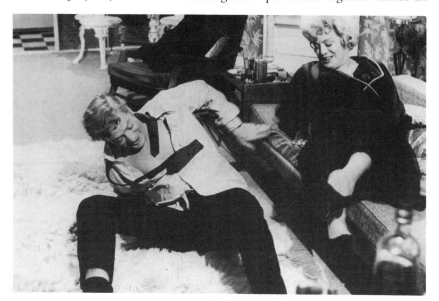

over London shouting 'Rape!', but we know that nothing has really happened to her. Wimpish little teacher Colin (Michael Craw-ford) fails to discover the 'knack' but can look forward to sharing his vast Gothic folly of a bed with Tushingham in monogamous bliss.

Nearly 20 years after it was made, *The Knack* remains a monument to Lester's ability to apply the slickest of finishes to the most inconsequential material. Its self-conscious modishness is perfectly caught during a long chase as Tolen's bike slides past a row of condemned buildings in whose gaping upper floors models are posing in evening dress for the photographer in the street below. The film's eclectic humour happily plunders everything from Godard to Lester's old associates, the Goons. The bleached-out sets of *It's Trad, Dad* are transformed into Donal Donnelly's all-white room where the antics of Colin's ill-assorted household are picked out in sharp relief and angular detail. A game in which everyone pretends to be lions under Tolen's whip threatens to turn nasty until the over-excited Colin, charging around on all fours with a paper bag rammed over his head, crashes straight through a plywood partition in a moment of pure slapstick. As Colin's absurd bed is wheeled through the streets of London, a censorious Greek chorus of glum middle-aged passers-by vent their grumpy disapproval of the 'spontaneity' of youth. Occasionally, a marvellously surreal touch is inserted – a middle-aged woman's plummy voice remarks *à propos* of nothing in par-ticular, 'I was never given so much as the opportunity to breast stroke before I went to sea – and I'm much better for it.'

The film closes with Tolen joining the ranks of the middle-aged, having been trampled underfoot by his former admirers at friend Rory's Albert Hall benefit night. With his vestigial Teddy Boy quiff, all-black out-fit, dark glasses and passion for Thelonius Monk, poor old Tolen is already a figure from the past, a redundant casualty of late 50s cool. A similar fate is suffered by Michael Caine's East End philanderer at the end of Lewis Gilbert's *Alfie* (1966). His snappy flannels and blazer sporting a phoney regi-mental badge mark him out not so much as a representative of 'Swinging London' than as a distant relative of Dennis Price's bogus fighter ace in Ken Annakin's *Holiday Camp* (1947). His humiliation comes at the hands of buxom regular lay Shelley Winters, whom he finds cavorting in bed with a young musician whose guitar, like a phallic symbol, is propped up by the bedroom door.

164

Enviable Lives

One of the most overworked items of journalistic shorthand employed to evoke the spirit of 'Swinging London' was the word 'classless'. Most 'classless' of all was the small coterie of successful photographers whose work papered the walls of the new pleasure dome. In the early summer of 1964 Francis Wyndham contributed an extremely influential article to the *Sunday Times* colour supplement, entitled 'The Model Makers'. In it he wrote: 'The London idea of style in the 1960s has been adjusted to a certain way of looking which is, to some extent, the creation of three young men, all from the East End. These are the fashion photographers Brian Duffy, Terence Donovan, David Bailey. Between

them they make more than £100,000 a year and they are usually accompanied by some of the most beautiful models in the world: they appear to lead enviable lives.'

Perhaps it was the £100,000 a year which conferred the seal of 'classlessness' on the upwardly mobile; or perhaps it was the camera, the tool of the photographer's trade and objective recorder of the world and the beautiful people around him that was the important factor. For the camera, after all, cannot lie. The mystique of the profession was so great that the Italian director Michelangelo Antonioni chose London as the location for a film, *Blow Up* (1967), whose central figure was a fashion photographer.

Dawn in London. A group of down-and-outs leave a dosshouse. One of them, a shabby young man clutching a brown paper

Blown up: Paul Jones' pop star parades before the faithful in Peter Watkins' *Privilege* (1967). (*Left*), David Hemmings' photographer finds a body in Antonioni's *Blow-Up* (1967). (*Above*), Monica Vitti's life-size cartoon heroine is imprisoned in an op-art dungeon in Joseph Losey's *Modesty Blaise* (1966).

parcel, walks round the corner and climbs into a Rolls Royce. The parcel is unwrapped to reveal a camera. Tom (David Hemmings) is a photographer and has spent the night taking pictures for a coffee table collection of his work soon to be published. Later, in a park, he takes some mood shots of a middle-aged man and a young woman embracing. After the woman (Vanessa Redgrave) has pursued him to his studio to demand the return of the roll of film, Tom develops it and studies the results closely. A disturbing detail catches his eye and, in order to isolate it, he produces an increasingly large series of blow-ups. Hung up in sequence like an enormous grainy comic strip, they reveal a man with a gun lurking in some bushes and, in a later shot, a body. The process recalls a conversation he has had with a neighbour, an artist, who remarks of his abstract paintings, 'They don't mean anything when I do them, just a mess. Then it all sorts itself out...it's like finding a clue in a detective story.' Tom goes back to the park at night and finds the body, which is shown stretched out in a strange, foreshortened perspective reminiscent of the dead soldier lying in the centre of Uccello's *The Rout of San Romano*. As he stares down at the body he hears a click – someone else's camera or a cocking gun? When he returns to his studio he finds it ransacked and all of his 'evidence' destroyed with the exception of the largest blow-up, whose blurry white body is too abstract to reveal its secret. Back in the park at dawn, he finds the body gone, only the flattened grass hinting at its former presence. As he walks away, a group of pantomime figures (glimpsed at the beginning of the film and more Commedia Dell' Arte than Kings Road) drive up in a jeep. They scamper over to a tennis court and two of them begin to play a game without rackets or balls. An imaginary ball is sent sailing over the wire mesh surrounding the court to land at Tom's feet. He is mutely requested to throw it back. He does so and, as the camera moves in on his face, we hear the gentle 'pick, pock' of the ball on the soundtrack. Then Tom, like the body, simply disappears from the screen and we are left to contemplate the empty space where he was standing.

In *Blow Up*, the real and the imaginary eventually become inseparable. The corpse disappears, while at the end the imaginary tennis ball – or at least its sound – has been willed into existence. In his studio Tom examines the enlargements and we hear the rustling of the park's trees on the soundtrack. Meeting the model Verushka at a drugs

party, Tom tells her, 'I thought you were in Paris,' to which she replies, 'I *am* in Paris.' In the end, *Blow Up* is open to as many interpretations as people who see it: the fallibility of modern communications; the role of chance in art and the ability of the disciplined artist to exploit it – Tom's skill as a photographer enables him to isolate and reconstruct the apparent murder of Redgrave's companion; and the distractions and aimlessness of London's 'magic village'. A girl in an antique shop talks idly of 'getting away' to Nepal until sharply reminded by Tom that Nepal is 'all antiques'. Tom himself is constantly being diverted from his pursuit of the truth. He tumbles around in a sea of crumpled mauve colour drops with a pair of nymphets who have sneaked into his studio. He allows himself to be trapped at the drugs party after he fails to make any impression with his story on his stoned writer friend (Peter Bowles). The sense of drifting is embodied in the wooden aircraft propeller Tom buys at the antique shop near the park. Lying on the floor of the studio, it becomes a symbol of form divorced from function, going nowhere.

David Hemmings, in a long and extremely exacting role, was perfectly cast as a member of London's new élite, a battered cherub whose entrepreneurial skill equals his flair as a photographer. Cruising in his open-top Rolls past the brightly painted façades of fashionable terraces, he re-enacts the dreams he pushes in the colour supplements. Hemmings later recalled that throughout the filming of *Blow Up* Antonioni directed him 'like an object'. He might have run the risk of delivering a performance as immobile as the models he poses between sheets of glass, like op-art butterflies. The freshness of his approach is caught in the agile little leap that Tom makes when he walks into the park for the first time, drawn into that strangely unreal and sensuously realized environment, the image of which lingers long after much else in *Blow Up* has faded from the memory.

Licensed to Print Money

The most potent, and enduring, fantasy figure of the 60s was not the man with a camera but the man with a licence to kill – James Bond, alias 007, the suave super-scoundrel who, in Raymond Durgnat's memorable phrase, is 'last to bat in the British Superman's XI'. Apart from his phenomenal success, the most remarkable thing about Bond is the length of time he took in getting to the screen. Ian Fleming published his first

Hardboiled stuff.
Richard Todd played an
insurance salesman at the end of
his tether after his car is stolen in
John Guillermin's *Never Let Go*
(1963), but looked ill at ease out
of uniform. Peter Sellers went
over the top as a sadistic
racketeer. The hired muscle is
David Lodge.

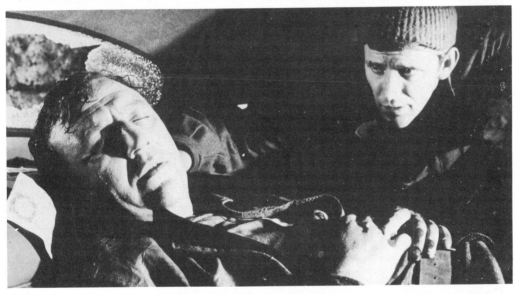

The best-laid plans…Tom Bell
finds a fatally-wounded
companion during the
armoured car robbery in
Sidney Hayers' *Payroll* (1961).

The real thing. *Robbery* (1967),
Peter Yates' fictionalised
reconstruction of the Great
Train Robbery. It opens with a
furious car chase which both
looks back to *The Blue Lamp*
and anticipates Yates'
American thriller *Bullitt* (1968).
Stanley Baker played the 'Mr
Big' of newspaper legend and,
among a cast of hand-picked
heavies, George Sewell and
William Marlowe were
outstanding.

Ursula Andress and Sean Connery's originally more rough-hewn Action Man in *Dr No* (1962), directed by Terence Young.

Bond thriller, *Casino Royale*, in 1951 but, despite endorsements from Raymond Chandler and later President Kennedy (who named *From Russia with Love* as one of his 10 favourite books), the film industry remained indifferent to 007.

Bond was in a backwater and there he might have remained but for the fact that in 1961 two North American producers decided to sever their connections with highly successful ventures in Britain and strike out on their own. Since the early 50s Albert (Cubby) Broccoli's Warwick Films – formed in partnership with former B director Irving Allen – had produced a stream of efficient action pictures beefed up with fading or second-rank American stars – Alan Ladd, Ray Milland, Victor Mature – and a stock company of British stalwarts, of whom Nigel Patrick and Anthony Newley were the most prominent. Harry Saltzman had played a vital role as the money man behind Woodfall's success but, after the completion of *Saturday Night and Sunday 'Morning*, he decided to move on, a decision prompted in part by a desire to make films on a wider, 'international' scale than that provided by social realism. Significantly, Saltzman had fallen out with Tony Richardson over the casting of *A Taste of Honey*, suggesting that it should be set in France, with Leslie Caron in the Tushingham role and Simone Signoret as her mother.

Broccoli and Saltzman had plenty in common, a hard-nosed attitude towards making films and an interest in James Bond. Their partnership was formed after Saltzman acquired from Ian Fleming an option on all the available Bond novels. Broccoli's old partners, Columbia, viewed the proposal for a film of *Dr No* or *Thunderball* as a strictly low-budget venture and it was left to United Artists to provide a million-dollar budget for *Dr No*, which eventually came in at $1,250,000.

As had happened with *Saturday Night and Sunday Morning* and *Tom Jones* no-one involved in the first Bond film had the slightest intimation of the bonanza which lay ahead. Part of *Dr No*'s appeal, however fanciful, lay in its correspondence with events in the real world. As Christopher Booker has observed, the spy was a 'shadow for the history of the age': in Britain there were the Vassall and Profumo scandals; the Cuban missile crisis pushed the superpowers close to an irreversible confrontation. In this context, Dr No's hijacking of American space probes from his computerized Jamaican tracking station acquired a crazy plausibility. The clinching factor was the casting of Sean Connery as James Bond. According to Richard Maibaum, *Dr. No*'s screenwriter, '...his close-up was magnificient. The only one I recall in any way comparable was Gable's'. Until the break, Connery had not had a particularly distinguished career in films, bouncing between hard-boiled British actioners like Cy Endfield's *Hell Drivers* (1957) and Disney whimsy in *Darby O'Gill and the Little People* (1959). His Bond, however, had the perfect combination of physical grace and a hint of sadism – emphasized by the soft Scots/Irish burr – to put flesh on the bones of a universal fantasy. Bond is utterly decisive, never afflicted with self-doubt, moving purposefully though a world in which he is able to experience instant gratification, whether in

helping himself to sex or dealing out death. At the same time he is tethered to a system of benign authority, represented by Bernard Lee's M, Lois Maxwell's Miss Moneypenny and Desmond Llewelyn's Q, which operates as an equal partner in our 'special relationship' with the United States while safeguarding what's left of the Empire. Bond is the Big White Carstairs of the free world, programmed to operate with the idiotic certainty of Beachcomber's original in a joke which the audience can share. If, as Dean Acheson remarked, 'Britain had lost an empire' and was 'looking for a role', then the British found a partial answer in the exploits of 007. Like Carstairs, Bond is a stickler for form and can be relied on to draw the correct conclusion when a heavy orders red wine with fish, as happens in *From Russia with Love* (1963). The exquisitely detailed brand-name snobbery in which the novels were saturated was carried over into the films. In *Goldfinger* (1964) Bond reminds a female companion that 'one doesn't drink Dom Perignon '55 above 38° Fahrenheit'. Bond was an adman's dream and, as the series continued, the films partook of the source of television commercials, echoing the fantasy world conjured up by by advertisements for cigarettes or aperitifs.

Dr No laid down the ground rules for the subsequent films. A preposterous villain (played by Joseph Wiseman) with an unbridled lust for world domination; the first in the long line of 'Bond girls', Ursula Andress as Honeychile Rider, rising glistening from the sea; a hint of the complex gadgetry to come; and Bond's throwaway comments as his enemies bite the dust – 'I think they must

have been going to a funeral', he drawls as a pursuing Cadillac hearse packed with SPECTRE hit men explodes in a sheet of flame.

The Bond films quickly developed a streak of self-parody which audiences could anticipate and savour when it came. It was already apparent in the small touch which provided *Dr No* with the Goya portrait of the Duke of Wellington which had recently been stolen from the National Gallery. Its ultimate expression was the pre-title sequence which, in *Goldfinger*, provided a three-minute précis of the complete Bond iconography. A seagull bobbing on the water of a harbour is revealed as a stuffed decoy strapped to the hood of Bond's frogman outfit. He swims ashore, scales a wall and lays a carefully placed charge in an industrial plant. Vaulting back to safety, he peels open his wetsuit, stepping out in a spotless white tuxedo, complete with carnation buttonhole, and then moves into a nearby bar to await the explosion. A rendezvous in the back room with a sultry temptress is interrupted when 007 glimpses an assassin reflected in her eye. In an instant his treacherous partner is twirled round to receive the brunt of the attack, while the assassin is flipped into a bath to which Bond thoughtfully adds an electric fire with the deadpan comment, 'Shocking'.

Goldfinger also contained the series' finest villain, Gert Frobe's tweedy megalomaniac, plotting to explode a 'dirty' nuclear device in the gold vaults of Fort Knox. As he threatens some rather drastic laser surgery on the pinioned 007's crotch, Connery reflects, 'I suppose you want me to talk.' The unruffled reply comes back, 'No Mr Bond, I just want you to die.'

Richard Burton in *The Spy Who Came in from the Cold* (1965), directed by Martin Ritt, whose painstaking translation to the screen of John Le Carré's shabby world of intelligence triple-bluffs was more in tune with the early 80s than the mid-60s.

Above left
Michael Caine showed that girls often make passes at men wearing glasses in *The Ipcress File* (1965), a downbeat espionage thriller from the Saltzman-Broccoli stable directed by Sidney J. Furie.

Such candid villainy, coupled with a fiendish device, is redolent of the old Saturday morning movie serials. The laser beam which sizzles its way towards the helpless Bond is merely an updated version of the whirling saw which menaced Rod Cameron in Republic's *Secret Service in Darkest Africa* (1943). Dr No is an alternative Fu Manchu, his metal hands recalling the claws of countless serial robots. Like Tarzan and Flash Gordon, Bond always escapes, and like Johnny Weissmuller and Buster Crabbe, Connery became completely identified with the role he had made famous.

By the time *Goldfinger* was released, the gadgets were beginning to take over. Bond is provided with an Aston Martin incorporating radar, machine-gun, ejector seat for unwelcome guests and a more old-fashioned attachment of which Boudicca would have approved – a spike which springs out from the hub cap to slash the tyres of pursuing vehicles. Dominating the film were the superb sets of German-born designer Ken Adam. The gold vaults at Fort Knox, with their towering arches, gliding elevators and limitless vistas of gold pyramids, conjure up memories of *Metropolis* and *Triumph of the Will*. The importance of Connery and Adam was underlined by their absence from the 1969 *On Her Majesty's Secret Service* in which George Lazenby – TV's Mr Big Fry – took over the Bond role under the direction of Peter Hunt who had edited all the preceding Bond features. The disappointing results led to Connery and Adam's recall for the 1971 *Diamonds Are Forever*, directed by Peter Hunt.

Bond had his imitators and competitors but it was hard to parody a series that was expert at parodying itself. *Hot Enough for June* (1964) began promisingly with civil servant John Le Mesurier strolling down a Whitehall corridor to file the effects of a deceased agent – 007 – but soon went downhill. Daniel Petrie's *The Spy with a Cold Nose* (1966) was a laboured farce in which British Intelligence plant a bug in a bulldog presented to the Russian premier as a gesture of goodwill. The mood of the film was not unlike that of Mario Zampi's cold war frolic of the 50s, *Top Secret* (1952), in which George Cole's sanitary engineer is kidnapped by the Russians under the impression that he is a top nuclear scientist. At the opposite end of the spectrum was the 1963 *Ring of Spies,* directed by Robert Tronson for Launder and Gilliat. A sober documentary account of the Gordon Lonsdale-Harry Houghton Portland spy case, its mood of seedy verisimilitude antici-

pated Martin Ritt's version of John Le Carré's *The Spy Who Came in from the Cold* (1965), and Sidney Lumet's *The Deadly Affair* (1966), adapted from the same author's *Call for the Dead*.

Saltzman and Broccoli provided Bond with some downmarket competition of their own devising in *The Ipcress File* (1965), starring Michael Caine as Len Deighton's reluctant agent Harry Palmer. A former NCO stationed in Berlin, Palmer has been press-ganged into intelligence work as an alternative to serving time in a military prison for his black market activities. His two upper-class superiors, Ross (Guy Doleman) and Dalby (Nigel Green) are officer types who treat Palmer with the offhand disdain reserved by the head of house for a troublesome errand boy. Palmer and his fellow agents are just civil servants in another guise, ploughing their way through an endless mound of forms in triplicate. There are no Aston Martins, maybe a Ford Zephyr from the car pool if you are lucky. The Bond glamour was stripped away but there was still a residue of fantasy in a plot involving the abduction and brainwashing of a number of leading British scientists. Inevitably, Palmer got the treatment himself, strapped inside a psychedelic box whose mind-numbing light show might have left even Bond a little confused about the correct serving temperature for Dom Perignon '55.

The most extravagant parody of the Bond films was Joseph Losey's *Modesty Blaise* (1966), based on Peter O'Donnell's heroine of novel and comic strip. It even boasted a pre-credits 'surprise' sequence in which a bowler-hatted British agent uses his umbrella to ring an Amsterdam doorbell and is promptly blown to smithereens. *Modesty Blaise* is packed with ludicrous gadgetry, op-art follies and charming conceits. An oil sheikh sporting an MCC tie hurls daggers at passing pigeons from his London hotel suite. Umbrellas spurt bullets, Gauloise packets billow elegant pink clouds of knockout gas. Modesty peels away confederate Willie Garvin's back to reveal an inflatable seagull equipped with a radio direction finder. Terence Stamp had the right kind of cockney nonchalance for Garvin but Monica Vitti lacked the strong physical presence to give the Amazonian Modesty a convincing edge. The film's chief delight was Dirk Bogarde's Gabriel. The most stylish of 60s villains, he sips cocktails from a glass size of a goldfish bowl, complete with goldfish. He consigns agents to their deaths with a petulant snap of the fingers but covers his ears when he hears the thin screams of the lobsters boiling for his lunch. As soon as Modesty falls into his hands, he locks her up in an op-art dungeon. Later, when the going gets rough, he signals his determination by snatching off his silver wig.

Otley (1969), with a witty script from Dick Clement and Ian La Frenais, waved an affectionate goodbye to the spy cycle. Tom Courtenay played a scruffy hanger-on at the shady end of the Portobello Road antiques racket who finds himself pitched into the double- and triple-crosses of the espionage world. Courtenay gave an engaging performance as a bewildered scuffler hopelessly out of his depth. When he tries to don the mantle of Richard Hannay and lose himself in a crowd – just like Robert Donat in *The Thirty-Nine Steps* – he finds himself the sole white man in a Black Power demonstration whose marchers tote an alarming array of banners urging the swift despatch of the white trash and all their works.

Games People Play

'Swinging Britain' was a shortlived affair, lasting a bare three years, from 1963 to 1966. At this point its crisp, op-art style, sent-up in *Modesty Blaise* and coolly observed in *Blow Up*, gave way to the grab-bag of drug-induced Oriental fantasies and role-playing of hippy culture, celebrated by *Oz* magazine and *International Times* and turned to a healthy profit by more traditional entrepreneurs. The obsession with increasingly fanciful games, the players decked out in ever more weird costumes, led to a series of films which were already living fossils by the time they were released. At an art gallery 'happening' in David Miller's spy thriller *Hammerhead* (1967), a model is smeared with ketchup and wrapped up inside a giant hot dog roll. In Robert Freeman's *The Touchables* (1969) four nymphets find a 'temporary solution to their leisure problem' by kidnapping a rock star and holding him prisoner in their plastic pleasure dome, which bulges with the inevitable pin-ball machines. Peter McEnery and Glenda Jackson while away their time in Peter Medak's *Negatives* (1969) by pretending to be Dr Crippen and Ethel Le Neve until German photographer Diane Cilento turns up to change the name of the game to a Baron von Richtofen fantasy, with a Fokker triplane anchored to the roof. 'Sapper' must have been whirling in his grave when Carl Peterssen

(James Villiers) dressed up for dinner as the Duke of Wellington in Ralph Thomas' updated Bulldog Drummond adventure, *Some Girls Do* (1969). Even the hirsute Viking berserkers of Clive Donner's disastrous 'youth epic' *Alfred the Great* (1969) seemed more like refugees from an open-air rock festival than proud warriors of the longships. When Norman Wisdom got around to prancing about in a kaftan in *What's Good for the Goose* (1969) it was time to ring down the curtain on flower power.

The rot had already set in three years before in Desmond Davies' *Smashing Time* (1966), in which Lynn Redgrave and Rita Tushingham played a 'swinging' version of Laurel and Hardy adrift among the picaresque tramps, trendy media folk and beautiful people who,

Lynn Redgrave and Rita Tushingham as Yvonne and Brenda, the 60s answer to Laurel and Hardy, in Desmond Davies' *Smashing Time* (1967). George Melly's screenplay suggested that Swinging London was a creation of the media but nevertheless displayed a frantic eagerness to exploit the myth it was attempting to explode.

Barry Evans and Judy Geeson in a bucolic fantasy from Clive Donner's *Here We Go Round the Mulberry Bush* (1967), an updated version of *The Knack* transposed to the rather less than swinging milieu of Stevenage.

Running, jumping and never standing still. The Beatles in Richard Lester's *A Hard Day's Night* (1964), whose release coincided exactly with the moment at which Beatlemania began to lift off. The freewheeling screenplay was by Alun Owen. By the time Lester made *Help!* (1965), the freshness was already beginning to fade. Despite, or perhaps because of, its big budget and exotic locations (moving from the Alps to the West Indies via the tank training ground on Salisbury Plain), the result was glossy, cluttered and confused. Michael Lindsay Hogg's *Let It Be* (1970), made when the Beatles were on the point of breaking up, provided a grumpy coda to the decade.

Gerry and the Pacemakers in a poor man's version of *A Hard Day's Night*, *Ferry Cross the Mersey* (1964), in which they win the European Beat Contest. The director was Jeremy Summers.

Stuntman Dave Clark and top model Barbara Ferris try to escape their artificial worlds by running along a beach in John Boorman's *Catch Us If You Can* (1965). They are pursued by the other members of the Dave Clark Five, who provided the film's soundtrack but did not play on screen, which was probably just as well.

in the mid-60s, seemed to be the only inhabitants of the nation's capital. Doubtless the rest of the population – driven to distraction by their fey antics – had taken to the hills. With prophetic irony Rita Tushingham succeeds in blowing up the revolving restaurant on top of the GPO Tower at the height of one of those parties that were *de rigueur* in films of the period. What better symbol of the transitory nature of 'swinging London' than the auto-destruction of its all-purpose totem pole and virility symbol?

Performers

To show the flower-children just what the grown-ups can really do, screenwriter Donald Cammell and cameraman Nicolas Roeg combined in 1968 to produce *Performance*, a film whose complexity and fitful brilliance is only matched in the post-war period by Michael Powell's *Peeping Tom*. Roeg, an immensely experienced film maker, had been in the business since 1947, taking the time-honoured route from clapper boy and assistant editor to director of photography on a number of key films of the 60s, including Clive Donner's *Nothing but the Best* (1964) and Roger Corman's *The Masque of the Red Death* (1964), and some interesting failures – Truffaut's *Fahrenheit 451* (1966) and Schlesinger's *Far from the Madding Crowd* (1967). Cammell had been the screenwriter on a Warner-financed caper movie, *Duffy* (1968), with James Fox. *Performance* was developed by Cammell as a vehicle for rock star Mick Jagger, and the backing was provided by Warner-Seven Arts. It was shot in 1968 but on its completion was 'locked up' by its American financiers until 1970, when it was released in a heavily re-edited version.

The film's two central characters are both performers and, when they meet, both are burnt-out cases. Chas (James Fox) is hired muscle of the most brutal kind, employed by a protection racket to 'put the frighteners on flash little twerps', a task he performs with studied relish. In a remarkably choreographed sequence, a troublesome barrister's Rolls is bathed in acid while his liveried chauffeur is tied to the bumper and has his head shaved. Pinkie's little race track gang would last about two minutes with our Chas. But times are changing in the underworld and the bosses bask in a rancid respectability which mirrors the 'straight' world of business. 'You was merged, my son,' Chas's boss tells small-time bookie Anthony Valentine

with sinister amiability, before going on to propose a toast to 'Olde England'. Chas's strong-arm tactics are becoming an embarrassment to the corporate moguls of crime. He is an 'ignorant boy, an out of date boy', and when he kills Valentine after the latter has him savagely beaten up in his flat, he is forced to go into hiding from the police and his former employers. It is during the beating-up sequence that we catch the first, almost subliminal, glimpse of Turner (Mick Jagger), another 'out of date boy', a played-out rock star who has withdrawn from the world into a Notting Hill dream palace. As Chas batters an assailant in his bathroom, we catch intercut flashes of Turner stepping under the jets of his shower. Later, as the fleeing Chas sits in his Jag dyeing his hair red, we watch Turner spraying a room the same colour.

A curiosity, *Gonks Go Beat* (1965): Terry Scott as the prime minister of Balladisle who is reconciled to his sworn enemy, Beatland, by the intervention of Kenneth Connor's intergalactic ambassador. Veterans of the music business will be amused by Frank Thornton's performance as Mr A & R.

Performers. James Fox's played-out hard man meets Mick Jagger's zonked-out rock star in Cammell and Roeg's *Performance* (1970).

173

Opposite top
Sailors two. Dirk Bogarde as the sadistic Scott Padgett and Alec Guinness as the captain of Lewis Gilbert's *HMS Defiant* (1962). With its mutiny organised like a modern strike by Anthony Quayle and Murray Melvin, the film can be seen as an eighteenth-century second cousin to *The Angry Silence*.

Opposite centre
Goaded beyond endurance, Terence Stamp's saintly seaman lashes out at Robert Ryan's evil master-at-arms in *Billy Budd* (1962), directed by Peter Ustinov. Ustinov played Captain Vere, but the acting honours went to newcomer Stamp and Hollywood veteran Melvyn Douglas.

Opposite bottom
John Gielgud's Lord Raglan listens to the impetuous advice offered by David Hemmings' Captain Nolan in *The Charge of the Light Brigade* (1968), directed by Tony Richardson. Like the Crimean military disaster which inspired Richardson, his film spent most of its time charging energetically in the wrong direction against the massed gun emplacements of the critics.

An overheard conversation leads Chas to seek refuge in Turner's house where, claiming to be a juggler, he rents a flat in the basement. His first sight of his new landlord is in a mirror. Mirrors have subsequently provided Nicolas Roeg with a constant source of inspiration and, significantly, it was after seeing his 'daemon' in a mirror that Turner went into retreat and the hits dried up. Chas is sucked into the bizarre routines of Turner's household – with its androgynous *ménage à trois*, magic mushrooms and scruffy little street Arab running messages to the outside world – first playing a bemused Caliban to his host's zonked-out Prospero, then slowly surrendering his own personality as Turner – as surely one of the undead as Count Dracula – perceives a way of refreshing himself before making a return to the world.

A photograph of a new Chas is required for his forged passport. He poses for Turner in wig and borrowed velvet trappings. Turner is suddenly framed in front of a huge blow-up of Ray Danton playing the gangster hero/villain of Budd Boetticher's *The Rise and Fall of Legs Diamond*. In the world outside Turner's refuge, Chas's boss busily pursues his 'mergers' while, inside, the personalities of the two men – at the outset apparently so different – are merged into one. When Chas's former associates turn up at the front door, it is Turner's face we glimpse in the window of their limousine as it pulls away, while inside No 81 Powys Square a crumpled body is found stuffed in a cupboard.

The *mise en scène* of this Borgesian parable was perfectly realized. The rot and aimlessness at the heart of Turner's dream world, with its gently degrading banks of electronic playthings and dust-laden piles of Oriental bric-à-brac, is paralleled in the torpor of the racketeers' headquarters, where a tableau of gangsters sit around, bathed in a sickly green light, under the portrait of the boss dressed up in his hunting gear. The two worlds come together in a sequence in which Jagger takes over the boss's chair, sings 'Memo to Turner' and compels his porky henchmen to indulge in a striptease which leaves them like so many raw slabs of flesh wrenched from a painting by Francis Bacon.

The Yanks Go Home

For a brief period in the mid-60s, American confidence in British films was justified by results. Mainly as a result of the success of *Tom Jones*, *A Hard Day's Night* and *Help!*, United Artists were able to transform a loss in 1963 of $800,000 to a 1965 profit of $12,800,000. In the general euphoria of the time, a modest film like Silvio Narizzano's *Georgy Girl* (1966) could become an international success simply by following the instructions on the 'swinging London' packet. Drop working class ugly duckling Lynn Redgrave into a trendy ménage à trois with Alan Bates and Charlotte Rampling; wind up self-made business tycoon James Mason in pursuit of Redgrave's lumpen Cinderella; set it all to a catchy pop tune and make sure that everyone spends a lot of time dancing around in the rain and being wistful in children's playgrounds – and you have a hit on your hands. The net result was one of Columbia's highest-grossing films of 1967. David Greene's spy thriller *Sebastian* (1968) provided a colourful, cluttered example of

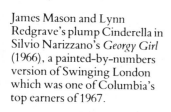

James Mason and Lynn Redgrave's plump Cinderella in Silvio Narizzano's *Georgy Girl* (1966), a painted-by-numbers version of Swinging London which was one of Columbia's top earners of 1967.

the slavish following of fashion. Codebreaker Dirk Bogarde's gleaming office is staffed entirely by pert, mini-skirted acolytes.

The most enthusiastic investors in the British film industry were Universal, who in November 1965 launched one of the most ambitious programmes by an American major to make films in Britain. Under the direction of the head of their London office, Jay Kantner, their total financial involvement in British films amounted to some $30 million and resulted in a fascinating range of late-60s box-office failures.

In 1967, Universal backed three films: Peter Watkins' *Privilege*, Chaplin's *A Countess from Hong Kong* and Francois Truffaut's muted adaptation of a Ray Bradbury story, *Fahrenheit 451*. The following year produced a more costly and equally unsuccessful series of investments: Albert Finney's *Charlie Bubbles*; two films from theatre director Peter Hall, *Work is a Four-Letter Word*, with David Warner as a drop-out growing psychedelic mushrooms in an automated world of the future, and *Three into Two Won't Go*, in which footloose nymphet Judy Geeson destroys Claire Bloom and Rod Steiger's marriage. In the same year, Joseph Losey's two ventures with Elizabeth Taylor – *Boom!* and *Secret Ceremony* – displayed his tendency to baroque over-elaboration and remain among his least satisfying films; Jack Gold's excellent *The Bofors Gun* proved unclassifiable for the overseas market; and Karel Reisz's *Isadora* proved to be simply a great disappointment. In 1969 Universal provided Anthony Newley with a chance to ape Fellini in the truly awful *Can Hieronymus Merkin Ever Forget Mercy Humpe and Find True Happiness?*, which achieved the signal distinction of being even worse than its title. After this débâcle it was with some irony that shell-shocked Universal executives contemplated their final British film, *The Adding Machine*, which, as cynics remarked, would at least help them to tot up their losses.

By the end of the decade, the American tap had been turned off. The decision to beat a strategic retreat from Britain was made easier by the success of indigenously produced films like *Bonnie and Clyde*, *The Graduate* and *Rosemary's Baby*. The Hollywood majors rediscovered their own 'youth market' with *Easy Rider* and *Woodstock* at the same time as the touch of directors like Richard Lester was beginning to fail. The end of the decade echoed with the grinding of wheels coming judderingly full circle. Lester himself returned to the world of the Goons which in

1959 had launched him on his way with the 11-minute *jeu d'esprit*, *The Running, Jumping and Standing Still Film*. His 1969 adaptation of John Antrobus' and Spike Milligan's *The Bed-Sitting Room* – a surreal view of Britain after a nuclear holocaust – was a doomed attempt to recapture on celluloid the free-wheeling radio humour of the classic Goon shows of the 50s.

From Realism to Pantomime

Social realism was translated into debased historical pantomime. Tony Richardson's *The Charge of the Light Brigade* (1968) combined pre-Raphaelite soft-focus and a laboured exposure of the 'two worlds' of Victorian Britain. The shades of *Tom Jones* were briefly evoked in a speeded-up seduction in which Trevor Howard's Lord Cardigan battled his

The anti-war film.
By the 60s the simplistic certainties of the 50s war film were ripe for subversion and parody. Richard Todd and Kenneth More had been permanently grounded. The balloon no longer went up as it had, in effect, been exploded. Tom Courtenay and his defending counsel face the court martial in Joseph Losey's *King and Country* (1964).

Ian Hendry's psychopathic military policeman looms over Jack Watson in Sidney Lumet's *The Hill* (1965), which was set in a North African military prison during World War II.

If war was hell, then so was peace. David Warner and Nicol Williamson in Jack Gold's *The Bofors Gun* (1968).

way through the thickets of stays and undergarments worn by Jill Bennett's Mrs Duberley. Howard, at least, seized his chance to give a spirited impersonation of one of the greatest swaggerers in military history, relishing such authentic period slang as 'Had me cherrybums out today – always makes me randified'. The charge itself was almost an afterthought, a miscalculation which cost United Artists dear at the box office. By the time Richardson came to set up his last film of the 60s – Vladimir Nabokov's *Laughter in the Dark* (1969) – the flight of American capital, and the replacement of Richard Burton by Nicol Williamson in the cast, forced the director to surrender his percentage in *Tom Jones* to secure backing from United Artists.

The biggest costume pantomime of the period was Richard Attenborough's first film

as a director, *Oh! What a Lovely War* (1969), an ambitious attempt to translate to the screen Joan Littlewood's scathing history of World War I. Her Stratford East production had combined popular songs, diaries and contemporary commentary in a withering attack on the folly of war and the fatuity of the ruling class. Attenborough's film retained the original's basic structure, which had been anchored in a seaside pierrot show, but opened out the action to take in the whole of Brighton pier and also the South Downs, which stood in for the Western Front. *Oh! What a Lovely War* is full of marvellous touches and small miracles of production design. Joe Melia's photographer takes a group portrait of European royalty and, as the flash bulb explodes, the Archduke Franz Ferdinand and his wife fall dead. Maggie

Smith's soubrette, urging the boys on to the stage and into the arms of the recruiting sergeant with the promise of 'I'll Make a Man of You', turns from a distant figure of glamour into a raddled old whore. Maurice Roeves, a member of the film's representative Smith family, gets on the pier's miniature railway and leaves for the front. John Mills' Field Marshal Haig directs the battle of the Somme from the top of a helter skelter while the mounting losses are posted on a cricket scoreboard. At the end of the film the last surviving Smith boy follows a red tape from the trenches into the room where the armistice is being signed. Unfortunately, the cumulative effect of art direction, logistics and the presence of so many stars in cameo roles transformed a scalding Brechtian indictment into a mere entertainment, losing the message

Above
Maggie Smith's raddled old soubrette lures the young men on stage and into the arms of the recruiting sergeant in Richard Attenborough's *Oh! What a Lovely War* (1968).

Above left
Richard Lester despatched Roy Kinnear and John Lennon to build a cricket pitch 400 miles behind enemy lines in the Western Desert in *How I Won the War* (1967).

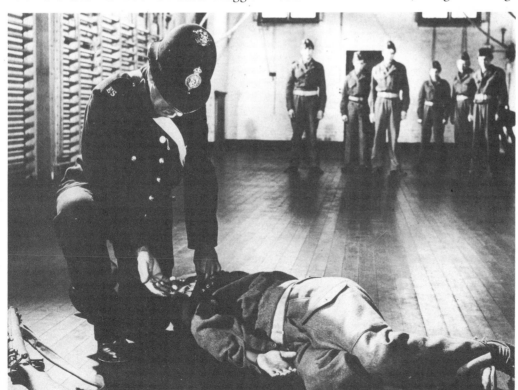

The tragic end to childish war games in Philip Leacock's sensitive *Reach for Glory* (1962).

Michael Caine discovers that his African enemy can run fifty miles a day, and then fight a battle at the end of it, in Cy Endfield's unfashionable, and hugely successful, evocation of Empire, *Zulu* (1963), based on the heroic defence of Rorke's Drift in 1879 during the Zulu Wars. Caine, in his first big role, was badly miscast as the languid Captain Bromhead. Nigel Green gave a definitive performance as a massively calm and imposing sergeant major of the old school.

Above right
Richard Attenborough played the last of the breed, the bull-necked, brass-lunged, copper-bottomed Sergeant Lauderdale of John Guillermin's *Guns at Batasi* (1964), caught up in the muddled politics of a newly-independent African state.

Terence Stamp as Sergeant Troy salutes Julie Christie's Bathsheba Everdene during the Maiden Castle interlude in John Schlesinger's *Far from the Madding Crowd* (1967).

somewhere between the South Downs and Brighton Pier.

Production values also came between John Schlesinger and his 1967 adaptation of Thomas Hardy's *Far from the Madding Crowd*. Stunningly mounted, with Nicolas Roeg's camera coaxing images of Courbet and Breughel from the Dorset countryside, the film was nevertheless undermined by errors of casting. Julie Christie reduced Bathsheba Everdene to a nineteenth-century 'Darling' – Googie Withers at the height of her powers in the 40s would have been magnificent in the role. Terence Stamp made a dashing Sergeant Troy, particularly in the film's most impressive sequence, a bravura passage shot in the strange undulations and buried ramparts of Maiden Castle. Troy woos Bathsheba with an intricately choreographed series of sabre

cuts, thrusts and passes as she sits passively on the grass. Peter Finch's Squire Boldwood had the right degree of doomed obsession but Alan Bates' shepherd Gabriel Oak looked as if he might have had some difficulty telling one end of a sheep from the other. The same could be said of the film's gallery of familiar character actors, dressed in their picturesque country togs and experimenting with an intriguing variety of Mummerset accents. Schlesinger's failure to get under the skin of his principal characters reduced them to little more than the tinkling automata which close the film. After the commercial and critical failure of *Far from the Madding Crowd*, he went to the United States to repair his reputation with *Midnight Cowboy* (1969).

A far more successful literary adaptation was Ken Russell's *Women in Love* (1969), which followed the director's disastrous handling of United Artist's third Len Deighton thriller *Billion Dollar Brain* (1967). With a degree of restraint not much in evidence in his later films, Russell succeeded in getting at the heart of Lawrence's novel – the conflict between Rupert Birkin's (Alan Bates) fanciful notions of a world of pure love ('uninterrupted grass and just a rabbit sitting up') and the bull-like potency of Gerald Crich (Oliver Reed) who is driven to pummel love from Gudrun Brangwen (Glenda Jackson), a woman whose willpower ultimately proves stronger than his own. Gerald is forced to seek fulfilment by crushing everything around him – his horse, his father's paternal style of management in the family mine, even his friend Birkin in the film's celebrated nude wrestling scene. The contrast between Gerald's overbearing presence in the dark bowels of the pit and his lonely, bewildered death in the Alpine snows is thus made particularly poignant.

Russell's use of 'I'm Forever Blowing Bubbles' thoroughly outraged F.R. Leavis but provided an authentic and appropriate touch. In similar fashion Gudrun's ecstatic dance to a herd of Highland cattle is both an ironic comment on her artistic pretensions and an affectionate tribute to the dotty notions of Isadora Duncan, about whom Russell had made an outstanding television documentary. The wrestling scene not only provides a perfect metaphor for the film's sexual message but also remains, with its rich *chiaroscuro*, a brilliantly handled set piece.

Loach, Anderson and *If...*

Part of producer Joseph Janni's 'penance' for *Far from the Madding Crowd*'s extravagant failure was his work on Ken Loach's *Poor Cow* (1968), which cost a mere £200,000 compared with the Hardy epic's $2,750,000. Together with his collaborator Tony Garnett, Loach had been responsible for two of the most celebrated television dramas of the 60s, *Up the Junction* and *Cathy Come Home*. Loach's dramatized documentary style was perfectly suited to a subject like *Cathy Come Home*, which focused on the plight of a young, homeless mother in London, played by Carol White. The play had an enormous impact when it was first broadcast but – such is the ephemeral nature of television – its social message fell on the deaf ears of the government of the day. When it was shown again, two years after its first transmission, there were more homeless people in London than ever before.

Poor Cow, scripted by *Up the Junction*'s author Nell Dunn, starred Carol White as another passive victim of circumstance, a working-class mother who takes up with a 'Jack the Lad' type (Terence Stamp) when her husband (John Bindon) is sent down for a prison stretch. Before long Stamp himself gets a twelve-year sentence for armed robbery, and on her husband's release White returns to him, although her life is now centred solely on her child. *Poor Cow* is an uncertain first film and, with the help of some fey songs by Donovan and an ill-judged rural idyll in Wales in which Stamp and White make love under a waterfall, it slides inexorably into sentimentality. Loach was on firmer ground when he renewed his partnership with Tony Garnett to make *Kes* (1969). The film selects a specific target – an edu-

Eleanor Bron, Jenny Linden and Glenda Jackson perform in the style of Isadora Duncan in Ken Russell's *Women in Love* (1969).

cation system geared to turning out docile factory fodder – but places its didactic concern inside a straightforward and warmly observed narrative. A young working-class boy (David Bradley) is rejected by family and school but finds release and purpose in nursing back to health, and then training, an injured kestrel, the only bird of prey which lower orders of the Middle Ages were allowed to hunt. At the end of the film the bird is killed by the boy's elder brother and the question is left open as to whether the loss of the kestrel will bring the shades of the prison house closing in once more on the young lad.

After *This Sporting Life* Lindsay Anderson limited his output in the 60s to three films, only one of which was a full-length feature. *The White Bus* (1966) was a 40-minute segment from an aborted three-part feature, the other contributors being Tony Richardson and Peter Brook. Shelagh Delaney's screenplay, taken from one of her short stories, was built around a young girl's return to her northern home town, where she encounters the white bus of the title taking a group of VIPs on a guided tour. A surrealistic satire on provincial life, its autobiographical flavour and elements of fantasy anticipate Delaney's screenplay for Albert Finney's directorial debut, *Charlie Bubbles* (1968), in which a successful but disillusioned novelist (played by Finney) returns to the north to cast around for his roots. In an enigmatic ending he floats away in a hot-air balloon.

After making a documentary in Poland, *The Singing Lesson* (1967), Anderson turned his attention to an original screenplay entitled 'Crusaders' which had been written in 1960

The happiest days of their lives: (*Top left*), Laurence Olivier and Terence Stamp in *Term of Trial* (1962), directed by Peter Glenville. (*Top right*), Maggie Smith's Miss Jean Brodie and her young acolytes in Ronald Neame's *The Prime of Miss Jean Brodie* (1968), the film of the play of the book. (*Above*), David Wood, Richard Warwick and Malcolm McDowell swig vodka and plot revolution in Lindsay Anderson's *If...* (1968).

by two former public school boys, David Sherwin and John Howlett, and originally developed by the director Seth Holt.

The resulting film, *If...*, enabled Anderson to make a semi-autobiographical journey of his own, to explore his middle-class background at public school. Much of the film was shot on location at Anderson's old school, Cheltenham College, and displays in its superbly detailed picture of the rituals of public school life that ambivalent love-hate relationship which a public school rebel inevitably has with his *alma mater*.

If... is a story of rebellion, and its release in 1968 coincided with a tidal wave of revolt and

insurrection by the young in Europe and the United States. However, the film's three rebels are conservative romantics who seal their brotherhood in a blood oath and in a mock duel in the gymnasium give vent to such sentiments as 'Some love England and her honour yet' and 'Death to tyrants'. Byron and Missolonghi are more apt models for their revolt than Marcuse and Berkely.

The 'tyranny' at the school is carefully presented at two levels. Old-fashioned authoritarianism is the prerogative of the prefects, the 'whips' resplendent and ludicrous in their dandified patterned waistcoats. Rowntree, the head of house, is an older version of Jack in *Lord of the Flies*. He makes the decisions on behalf of Arthur Lowe's feeble housemaster, whose inert resignation is reminiscent of Norman Bird's absentee CO in Sidney Lumet's *The Hill* (1966), who allows the NCOs to run a military prison. Rowntree is hot on discipline – 'I wouldn't like the house to get a reputation for decadence,' he remarks, *à propos* of a string of failures on the games field. But his own decadence extends to the bartering of pretty fags among his fellow 'whips'. On the other level is the school's headmaster, a superb caricature of repressive liberal tolerance by Peter Jeffrey as he waffles on about Britain being 'a powerhouse of ideas' and suggests linking the college with the 'high standards in the television and entertainment industry'.

The conflict is resolved in the poetic fantasy of the film's conclusion. The rebels and their confederates discover a long-forgotten cache of arms and ammunition. At the school's speech day a pompous general, flanked by two school servants in suits of armour, delivers a suitably Blimpish address to the assembled boys, parents and staff – 'There's nothing the matter with privilege so long as we're prepared to pay for it.' Flushed out of the hall by the rebels' smoke bomb they are met with a hail of fire from the roof-tops, a conscious borrowing from Vigo's *Zéro de Conduite*. The headmaster steps forward: 'Boys, boys, I understand you,' he cries before receiving a bullet smack between the eyes. As the bourgeoisie fight back, the camera moves in on the rebel leader, Malcolm McDowell's Travis, who turns his chattering submachine gun on the audience. It is a peculiarly British ending to one of the key films of the decade, for – like Anderson himself – we are given the chance to experience the feeling of alarm and guilt without suffering any of the consequences.

AFTERWORD

What are the themes which run through the thirty years of cinema which this book has reviewed? Three emerge quite clearly: the recurrent dawn of false hopes; the intermittent role played by American finance; and the fossilization or self-destruction of the principal talents thrown up in each of the decades under review.

False hopes of a British assault on the world market were first raised by Korda's success in the 30s. In the immediate post-war period, J. Arthur Rank, like Korda before him, sank beneath the weight of his own missionary zeal and *folie de grandeur*. In the late 50s the illusory breakthrough of 'social realism' encouraged equally illusory notions of artistic maturity. Close on its heels came the brief summer of 'Swinging London', a bubble which burst wetly in the faces of the Hollywood majors and the native industry, which was too narrowly based to survive the flight of American capital. Ironically, in 1969 the ailing British film industry's response was to evoke the ghosts of moguls long dead by appointing Bryan Forbes as head of production at Elstree, a position he held for two years. On the plus side of the balance sheet during his tenure was *The Railway Children* (1970). On the debit side was a string of limp, middle-of-the-road flops which included *Hoffman* (1970), *The Breaking of Bumbo* (1970), Forbes' own *The Raging Moon* (1971) and *The Man Who Haunted Himself* (1970), directed by Basil Dearden.

Basil Dearden is the archetypal figure of the post-war film industry, a position which can be confirmed by a glance at the number of entries against his name in the index. A long-serving Ealing man, proficient technician and exponent of the cinema of bureaucracy, his films move from the rough, energetic first solo effort, *The Bells Go Down* (1943), to the increasingly inert, bloodless rehearsals of liberal social conscience of the early 60s – *Sapphire* (1959), *Victim* (1961) and *Life For Ruth* (1962). Dearden, of course, directed *The Blue Lamp*, a film which lies at the heart of Ealing's receding fantasy of a wartime solidarity projected into an uncertain future. The Ealing tradition was subverted by Alexander Mackendrick and Robert Hamer, but the former left for America in the mid-50s, while at the same time the latter was burying himself under a bottle every bit as large as the one which loomed over David Farrar in Michael Powell's *The Small Back Room* (1949).

In the 50s Anthony Asquith retreated into a purely theatrical cinema and Carol Reed ran up the confused cul-de-sac of *Our Man in Havana* (1959). David Lean increasingly confused anal retention with making films. Launder and Gilliat's work described a gently descending curve from the poignant social observation of *Millions Like Us* (1943) to the cosy anarchy of the St Trinians series. The Boultings, too, after *Brighton Rock* (1947) and *Seven Days to Noon* (1950), settled for the celebration of the curiously muddled and slapdash view of themselves which the British hold so dear. By contrast, Michael Powell's complex exploration of 'Englishness' in *The Life and Death of Colonel Blimp* (1943) was completely misunderstood. It is hardly surprising, therefore, that *Peeping Tom* (1959), the summation of a life's work and one of the few British films of the 50s to display an uninhibited feel for cinema, virtually finished Powell's career amid howls of critical execration. Other directors took a spectacular course of auto-destruction: David Macdonald descended from *This Man is News* (1938) and distinguished wartime documentary to *Devil Girl from Mars* (1954). In the 60s, Tony Richardson plummeted from the heights of *Tom Jones* to the botched Nabokov adaptation *Laughter in the Dark* (1969).

History has a habit of repeating itself, and the cyclical ups and downs of the British film industry are no exception. Significantly, the celebrations over *Gandhi* came exactly fifty years after Korda's triumph with *The Private Life of Henry VIII*.

FINALLY

A tribute to some of the players who provided British cinema with a host of comforting stereotypes and saved hard-pressed screenwriters pages of dialogue: shifty wide boys, long-suffering barmaids, busty ingenues, flustered civil servants and chirpy Cockney privates.

Jane Hylton, an undervalued supporting player of the 40s and 50s, as she appeared in *My Brother's Keeper* (1948). A graduate of the Rank Charm School, she made her screen début, as a barmaid, in *Daybreak* (1947).

Stately Margaret Leighton, all set to do some 'business' with her fan in Powell and Pressburger's *The Elusive Pimpernel* (1951).

Diana Decker, a breezy American leading lady in British films, who leapt to fame in a toothpaste commercial ('Irium, Miriam?') and went on to adorn homely domestic thrillers like *Murder at the Windmill* (1948), in which a body is found slumped in the stalls of London's famous revue theatre.

The lovely Kathleen Byron, under whose calm exterior hidden passion bubbled away in *The Small Back Room* (1949) and erupted in *Black Narcissus* (1947). She made her debut in 1942 in *The Young Mr Pitt*.

Anne Crawford, who combined a light touch with a nice sense of irony. She made her screen debut in 1942 in *They Flew Alone* and followed it a year later with a memorable performance as the stuck-up model who falls in love with Eric Portman's factory foreman in *Millions Like Us* (1943). She died in 1956.

Belinda Lee got her first break in a Frankie Howerd comedy, *The Runaway Bus* (1953), a sadly prophetic title as she was to die in a car accident eight years later. Despite beauty and talent, she never quite made it in Britain and ended her career in a series of Italian muscleman epics.

Virginia McKenna, Ann Todd's successor as No.1 Ice Maiden, whose passive suffering in *Carve Her Name with Pride* (1958), was one of the keynote performances of 50s British cinema.

Carole Leslie – whose real name was Maureen Rippingdale – lent a sexy presence to a number of 50s features, including *Woman in a Dressing Gown* (1957).

Hazel Court in the pert little utility number she wore as the young war widow in *Holiday Camp* (1947). Her first screen appearance was in *Champagne Charlie* (1944), but later in her career the goblets were filled with blood rather than bubbly in a string of horror features – *The Curse of Frankenstein* (1957), *The Man Who Could Cheat Death* (1959), *Dr Blood's Coffin* (1961) and *The Masque of the Red Death* (1964).

Left
Jennifer Jayne, perennial starlet of the mid-50s, poses with a tasteful array of musical instruments for the rather less tastefully titled *Raising the Wind* (1961), in which she played a music student, naturally.

Shirley Ann Field, an actress of some beauty but limited range, who nevertheless gave some telling performances. She was the young beauty queen seduced by Olivier's Archie Rice in *The Entertainer* (1960), and the calculating tease Doreen, who traps Albert Finney's Arthur Seaton in *Saturday Night and Sunday Morning* (1960). She also appeared briefly, but unforgettably, as the ultimate dumb actress in Michael Powell's *Peeping Tom* (1959). With red hair, of course.

183

Gladys Henson is permanently fixed in the memory making cups of tea for hubby Jack Warner in *The Captive Heart* (1946) and *The Blue Lamp* (1949). In the latter film, as PC George Dixon's widow, she gave an understated performance of quiet poignancy which went unerringly to the heart of the Ealing tradition.

Joyce Grenfell's fluttering charms were confined to roles which aped the angular gaucherie of the chirpy games mistress, Miss Gossage, she played in Launder and Gilliat's *The Happiest Days of Your Life* (1950).

Liz Fraser, a generously proportioned dizzy blonde who provided a lingering image of the Macmillan era when, in the Boultings' *I'm All Right, Jack* (1959), she swarmed all over Ian Carmichael in his swaying white bubble car, parked on the edge of the municipal rubbish tip.

The 'Carry On' series' very own bombshell, petite but perfectly formed Barbara Windsor, whose ability to act from the neck downwards has no rival in British cinema.

A characteristically dowdy Brenda de Banzie, struggling home with the laundry in Anthony Bushell's *The Long, Dark Hall* (1951). She came into films in middle age and has left two indelible performances, in David Lean's *Hobson's Choice* (1954) and as Archie Rice's pathetic, alcoholic wife in *The Entertainer* (1960).

Sylvia Syms and Herbert Lom in *No Trees in the Street* (1958), Ted Willis's glum working class drama set in the 1930s. When he was not playing mid-European psychiatrists (most notably in *The Seventh Veil*), Lom was applying a silky-smooth varnish of villainy to films like *Snowbound* (1947) and *Dual Alibi* (1947), in which audiences were treated to two Loms for the price of one as he played identical twins, one of whom commits a murder.

Kathleen Harrison's French patriot provides Tony Wright's escaped PoW with hastily improvized cover in *Seven Thunders* (1957).

Kenneth Williams and Charles Hawtrey seem perfectly at home masquerading as store detectives in *Carry on Constable* (1960), one of the 27 'Carry On' films Gerald Thomas directed between 1958 and 1978.

Nice young people: Joan Rice and James Donald in Compton Bennett's *The Gift Horse* (1951).

Joan Greenwood and Nigel Patrick as Sabina and Rodney Pennant, the bohemian couple who plant themselves on Derek Farr and Helen Cherry in *Young Wives' Tale* (1950), a suburban marital comedy directed by Henry Cass. Greenwood's inimitably sexy voice was one of the great siren calls of the 40s, and in the 60s she was still applying the husky charm to Albert Finney's young hero in *Tom Jones*.

Eccentric dodderer Miles Malleson strikes up the band in the Boultings' *The Magic Box* (1951). Malleson's film career stretched from the 1921 silent *The Headmaster* to Michael Winner's 60s comedy *You Must Be Joking* (1965). As an accomplished screenwriter, his credits included *Nell Gwynn* (1934), *Victoria the Great* (1937) and *The Thief of Bagdad* (1940).

Left
Felix Aylmer in *The Calendar* (1948), a Gainsborough film based on an Edgar Wallace story. His air of benign authority was lent to a succession of bankers, bishops, businessmen and the occasional peppery headmaster. He was the unworldly but fiendishly efficient captain of the shipbuilding industry in Anthony Asquith's *The Demi Paradise* (1944).

Right
Eric Pohlman, the British film industry's all-purpose oily Levantine, the black marketeer in the crumpled white suit.

Edward Chapman, perennial bluff northerner, Labour MP, corrupt alderman and wartime working class Everyman. When he was allowed to keep the "ee bah gooms' under control, Chapman proved a capable actor, as the choirmaster in Penrose Tennyson's *The Proud Valley* (1940) and as Googie Withers' portly, darts-loving husband in *It Always Rains on Sunday* (1947). A less distinguished Ealing film, *Ships with Wings* (1942), gave him the chance to step out of character and play the excitable Greek owner of the world's smallest airline.

Sidney Tafler as Morrie Hyams, record shop proprietor and part-time musician ('the man with sax appeal') in Robert Hamer's *It Always Rains on Sunday* (1947). The perfect spiv, usually dumber than the punters he was trying to con, Tafler made his screen debut in *The Little Ballerina* (1946) and went on to star in the 1952 *Wide Boy*, in which he graduated from selling black market nylons to blackmail and murder before coming to a sticky end.

Caught in an uncharacteristically shifty mood, Bernard Lee spent most of his career playing stolid NCOs, incorruptible policemen and persistently inquisitive customs men, which led to his murder in Basil Dearden's *The Ship That Died of Shame* (1955). His reward was the role of the down-to-earth intelligence mandarin and father figure 'M' in the James Bond films.

Boy next door Jimmy Hanley turns to crime as 'Whitey' in *It Always Rains on Sunday* (1947), playing a tame South London version of Richard Attenborough's 'Pinkie' in *Brighton Rock*. After an eternity spent hovering around adolescence, Hanley's career took a nose dive in the 1950s.

Two civil servants, Arthur Howard and Richard Wattis, the permanently embattled agents of the post-war Welfare State whose long careers spent grappling with Launder and Gilliat's special form of educational anarchy began with *The Happiest Days of Your Life* (1950).

Denholm Elliott, a well-groomed and rather bloodless juvenile lead in the early 50s, seen here in David Lean's *The Sound Barrier* (1952), but more successful in his 1960s incarnation as a seedy remittance man (*Nothing But the Best*) and permanently sozzled parent (*Here We Go Round the Mulberry Bush*).

Kieron Moore, an Irish-born leading man whose youthful good looks became set and morose as he grew older. Early success in *A Man About the House* (1947) and *Mine Own Executioner* (1947) led to a disastrous miscasting as Vronsky in Alexander Korda's *Anna Karenina* (1948). Thereafter he remained a familiar face in more routine features with the occasional foray into low-budget horror and science fiction – *Dr Blood's Coffin* (1961) and *The Day of the Triffids* (1962).

Clive Morton as he appeared in Harold French's *The Blind Goddess* (1948). He played the photographer Herbert Ponting in Ealing's *Scott of the Antarctic* (1949), surprising the hearty Edwardian explorers with a remarkable party turn with his sleeping bag at a base camp Christmas concert. Later he swapped photography for an extended legal career at Ealing, playing the obsequious prison governor in *Kind Hearts and Coronets* (1949) and a typically solid desk sergeant in *The Blue Lamp* (1949) and *The Lavender Hill Mob* (1951).

187

Robert Beatty, rugged general-purpose hero of the 1940s and 50s, memorable as the cynical American seaman in *San Demetrio, London* (1943) who is won over by the quiet good humour and determination of his shipmates. Here he is in pensive mood in Guy Green's *Portrait of Alison* (1955), Alison being the American actress Terry Moore.

Victor Maddern, chirpy steward, Cockney rating, Cockleshell Hero and occasionally panic-stricken private – in his screen debut he shot Barry Jones' mad scientist at the climax of *Seven Days to Noon* (1950). This is how he appeared in Harry Watt's *The Siege of Pinchgut* (1959), a thriller set in Australia and the last film made by Ealing.

Guy Middleton, an accomplished silly ass or edgy man about town with a shady past, a role he played in David Macdonald's *Snowbound* (1947). A raffish figure in the cinema of austerity Britain, he was at his best behind the wheel of a sports car (*Laughter in Paradise*), or plying his friends with black market whisky (*The Young Wives' Tale*).

Maxwell Reed, a Rank Charm School success and brooding heavy of the 40s, whose career sputtered out in the mid-50s. Tall and languid of movement and delivery, Reed left most of the acting to his eyebrows and an increasingly baroque hairstyle which constantly threatened to take on a life of its own. He was at his best being beastly to the infatuated Sonia Dresdel in *The Clouded Yellow* (1950) or as a psychopath in *The Brain Machine* (1954), directed by Ken Hughes. He was briefly and tempestuously married to Joan Collins.

Guy Rolfe, a former racing driver and elegant leading man of the 40s, in Terence Fisher's 1948 *Portrait from Life*, in which he searched the refugee camps of post-war Europe for amnesiac Mai Zetterling.

No war film of the 1950s was complete without the solid presence of Percy Herbert as a grizzled NCO or disgruntled private. His round, potato face pops out of the ranks in *The Baby and the Battleship* (1956), *A Hill in Korea* (1956), *Bridge on the River Kwai* (1957) and *Yesterday's Enemy* (1959).

AUTHOR'S ACKNOWLEDGMENT

The author would like to thank the staff of the British Film Institute for their help with this book, particularly Michelle Snapes of the stills library. Additional illustration material was provided by the John Kobal Collection and Tom Graves.

BIBLIOGRAPHY

Aspinall, Sue and Murphy, Robert, *Gainsborough Melodrama*. BFI Dossier 18, 1982.
Balcon, Michael, *Michael Balcon Presents . . . A Lifetime in Films*. Hutchinson, 1969.
Barr, Charles, *Ealing Studios*. David and Charles, 1977.
Booker, Christopher, *The Neophiliacs*. Fontana, 1970.
Brown, Geoff, *Launder and Gilliat*. BFI, 1977.
Calder, Angus, *The People's War*. Panther, 1971.
Christie, Ian (ed.), *Powell, Pressburger and Others*. BFI, 1978.
Dors, Diana, *Dors By Diana, An Intimate Self-Portrait*. Queen Anne Press, 1981.
Durgnat, Raymond, *A Mirror for England*. Faber and Faber, 1970.
Gifford, Denis, *The British Film Catalogue*. David and Charles, 1973.
Korda, Michael, *Charmed Lives. A Family Romance*. Allen Lane, 1980.
Kulik, Karol, *Alexander Korda – The Man Who Could Work Miracles*. W.H. Allen, 1975.
Marwick, Arthur, *The Explosion of British Society*. Macmillan, 1971.
Melly, George, *Revolt into Style*. Allen Lane, 1970.
Perry, George, *The Great British Picture Show*. Hart Davis/MacGibbon, 1974.
— *Movies from the Mansion. A History of Pinewood Studios*. Elm Tree, 1982.
— *Forever Ealing*. Pavilion/Michael Joseph, 1981.
Pirie, David, *A Heritage of Horror*. Gordon Fraser, 1973.
Richards, Jeffrey, *Visions of Yesterday*. Routledge and Kegan Paul, 1973.
Sussex, Elizabeth, *The Rise and Fall of the British Documentary*. University of California Press, 1975.
— *Lindsay Anderson*. Studio Vista, 1969.
Thomson, David, *A Biographical Dictionary of the Cinema*. Secker and Warburg, 1980.
Walker, Alexander, *Hollywood, England*. Michael Joseph, 1974.
Warren, Patricia, *Elstree, The British Hollywood*. Elm Tree, 1983.
Watt, Harry, *Don't Look at the Camera*. Elek, 1974.
Wood, Alan, *Mr Rank*. Hodder and Stoughton, 1952.
Wright, Basil, *The Long View*. Secker and Warburg, 1974.

INDEX

Page numbers in italics refer to illustrations.

ABC — see Associated British Picture Corporation
Above Us the Waves 101
Accident 148
Adam, Ken 170
Adams, Robert *104*
Adding Machine, The 175
Addinsell, Richard 16, 17
Admirable Crichton, The 159
Adventures of Tartu, The 15
Against the Wind 112
Aked, Jean *39*
Albert RN 115–16, *115*
Alexander, Terence 97, *97, 118*
Alexander Nevsky 57
Alfie 164, *164*
Alfred the Great 171
Allen, Irving 120, 138
Allen, Patrick 129
Allied Film Makers 145–6, 159
Ambler, Eric 32, 105
Amis, Kingsley 106, 138
Anderson, Lindsay 93, 138, 140, 152, 179–81
Anderson, Michael 118–21
Andress, Ursula *168*, 169
Andrews, Harry *118*
Angeli, Pier 146
Angels One Five 112, 119, *127*
Anglo-Amalgamated 55, 135
Angry Silence, The 101, 145–6, *145*, 174
Anna Karenina 85, 187
Annakin, Ken 65, 76–7, 164
Anniversary, The 134
Anstey, Edgar 26
Antonioni, Michelangelo 165–6
Antrobus, John 175
Appointment with Crime 71
Archers, The 58, 80–3, 137
Arden, Bob 31
Ardizzone, Edward 97
Arliss, Leslie 42–3, 61
Arsenal Stadium Mystery, The 9
Asherson, Renee 47
Askey, Arthur 49, *49*, 53
Asquith, Anthony 14–17, 24, 35, 39–41, 43, 44–46, 85, 121–3, 149, 181, 186
Associated British Picture Corporation 55, 68, 101, 129, 141, 154
Astonished Heart, The 134
Attenborough, Richard 62–3, 68–9, *69, 70–1*, 71–2, 97, 106–7, 114–16, 144–6, *145*, 158, *159*, 176–7, *178*, 187
Aubrey, Anne *139*
Audley, Maxine 136–7
Aylmer, Felix 40, 49, 61, *186*

Baby and the Battleship, The 188
Back Room Boy 49
Baddeley, Hermione 72, 105
Bad Lord Byron 63, 64–5
Baker, George 114–15, *114*
Baker, Hylda *143*
Baker, Roy 103, 113, 118, 128
Baker, Stanley *102, 148*, 149, *167*
Balchin, Nigel 85
Balcon, Jill 60, 71
Balcon, Michael 7–10, 19, 32, 35, 51, 55, 58, 74, 83, 87–8, 90, 95–7, 99, 128, 142
Balfour, Michael *115*
Bancroft, Ann 161
Bank Holiday 9
Banks, Leslie 9, 21, 37, 39
Bannen, Ian 106–7
Baranova, Irina 75
Bardot, Brigitte 102, *103*
Barnacle Bill 98, *99*
Barnes, Barry K. 28, *78*, 79
Barr, Douglas 76
Barrett, Sean 121
Bartlett, Lucy *164*
Bartok, Eva *132*
Bass, Alfie *42*, 69, *69, 94, 135*
Bates, Alan, *151*, 152, *160, 162*, 162, 174, 178
Battle of Britain, The 116
Battle of the River Plate, The 127, 135
Battle of the Sexes, The 96, 142
Baxter, Beryl *64*
Baxter, Jane 21
Baxter, John 18, 50, 100
Beat Girl 139
Beatles, The *172*
Beatty, Robert 34, *34*, 76, *76, 115, 188*
Beaudine, William 8
Beaver Films 145
Beckwith, Reginald *14*, 69, 90
Bedelia 78, *78*
Bedford, Brian 145, 146
Bed-Sitting Room, The 175
Bell, Tom *167*
Belles of St Trinians, The 109, *109*
Bells Go Down, The 33, *33*, 34, 95–6, 181
Bennett, Compton 61–2, 67, 79, 185
Bennett, Jill 176
Bentley, John *111*
Berger, Ludwig 8
Berkeley, Ballard *130*
Betjeman, John 27, 30
Beyond the Fringe 119
Big Blockade, The 13
Billington, Kevin 159
Billion Dollar Brain 178
Billy Budd 174
Billy Liar 153–4, *153*, 162
Binder, Sybilla *114*
Bird, Norman *97*, 180
Biro, Lajos 7, 8
Bitter Springs 102
Black, Edward 18, 45
Blackboard Jungle, The 142
Black Magic 97
Blackman, Honor 77, *126*
Black Narcissus 81, *81*, 128, 137, 182
Black Sheep of Whitehall, The 49
Blewitt, Bill *30*
Blind Date 148, 149
Blind Goddess 187
Blithe Spirit 54
Blood from the Mummy's Tomb 100
Bloom, Claire 124, 142, *142*, 175
Blow Up 165–6, *165*, 171
Blue Lamp, The 34, 70, 73, 75, 95–9, *95*, 113, 167, 181, 184, 187
Blue Murder at St Trinians 109
Blue Parrot, The 130
Blythe, John 69, *69*
Body and Soul 83
Boehm, Carl 136–7, *136*
Boelficher, Budd 174
Bofors Gun, The 158, 175, *176*
Bogarde, Dirk 66, 68–9, *69*, 77, 95, *95*, 101–3, *102–3*, 146–7, *148*, 149–50, 160, *161*, 163, 170, *174*, 175
Bond, Derek *24, 59*, 60, 74, *90*
Bonnie and Clyde 175
Bonnie Prince Charlie 84–5
Boom! 175
Boorman, John 172
Borchers, Cornell 114
Borehamwood Studios 88, 98, 99, 114
Bould, Beckett 146
Boulting Brothers 14, 15, 22–3, 28, 68–9, 71–2, 105–6, 145, 181, 184–5
Bowles, Peter 166
Box, Betty 67, 101, 103
Box, Muriel 62, 67
Box, Sydney 56, 61, 62, 64, 85
Boy, a Girl and a Bike, A 126
Boys in Brown, The 68–9, 113, 123
Boys Will Be Boys 8
Bradley, David 179
Brady, Scott 131
Braine, John 141
Brain Machine, The 188
Brand, Christianne 66
Brandon, Phil 52
Brandy for the Parson 100
Brave Don't Cry, The 100
Bray Studios 133
Breaking of Bumbo, The 181
Bredin, Patricia 112
Brent, George 131
Bresslaw, Bernard 158
Brides of Dracula 134
Bridge on the River Kwai, The 113, 116–17, *117*, 119, 124, 188
Bridie, James 108
Brief Encounter 58, 58–9, 61, 73, 90, 119, 124, 128, 142, 154
Brighton Rock 71, 72, 105, 181, 186
British Broadcasting Corporation 10, 159–60
British Lion 23, 83, 85
Broccoli, Albert (Cubby) 120, 138, 168–70
Broken Journey 65
Bron, Eleanor 179
Brook, Clive 15, *20*, 20
Brook, Lyndon *119*
Brook, Peter 160, 179
Brooke, Hillary 131
Brooks, Ray 164, *164*
Brothers, The 64
Brothers-in-Law 106
Brown, Janet 108, *109*
Browning Version, The 122, *123*
Bruce, Brenda 137
Brunel, Adrian 11
Bryan, Dora 151
Bryan, John 60–1, 142
Bryan, Peggy 75
Bryanston Films 142–3, 156–7
Bucholz, Horst 160
Bull, Peter 156
Bullitt 167
Bulloch, Jeremy 154
Bunuel, Luis 99
Burden, Hugh 20
Burford, Roger 30
Burke, Alfred 145–6
Burma Victory 28
Burton, Richard 142, *142*, 144, *169*, 176
Burtwell, Frederick 60
Bushell, Anthony 9, 184
Byrne, Eddie *115*
Byron, Kathleen 81, *81*, 128, 182
Cabot, Bruce 11
Cadell, Jean *17*
Caesar and Cleopatra 56, *57*
Caine, Michael *164*, 164, *169*, 170, *178*
Calendar, The 186
Calling Paul Temple 111
Calvert, Phyllis 18, *31, 35*, 42–5, *43–4, 48, 48, 63, 65*, 67, 67–8, 103, *104*
Cameron, Earl *76*
Cameron, Rod 170
Cammell, Donald 173
Campbell, Colin *147*
Campbell's Kingdom 101, *102*
Campion, Gerald 103
Camp on Blood Island, The 116
Can Hieronymus Merkin Ever Forget Mercy Humpe and Find True Happiness? 175
Cannon, Esme 77
Canterbury Tale, A 41
Captain Boycott 66
Captain Horatio Hornblower RN 114
Captive Heart, The 75, 112–13, *112*, 116, 184
Caravan 61, 63
Cardiff, Jack 28, 81–2, 105
Carey, Joyce *58*, 72, 104
Carlson, Richard 131
Carlton-Browne of the FO 107, *107*
Carmichael, Ian, 106, *106*, 112, 116, *145*, 184
Carney, George *23*, 76, *76*
Caron, Leslie *151*, 168
Carpenter, Paul *115*
Carrick, Edward 28
Carrington VC 122, *122*
Carry on Constable 185
Carry On Sergeant 103
Carstairs, John Paddy 48, 70, 100, 103
Carve Her Name With Pride 115, 121, 136, 183
Case for PC49, A 110, 130
Casino Royal 168
Caspary, Vera 78
Cass, Henry 185
Catch Us If You Can 172
Catherine the Great 7
Cattle Queen of Montana 74
Cavalcanti, Alberto 10, 23, 26, 32, 35–6, 51, 59, 60, 71, 74–5
Chaffey, Don 116
Champagne Charlie 51, 183
Chaplin, Charles 175
Chapman, Edward *19*, 20, 72, *186*
Chance of a Lifetime 144, 145
Charge of The Light Brigade, The 174, 175
Charlie Bubbles 175, 179
Charter Films 14
Cheer Boys Cheer 88
Cherry, Helen 185
Children's Film Foundation 100
Chiltern Hundreds, The 100
Christie, Julie 154, 162, 163, *163*, 178, *178*
Christopher Columbus 64
Cilento, Diane 156, 171
Cineguild 58, 122
Circus of Horrors 135, *136*
Citadel, The 7
Clair, René 8
Clare, Mary 35, *36*
Clark, Dane 131
Clark, Petula 75–6, *110*
Clarke, T.E.B. 90, 94–5, 98
Clayton, Jack 95, 140–1, 144, 161
Clements, John 17, 20–1, *20–1*, 75
Clifton-James, M.E. 121
Close Quarters 27
Cloudburst 131, 136
Clouded Yellow, The 101, *101*, 188
Coastal Command 25, 27
Cockleshell Heroes 97, 120, *120*
Colditz Story, The 112, 116, *116*
Cole, George *39*, 71, *71*, 109, *109*, 170
Cole, Sidney 75
Coleridge, Ethel *130*
Colleano, Bonar 47, 71, 76, *76*
Collins, Joan *70*, 128, 188
Collins, Norman 72
Columbia Pictures 155, 168, 174
Comfort, Lance 17, 35, 78, 113
Compton, Fay 17, *60*
Connor, Kenneth *173*
Connery, Sean *168*, 168–70
Constanduros, Mabel *39*
Constantine, Eddie *127*
Contraband 11, *12*
Convoy 20, *20*
Conway, Tom 131
Corman, Roger 173
Cornelius, Henry 34, 87, 91, 96
Corri, Adrienne *131*
Cottage to Let 35, *39*
Cotten, Joseph *86*, 87
Counterspy 130
Countess from Hong Kong, A 175
Court, Hazel 130, *131, 183*
Courtenay, Tom 149–50, *150*, 153, *153*, 171, *176*
Courtneidge, Cicely *151*
Coward, Noel 23–4, 39, 54, 58, 87, 125, *125*, 159
Crabbe, Buster 170
Crabtree, Arthur 44, 68, 77, 79, 135
Craig, Michael *102*, 126, 144–6, *145*
Crawford, Andrew 65, 69, *69*
Crawford, Anne 30, 32, 44, 63, 69, *182*
Crawford, Howard Marion *94*
Crawford, Michael 164, *164*
Crazy Gang 50
Crichton, Charles 8, 30, 75, 76, 94, 96–7, 101, 112, 114, 160
Criminal, The 148, 149
Croft, Peter *49*
Crooks' Tour 49, *50*, 107
Cross, Hugh 105, 111
Crown Film Unit 25–6
Cruel Sea, The 127
Cry the Beloved Country 104
Cul de Sac 158, *159*
Culloden 159
Culver, Roland 15, 16, 91, 108, 115
Cummings, Constance 32, *54, 96*
Curran, Roland 163
Currie, Finlay *15*, 33, 60, 64, 154
Curse of Frankenstein, The 133, *133*, 183
Cushing, Peter 133–4, *133*

D & P Studios 55
Dalrymple, Ian 58
Dambusters, The 112, 118–20, *118*
Damned, The 132
Dance Hall 75–6
Dance of the Vampires 135
Dancing With Crime 70–1
Dangerous Moonlight 16–17
Danger Within, The 116
Danischewsky, Monja 88, 142
Danquah, Paul *150*, 151
Darby O'Gill and the Little People 168
Darling 162, *163*
Darnborough, Anthony 134
Dassin, Jules 129
Dave Clark Five 172
Davies, Desmond 171
Davis, John 83, 85, 99, 101
Davy 99, 100
Day, Robert 161
Daybreak 79, *79*, 182
Day of the Triffids, The 187
Day Will Dawn, The 15
Deadly Affair, The 170
Dead of Night 74, *74*, 89
Dean, Basil 9, 87
Dearden, Basil 33–4, 46, 49–50, 70, 73–6, 88–9, 95–7, 100, 112–14, 142, 146, 159, 181, 186
Dear Mr Prohack 100
Dear Murderer 79
de Banzie, Brenda *184*
de Cassalis, Jeanne *39*
Decker, Diana *182*
de Grunwald, Anatole 40
Dehn, Paul 105
Deighton, Len 170, 178
Delaney, Shelagh 150–1, 179
del Guidice, Filippo 23, 56, 85
de Marney, Derrick *111*
Demi-Paradise, The 40–1, *41*, 186
Deneuve, Catherine 158
Denham, Maurice 72, 125
Denham Studios 7, 8, 10, 55, 85
Denison, Michael 68
Desert Victory 26, 28
Desmond, Robert *69, 119*
Desmonde, Jerry 103
Desperate Moment 101
Destination Moon 132
Deutsch, Oscar 7, 55
Devil Girl from Mars 131, 181
Devil Ship Pirates 134
de Wolff, Francis 109
Diamonds are Forever 170
Diary For Timothy 30
Dick Barton at Bay 130
Dick Barton, Special Agent 110, 130
Dick Barton Strikes Back 130

Dickinson, Desmond 57
Dickinson, Thorold 9, 17, 35–6, 63, 85, 104
Diffring, Anton 116, 135, *136*
Dighton, John 35, 51, 60, 92, 107–8
Disney, Walt 56, 82–3, 168
Divided Heart, The 114
Dmytryk, Edward 71
Doctor at Large 103
Doctor at Sea 102, *103*
Doctor in Clover 103
Doctor in Distress 103
Doctor in Love 103
Doctor in the House 102–3
Doctor in Trouble 103
Doctor's Dilemma, The 122
Doctor Zhivago 116
Doleman, Guy 170
Donald, James *32*, *185*
Donat, Robert 6, 8, 15, 17–18, *17*, 85, 101, *105*, 171
Donlan, Yolande 102, *139*
Donlevy, Brian 131–2
Donnelly, Donal 164
Donner, Clive 162, 171, 173
Donovan 179
Doonan, Patrick 96
Dorleac, Françoise 158
Dors, Diana 52, 58, 70–1, 75–6, *76*, 108, 126–7, *126*, 131
Double Indemnity 78, 131
Douglas, Craig 155
Douglas, Melvyn 174
Douglas, Paul 98, *98*
Dover Frontline 26
Dowling, Joan 75
Dracula 133–4, *133*
Drayton, Alfred 49, 60
Dresdel, Sonia 86, 188
Dr Blood's Coffin 183, 187
Drifters 25, 27
Dr No 168, 168–9
Dr Terror's House of Horrors 74
Drum, The 7
Dual Alibi 184
Duff, Howard *132*
Duffy 173
Duke Wore Jeans, The 138
Dunkirk 121, 128
Dunn, Nell 179
Dupuis, Paul 91
Duvivier, Julien 85
Dwyer, Leslie *32*, *126*

Each Dawn I Die 71
Ealing Studios 8–10, 13, 19–20, 30, 32–6, 42, 46, 48–9, 51, 58, 60, 72–5, 85, 87–8, 90–102, 112–14, 127–8, 140, 158, 181, 184, 186, 188
Easdale, Brian 81–2
Easy Money 77
Easy Rider 175
Edge of the World, The 47, 80
Edwards, Meredith 95
Elephant Boy 8
Elliott, Denholm 104, *123*, *162*, *162*, *187*
Elstree Studios 55, 85, 181
Elusive Pimpernel, The 135, 182
Elvey, Maurice 14, 39
Emerton, Roy 17
Encore 77
Endfield, Cy 129, 168, 178
Entertainer, The 101, 142–3, *143*, 183–4
Esther Waters 66
Evans, Barry 171
Evans, Clifford 18, 32–3, *33*
Evans, Edith 63, 142, 156, 158
Evans, Peggy 96, *130*
Escape 71
Eureka Stockade 88, 102
Evergreen 9
Every Day Except Christmas 140
Expresso Bongo 138, *139*
Exterminating Angel 99
Exton, Clive 157

Fabrizi, Mario 155
Fahrenheit 451 173, 175
Fairbanks, Douglas Jr 101, 107
Faith, Adam *139*
Fallen Idol, The 86, *86*
Fanatic 134
Fanny By Gaslight 43–5, *43*
Far from the Madding Crowd 173, 178–9, *178*
Farr, Derek 185
Farrar, David 37, 80–1, *82*, 88, 89, 128, 181
Father Brown 93
Fellini, Federico 175

Ferrer, Jose 120
Ferris, Barbara *172*
Ferry Cross the Mersey 172
Feyder, Jacques 8
Field, Marjorie *100*
Field, Mary 56, 100
Field, Shirley Ann *132*, 136, *139*, 144, *183*
Field, Sid 56, 103
Fields, Gracie 8, 9, 47
Final Test, The 122
Finch, Peter 75, *75*, 146, 161, 178
Finney, Albert 143–4, *143*, 155–7, *156*–7, 175, 179, 183, 185
First A Girl 9
First Days, The 10, 26
First National Film Company 6
Fire Over England 8
Fires Were Started 29, *29*, 96
First of the Few, The 24, 25
Fisher, Terence 76, 114, 131, 132–4, 188
Fitzgerald, Geraldine 55
Flaherty, Robert 8
Flanagan and Allen 29, *50*
Ford, George 130
Ford, Glenn 142
Forde, Walter 49, 51, 88
Foreman, Carl 124
Foreman Went To France, The 32, *33*, 34, 48
For Freedom 14
Formby, George 8, 47–8, *48*, 53, 85, 103, 154
Forster, E.M. 30
49th Parallel 22–3, *22*, 40
Foster, Julia 160
Four Feathers, The 7
Four-Sided Triangle 131
Fowler, Harry 37
Fox, James *148*, 149, *150*, 173, *173*
Francis, Raymond 122
Franklin, Pamela 161
Fraser, John 128, 158
Fraser, Liz *184*
Frederick, Cecil *52*, 53
Free Cinema Group 138, 140–1
Freedom Radio 14, 15
Freeman, Robert 171
French, Harold 15, 16, *36*, 68, 77, 187
French Without Tears 122
Frend, Charles 13, 32–4, 42, 73, 89, 90, 99, 142
Frend, Philip *33*
Freud – the Secret Passion 136
Frieda 88–9, *88*
Freedom Radio 14
Frobe, Gert 169
From Russia with Love 168–9
From the Four Corners 27
Furie, Sidney J. 147, 169
Furse, Roger 57
Fyffe, Will 17, *64*

Gainsborough Studios 8, 9, 42–5, 49, 55, 60–5, 67, 74, 76–7, 85, 109, 126, 134, 186
Gandhi 181
Gardiner, Cyril 50
Garfield, John 140
Garnett, Tony 179
Garson, Greer 114
Garvin, Willie 170
Gasbags 50
Gaumont-British 7, 9, 11, 17, 55
Gaunt, Valerie 133
Geeson, Judy 171, 175
General Film Distributors 55, 85
Genevieve 96
Genn, Leo 115
Gentle Gunman, The 85, 101
Gentleman's Agreement 83
Gentle Sex, The 31
Geordie 109
George, Muriel *36*, 37
Georgy Girl 174, 174
Gerry and the Pacemakers 172
Ghost Goes West, The 8
Ghost of St Michaels, The 20, 49
Ghost Ship 130
Ghost Train, The 49, *49*
Gibbs, Gerald 132
Gielgud, John *17*, *174*
Gift Horse, The 185
Gilbert, Lewis 19, 115, 119, 121, 159, 164, 174
Gilliat, Sidney 12, 18, 27, 31, 45, 50, 58, 65, *66*, 72, 85, 105, 107, 109, 112, 170, 181, 184, 187
Gilling, John 134, 138–9
Glass Key, The 132

Glenville, Peter 44, *44*, 70, *70*, 152, 180
Godden, Rumer 81
Gold, Jack 158–9, 175–6
Gold, Jimmy *50*
Golden, Michael 95
Goldfinger 169–70
Golding, William 159–60
Goldner, Charles *13*
Gone to Earth 135
Gonks Go Beat 173
Goodbye Mr Chips 7
Good Companions, The 19
Goodliffe, Michael *118*
Good Morning, Boys 109
Good Time Girl 69, *70*, 130
Goodwin, Harry 119
Gordon, Colin 108–9
Goring, Marius 15, 80, *80*, 82
Gough, Michael *94*, 94
Goulding, Alfred 110
Graduate, The 175
Graham, William *111*
Granger, Stewart *20*, 42–5, *44–5*, *57*, *61*, 63, 66, 101
Gray, Dulcie 45, *68*, 79
Gray, Sally *16*, 17
Great Expectations 58–60, *59*
Great Mr Handel, The 17
Great St Trinians Train Robbery, The 109
Green, Danny 99
Green, F.L. 85
Green, Guy 144–6, *187*
Green, Janet 146
Green, Nigel 170, 178
Green, Teddy 154
Greene, David 174
Greene, Graham 9, 62, 72, 86, 87, 125
Greene, Richard *36*
Green For Danger 66
Green Man, The 109
Greenwood, Joan 62, 65, 92, 94, 128
Gregg, Evelyn 59
Gregg, Hubert 98
Gregson, John 96, 98, 119, *127*
Grenfell, Joyce 108, *184*
Greville, Edmond T. 139
Grex, Leo 35
Grey, Sally 113
Grierson, John 25–6, 100, 140
Griffith, Hugh 72, 156
Griffith, Kenneth 106, *136*
Group 3 100
Guest, Val 101, 111, 116, 131–2, 138–9
Guinea Pig, The 68, 69
Guillermin, John 121, 167, 178
Guinness, Alec *59*, 60, 92–3, *94*, 98–9, *99*, 116, *117*, 125, *125*, 174
Guns at Batasi 178
Gwynn, Nell 185
Gynt, Greta 51, 77
Gypsy and the Gentleman, The 149

Hale, Sonny 56
Halfway House 46
Hall, Peter 175
Hall, Willis 117, 153
Hallet, Mary 30
Hamer, Robert 72–4, 91–3, 181, 186
Hamilton, Guy 116, 128
Hamilton, Russ 138
Hamlet 57
Hammer, Will 129
Hammer Films 116–7, 129–34, 136, 182
Hammer-Exclusive Distribution Company 110, 129
Hammerhead 171
Hammer the Toff 111
Hammond, Kay *54*
Hanbury, Victor 147
Hancock, Tony *161*
Hand, David 56
Hand, Slim 130
Handl, Irene 27
Handley, Tommy 53, *53*
Hanley, Jimmy 19, *32*, 68–9, 95, *110*, 112, 113, *187*
Happidrome 52, 53
Happiest Days of Your Life 107–8, *184*, *187*
Harcourt, James 12
Hard Day's Night, A 164, *172*, 174
Harding, Gilbert 101
Hard Steel 145

Hardwicke, Cedric 27, 60
Hardy, Thomas 178
Hare, Robertson 49
Harker, Gordon 20, 35, *35*
Harlow, John 130
Harmer, Robert 51
Harris, Richard 117, 152, *152*
Harrison, Kathleen 23, 76–7, *110*, *185*
Harrison, Rex 12, 41, *54*, 65, 66, 71
Hartnell, William 32–3, *33*, 71–2, *71*, 103, *103*, 121
Harvey, Laurence 70, 138, *139*, 140–1, *141*, 144, 163, *163*
Hasty Heart, The 129
Havelock-Allan, Anthony 58
Havens above 107
Hawkins, Jack *97*, 117, 119, 127, 127, 128
Hawtrey, Charles 49, *49*, *185*
Hay, Will 8, 13, 47, 49, 49–50, 51, 109, 111
Hayakawa, Sessue 116, *117*
Hayers, Sidney 135–6, 167
Hayes, Melvyn 154
Hayward, Louis 131
Hayworth, Rita 61
Heart of Britain 28
Headmaster, The 185
Heavens Above 107
Hell Drivers 129, 168
Help! 164, *172*, 174
Helpmann, Robert 63, 82
Hemmings, David 165, *166*, 174
Hendry, Ian 153, *153*, 176
Henry V 56, 57, 128
Henson, Gladys 72, 75, 95, *184*
Henreid, Paul 131
Henrey, Bobby 86, *86*
Herbert, Percy 188
Here Come the Huggetts 76
Here We Go Round the Mulberry Bush 171, 187
Hibbert, Geoffrey 18
Hicks, Seymour 15
Highbury Studios 58, 130, 134, 150
High Treason 106
Hill in Korea, A 188
Hill, Jacqueline 130
Hill, The 176, 180
Hiller, Wendy 46, 80
Hills, Gillian *139*
Hird, Thora 114
Hitchcock, Alfred 9, 19
HMS Defiant 19, 174
Hobson, Valerie 11, *12*, 60, 67, 75, 92–3, 113
Hobson's Choice 122, 184
Hoffmann 181
Hogg, Michael Lindsay 172
Holden, William 116, 125, *125*
Holiday Camp 76, 77, 110, 164, *183*
Holloway, Stanley 24, 51, 57, 58, 60, 90, *91*, 94, 98, 101
Holm, Sonia 65
Holman, Vincent 38
Holmes, Jack 25, 27
Holt, Patrick 114, *126*
Holt, Seth 100, 180
Hood, Noel 50
Horniman, Roy 92
Horrors of the Black Museum 135
Hot Enough for June 170
House Across the Lake, The 131
House of Darkness 74
Housing Problems 26
Houston, Donald 76, 116
Houston, Renee 31
Howard, Arthur 187
Howard, Joyce *31*, 35
Howard, Leslie 12, 13, *13*, 22–4, *22*, 25, 27, 31
Howard, Michael 72
Howard, Ronald 71
Howard, Sydney 27
Howard, Trevor 58, 66, 71, 87, 101, 120–1, *120*, 124–5, *125*, 128, 175
Howard, William K. 8
Howe, James Wong 8
How Green Was My Valley 146
How I Won the War 177
Howlett, John 180
Howlett, Noel 146
Hue and Cry 90, 97
Huggetts Abroad, The 76, 110
Hughes, Ken 129, 131, 187
Hulbert, Claude 49, *50*, 51, *51*, 56
Hulbert, Jack 49
Hungry Hill 66, 130
Hunt, Martita *59*, 60, *109*, 134
Hunt, Peter 170
Hunted 101, 160
Hunter, Ian 78–9

Hunter, Kim 80
Huntington, Laurence 49, 67, 78–9
Huntley, Raymond 13, *32*, 35, 65, 90, 107, 125
Hurst, Brian Desmond 11, 16, 17, 66
Huston, John 136
Hutcheson, David 35
Hylton, Jane 71, 75, *136*, *182*

I Believe In You 70, 128
Ice Cold in Alex 118
I, Claudius 8
Ideal Husband, An 85
Idle on Parade 138, *139*
Idol of Paris 64
If... 180, *180*
I Know Where I'm Going 47, 80, 137
I Live in Grosvenor Square 41, *41*
Ill Met By Moonlight 135
I'll Never Forget Whatsisname 163
I'm All Right Jack 101, 106, 145, *145*, 184
Importance of Being Earnest, The 122
Independent Producers 58, 85
Individual Pictures 58, 65–6
Ingram, Rex 8
Innocents, The 161
Innocents in Paris 133
Inspector Hornleigh 35
Inspector Hornleigh Goes To It 35, *35*
Inspector Hornleigh on Holiday 35
Invasion of the Body Snatchers 37
In Which We Serve 23–4, *23*, 32, 56, 113, 159
Ipcress File, The 169
Isadora 175
I See a Dark Stranger 66, *66*
It Always Rains on Sunday 72–3, *72*, 75, 88–9, 144, 186, *186*–7
It's A Grand Life 52
It's That Man Again 53
It's Trad, Dad 155, *155*, 164
I Was Monty's Double 121

Jackson, Freda 114, 134
Jackson, Glenda 171, 178–9
Jackson, Gordon 30, *32*, 73, *102*, 132
Jackson, Pat 27–8, *28*
Jacques, Hattie 103, *144*
Jagger, Dean 41, *41*
Jagger, Mick 173, *173*
James, Barry 188
James, Sidney 76, *94*, *102*, 103, 131
Janni, Joseph 179
Jassy 63, 130
Javelin Films 85
Jayne, Jennifer *183*
Jeffrey, Peter 180
Jeffries, Lionel *116*
Jellicoe, Ann 164
Jenkins, Megs 30, *31*, 32, *126*
Jennings, Humphrey 26, 28–30, 77, *153*
John, Rosamund 46, 78
Johnny Frenchman 42, 88
John Smith Wakes Up 39
Johns, Glynis 22, 46, 65, 89, 107
Johns, Mervyn 33–5, *33*, 37, 46, *50*, 51, 74–5, 95, 112–13
Johnson, Celia 24, *58*, 58, 134
Johnson, Katie 66, 98, *99*
Johnson, Noel 130
Jones, Barry 105, *105*
Jones, Elwyn Brook *85*
Jones, Griffith 60, *65*, 71
Jones, Jonah 26
Jones, Paul 159, *165*
Jones, Peter 106
Journey into Yesterday 188
Joyce, Yootha 161
Justice, James Robertson 68, *102*, *102*, 108
Just William's Luck 111

Kanin, Garson 27–8
Kantner, Jay 175
Karas, Anton 87
Katzman, Sam 155
Kearins, Tommy 98
Keen, Geoffrey 101, 146
Kellino, Pamela 78
Kellner, William 92
Kelsall, Moultrie 115
Kempson, Rachel 113
Kendall, Kay 76, 96, 102
Kenny, James 121
Kent, Jean 43, 46, *51*, 61, *61*, 62–3, *63*, 65, 69–70, 70, 74, 122, *123*
Kerr, Deborah 15, 18, *18*, 38, 66, *66*, 81, *81*, 85, 161
Kes 179